Umm Kulthūm

LAURA LOHMAN

Umm Kulthūm

ARTISTIC AGENCY AND THE SHAPING OF AN ARAB LEGEND, 1967–2007

WESLEYAN UNIVERSITY PRESS
Middletown, Connecticut

WESLEYAN UNIVERSITY PRESS
Middletown, CT 06459
www.wesleyan.edu/wespress

First paperback edition 2013
Manufactured in the United States of America
ISBN for the paperback edition: 978-0-8195-7072-7

Portions of this book appeared previously in a different form as "'The Artist of the People in the Battle': Umm Kulthūm's Concerts for Egypt in Political Context," in *Music and the Play of Power in the Middle East, North Africa, and Central Asia*, ed. Laudan Nooshin, Ashgate Press, 2009, and "Preservation and Politicization: Umm Kulthūm's National and International Legacy," *Popular Music and Society* 33 (1), 2010, http://www.informaworld.com.

Wesleyan University Press is a member of the Green Press Initiative. The paper used in this book meets its minimum requirement for recycled paper.

Library of Congress Cataloging-in-Publication Data
Lohman, Laura, 1974–
Umm Kulthūm : artistic agency and the shaping of an Arab legend, 1967–2007 / Laura Lohman.
p. cm. — (Music/culture)
Includes bibliographical references and index.
ISBN 978-0-8195-7071-0 (cloth : alk. paper)
1. Umm Kulthum, 1898–1975. 2. Singers—Egypt—Biography. I. Title.
ML420.U46L65 2010
782.4216'3092—dc22
[B] 2010023311
5 4 3 2 1

We gratefully acknowledge the assistance of the AMS 75 PAYS Endowment of the American Musicological Society.

To my parents

Contents

Illustrations

Figures

Musical Examples

Acknowledgments

The research for this book was made possible by the generous financial support of several organizations. The National Endowment for the Humanities funded my research in Egypt through a fellowship at the American Research Center in Egypt. A Jacob K. Javits Graduate Fellowship from the U.S. Department of Education supported the early research that I conducted in the United States. A faculty stipend from California State University, Fullerton, assisted in my later research and writing. Although the views, findings, and conclusions expressed in this book do not necessarily represent those of the organizations that funded my research, I am especially grateful for their financial support.

In Egypt, I benefited greatly from the insight, assistance, and patience of the many journalists with whom I spoke. I am indebted to Farūq Ibrāhīm for his generosity in sharing his time, knowledge, and exquisite photographs. I am grateful to Muḥammad Wajdī Qandīl, Muḥammad Tabārak, 'Afāf Yaḥyá, Muḥammad Ṣāliḥ, Muḥammad Salmāwī, and Ḥasan Rajab for the insights they shared in their many helpful interviews. Aḥmad al-Ṣaghīr at Akhbār al-Yawm gave invaluable assistance in gaining access to many of these writers and photographers. Nadia Luṭfī at al-Ahrām and the staff at Dār al-Hilāl and Idhā'ah wa al-Tilīfizyūn generously provided essential aid in utilizing publishing house archives.

Outside these publishing houses, I received help from many other individuals in Egypt. Aḥmad 'Antar, director of the Umm Kulthūm Museum, helped me obtain numerous audio-visual records, provided valuable insight on her rarely heard songs, and granted me generous access to the museum's collections. In addition, I thank Umm Kulthūm's stepson, Muḥammad Ḥasan al-Ḥifnāwī, along with Nabīl Shūrah and Wajdī al-Ḥakīm, for their helpful discussions. My research in Egypt would not have been possible without help from the entire staff at the American Research Center in Egypt.

Special thanks go to Jere Bacharach, Amīrah Khattab, Amīr 'Abd al-Ḥamīd, and Amīrah Jamāl.

Many individuals offered invaluable assistance during the lengthy and challenging process of gaining access to the archives of the Egyptian State Radio and Television Union. In particular, I offer heartfelt thanks to Charles Dibble and Yūsuf Sharīf Rizq Allāh, the former president of Nile Television, for their help in gaining permission to utilize the resources of the state television archives. I also thank Nabīl 'Uṭhmān, chairman of State Information Services, for his help in accessing valuable audio recordings and video footage.

In the United States, I also have many to thank. I express my gratitude to Carol Muller and Scott Marcus, in whose stimulating seminars I first formulated and explored the idea behind this book. I also thank Dwight Reynolds, who provided a helpful forum for presenting and discussing my early research. I am indebted to the late Eugene Wolf for his model of meticulous scholarship and professionalism. At Wesleyan University Press, I owe many thanks to Parker Smathers, the series editors, and the anonymous readers, all of whom offered critical insight and guidance. Finally, I thank my parents for their unwavering support during the challenging times spent researching and writing this book.

Note on Transliteration

In transliterating Arabic, I have generally followed the system adopted by the American Library Association and the Library of Congress. I represent one Arabic consonant differently. Instead of using the symbol "ẓ" to represent the consonant pronounced like the "th" in "though," I use the symbol "ṭh." I have used this system of transliteration for most persons' names, including those of well-known figures such as Jamāl 'Abd al-Nāṣir. For well-known place names and organizations, however, I have used accepted English spellings, such as Beirut, Cairo, and Fatah. In references to titles of non-Arabic sources, I have retained the spelling of Arabic names used in the original documents. Thus, while in the body of the text I use "Umm Kulthūm," references to titles of English and French sources include various original spellings such as "Oum Kalthoum," "Om Kalthoum," and "Umm Kolthoum." When referring to Arab authors who have published work in English or French, I have adopted their preferred nonstandard transliterations of their names.

Chronology of Important Performances and Events

1967	June 1	Qaṣr al-Nīl (Cairo) concert
	June 5–10	Six-Day War
	August 17	Fundraising concert in Damanhūr
	August 31	Fundraising concert in Alexandria
	November 9–22	Paris trip
1968	February 1	Fundraising concert in al-Mansūrah
	March 1–21	Morocco trip
	April 18–27	Kuwait trip
	May 9	Qaṣr al-Nīl concert
	May 30–June 9	Tunisia trip
	July 10–17	Lebanon trip
	December 5	Qaṣr al-Nīl concert
	December 25–January 2	Sudan trip
1969	January 9	Qaṣr al-Nīl concert
	February 6	Qaṣr al-Nīl concert
	March 10–22	Libya trip
	May 8	Fundraising concert in Tanta
	June 19	Concert to rescue the Philae Temple
	October 23–November 3	Minor pilgrimage to Mecca
	December 4	Qaṣr al-Nīl concerts resume
1970	July 7–14	Lebanon trip
	September 25–30	USSR trip
	September 28	Death of Jamāl ʿAbd al-Nāṣir
1971	November 26–December 3	Abu Dhabi trip

Umm Kulthūm

Introduction

Just days before the fall of Ṣaddām Ḥussayn's statue during the Iraq war of 2003, cassettes of a song about Baghdad suddenly sold out in Cairo. Not surprising, perhaps, for a recent hit like Sha'bān 'Abd al-Raḥīm's "al-Ḍarb x al-'Irāq" (Attack on Iraq), but unusual for a song created nearly five decades earlier. Initially recorded after the overthrow of King Fayṣal II of Iraq, the song "Baghdad" lauded the Ba'th Party, glorified the city as a "lions' fortress," and called Arabs to "seize the torch of battle." A half-century later, at the outset of the Iraq war, its assurances of victory offered Egyptians inspiration and hope. The iconic voice singing the lyrics—that of Umm Kulthūm—only added to their allure.

Born in a small Egyptian village in 1904, Umm Kulthūm established herself as a singer in Cairo in the 1920s. Her popularity swelled during the next two decades as she took advantage of the burgeoning radio, recording, and film industries and developed a broad repertory of romantic, patriotic, and religious songs. Valuable social connections enhanced her artistic success. She forged long-lasting relationships with powerful cultural leaders, including leading journalists. She socialized with members of the elite, recorded songs honoring King Fārūq's ascension to the throne, and received a marriage proposal from his uncle. After the 1952 revolution, she recorded patriotic songs in support of Jamāl 'Abd al-Nāṣir. As 'Abd al-Nāṣir's wife, Taḥīyah, stayed out of the public eye, Umm Kulthūm acquired the status of a surrogate first lady. Distinguished musically by her improvisatory skills and vocal stamina, she sustained her career and her popularity through the 1960s despite the emergence of younger singers and listeners. She gave her final concert in 1972. When she died three years later, her funeral reportedly drew more than four million mourners.

In concluding her award-winning study of the singer, Virginia Danielson noted Umm Kulthūm's lingering presence in late twentieth-century Egyptian life (1997, 200–201). This presence continued into the twenty-first century, with her recordings accounting for 40 to 50 percent of Sono Cairo's sales (Farag 2000b). Encounters with her music in daily life support these statistics. In 2003, when I lived in Cairo, uses of her music ranged from the commercial to the personal. A television ad for the beverage company Juḥaynah turned "Ghannī Lī Shwayya Shwayya" into a catchy jingle appealing to the country's youngest viewers, and Egyptians of many generations turned to her music for personal entertainment. On separate occasions, I noticed an office assistant in his early thirties singing parts of "al-Aṭlāl" during his daily work, while a man in his twenties belted out selections from "Inta 'Umrī" in an internet café and a teenager sang along as one of her movies played in a grilled chicken shop. Listeners have also used her music for pragmatic reasons. For example, in an effort to demonstrate their "culturedness" to Westerners, Egyptian drivers at archaeological digs abandoned recent pop hits for Umm Kulthūm's recordings when escorting Western archaeologists.[1]

This continued consumption during the three and a half decades after Umm Kulthūm's death has been accompanied by a reverent reception that prompts important questions about her career and its representations. Years of hagiographic portrayals have shaped listeners' perceptions, leading an ordinary Egyptian in Michel Goldman's 1996 documentary, *Umm Kulthūm: A Voice Like Egypt*, to laud the singer as a pyramid and proclaim that "today no one can do what she did." Umm Kulthūm went from being described in the 1950s as a woman who "loves herself more than her art and refuses to extend a helping hand"[2] to being hailed after her death as "the possessor of the most devoted and most compassionate human heart, who dedicated her life and everything she possessed in artistic magnificence, the utmost effort, and the height of giving to her homeland and her Arabness" (Zakariyā 1983, 5). While her concerts were described during her lifetime as a "drug that leads Arabs to linger in truancy" and "one of the reasons for the defeat of 1967" (I. Saḥḥāb 1980, 19), she was praised by ordinary Egyptians after her death as an exemplary patriot. Exactly what caused these perceptions to change? How and why has she been remembered so reverently for more than three decades after her death?

The end of her career holds valuable answers to these questions. This part of an artist's career often risks being underestimated. Through the historiographical application of a metaphor of organic growth, periods of development and maturity may overshadow a later period that is seen to entail a process of decline, decay, or deterioration. This type of organic view shaped the reception of Beethoven in much of the nineteenth century. While his middle period works, such as the Fifth and Third symphonies, were praised as his greatest achievements, his late works were described in the decades immediately following his death as "decadent," "incoherent," "formless," and "chaotic" (Knittel 1998, 51–57). A similar midcareer peak was articulated in Umm Kulthūm's life by Egyptian music historian Maḥmūd Kāmil, whose valuation of the 1940s as her "Golden Age" gained wide influence, appearing in time lines of her career in the Umm Kulthūm museum as well as in Danielson's study (1997, 100, 199). The identification of this decade as constituting the pinnacle of her artistic achievement has rested in large part on her performance of the neoclassical *qaṣīdahs* of Aḥmad Shawqī and Riyāḍ al-Ṣunbāṭī and the more accessible populist songs of Bayram al-Tūnisī and Zakariyā Aḥmad. Taken together, these two contrasting bodies of songs garnered her strong appeal amongst a broad spectrum of Egyptian society. The articulation of such a Golden Age has an impact on perceptions of the rest of her career. The narration of Umm Kulthūm's transformation from a "backward" village singer to an urbanite moving fluidly among elites, coupled with her artistic success in the face of rivals like Munīrah al-Mahdīyah, casts her early years as a period of growth and triumph over adversity that led to a culminating Golden Age. Her later career may then be devalued because she produced patriotic songs seen to hold less value as "pure art," relied increasingly on dance rhythms in her romantic songs, turned to a diverse array of younger composers, lost vocal agility, or declined in health.

I demonstrate, to the contrary, that Umm Kulthūm's later career was not a period of decline but rather offered a valuable opportunity for her to redefine herself as an artist and to shape the way that she would be remembered after her death.[3] I focus on the period beginning in 1967, an era marked in Egyptian cultural and political history by the devastating defeat by Israel in the Six-Day War. The defeat and the era it launched were dubbed "al-Naksah," usually translated as "the setback."[4] Like other crises, the defeat spurred intensified creative effort in response to loss and destruction.[5] Physical, emotional, and conceptual losses gripped the nation, with the dream of Arab political unity, the goal of reclaiming Palestine, and total faith in the hero ʿAbd al-Nāṣir numbering among the casualties. The war prompted a cultural renaissance, motivated by and expressing grief, resolve, and disappointment. Resistance literature appeared, especially works of poetry and theater, and a defensive interest in cultural heritage, including traditional designs and clothing, emerged as a means of rejecting the West and its support of Israel (Stone 2008, 94; Makdisi 2006, 337). In music, Umm Kulthūm's contemporary Fayrūz and her collaborators ʿĀṣī and Manṣūr al-Raḥbānī entered a period of greater productivity and generated works of more realism and overt political content (Stone 2008, 95). Within Umm Kulthūm's career, the period is marked by the sudden prominence of her fundraising concerts (Danielson 1997, 185–86). As other periods in her career can be demarcated by new, distinctive groups of songs created in tandem with the changing needs and tastes of the Egyptian public, a final period beginning in 1967 may be marked by her sustained presentation of fundraising concerts to benefit the country's military reconstruction.[6] Through careful self-presentation, she prevented the decline and destruction of her image both during her lifetime—a fate suffered by other stars like Charlie Chaplin—and after her death (Maland 1991, 197–316).

By focusing on Umm Kulthūm's later career, I do not promote a teleological view like that which elevated Beethoven's late works as superior products of "transcendence" and ultimately supplanted the organic view of his career (Knittel 1998, 71). Instead, I argue that Umm Kulthūm's strategic decisions about her self-presentation from 1967 onward were essential to both her longevity and her hagiographic posthumous reception. The war's outcome would have presented anyone in her position with a dilemma. No longer able to expect an audience to patronize three-hour concerts of lengthy romantic songs, many artists would have seriously considered retirement. Although already in her sixties and past the age when most singers would have stopped performing, Umm Kulthūm continued singing and seized these years to redefine her relevance for Egyptian society, intensify her relationships with listeners abroad, and cultivate a multifaceted public persona that would influence strongly her reception in the decades following her death. She presented herself as a consummate patriot and an ordinary citizen, all while realizing previously conceived international performances and turning herself into a cultural and artistic ambassador. Her broad-ranging activities in response to the defeat solidified her transformation from singer to patriot and are essential to understanding the magnitude, intensity, and tenacity of her reverent reception. As Danielson noted, Umm Kulthūm began to craft a consistent public persona as early as the late 1930s (1997, 185). She honed this image in her later years in new political contexts. Although it was variously exaggerated, idealized, reduced, and simplified after her death, the persona that she continued to cultivate so effectively through her later career would enable her, posthumously, to serve a remarkable variety of political and cultural agendas, ranging from the reinforcement of conventional gender roles to the anti–George W. Bush rhetoric of Palestinian-American hip-hop artist Will Youmans, aka the Iron Sheik.

A close examination of Umm Kulthūm's later career offers insights not only into the durability of her reverent reception, but also its geographic and cultural scope. While her monthly concerts had long reached millions of listeners outside Egypt through radio broadcasts that spanned the Arab world, she harnessed her later career to solidify and intensify her relationships with her listeners. As a result, gold medals carrying her image were sold in the Arab world in 1969 (ʿĀrif 1969). Her fans also resided in Israel, Europe, and North America, and her increasing international renown brought her music to the attention of such American artists as Bob Dylan by 1971 (Cott 2006, 184, 213). Her death four years later was quickly cast as an Arab loss, and Arab authors claimed her musical contributions as part of an Arab musical heritage, rather than a strictly Egyptian one (Melligi 1975; *al-Idhāʿah wa al-talfazah* 1975; "Fannānūnā" 1975, 20). One Moroccan writer described her as "a believer in her Arabness and Egyptianness as if she were responsible for the destiny of Egypt and Arabism" (Banjulūn 1975, 239). She still earns the praise of ordinary Arabs, and a necklace given to her by the first president of the United Arab Emirates recently garnered more than a million dollars from a Middle Eastern buyer at a Dubai auction (Dirks 2007; Surk 2008). Echoing this regional attachment, an Egyptian government website identifies her as the "voice of Arabs" ("Umm Kolthoum"). These articulations of her value across the region and her self-awareness of that value call for a close examination of the ways in which she established and maintained such a lasting regional presence.

In focusing on one iconic singer, this study addresses issues of broader relevance and contributes to several noteworthy bodies of literature. My study of Umm Kulthūm's later career, which included a host of autobiographical acts—efforts to define herself through text and performance—is situated in a growing body of auto/biographical studies of important figures in the Middle East. Although a number of factors may be said to have worked historically against the production and criticism of auto/biography in the region, this literature has grown substantially during the past two decades, adding to what in fact is a long history of biography in the Arab-Islamic world.[7] In several collections, writers and critics using diverse disciplinary and evidentiary approaches to biography and autobiography have shown how the study of individual lives can enhance understanding of the region, how biography can be used to understand history and culture, and how biography constructs both personal and communal identity (Kramer 1991; Fay 2001a, 3–4). This increasing scholarly attention to the individual in the Middle East and in the humanities more generally comes as poststructuralist critique of metanarratives and universalism has spurred a focus on the local and the particular (Fay 2001a, 3).

Women's auto/biographies and their study have been important parts of this growing literature, as the poststructuralist critique has also given legitimacy to those positioned at the margins (Fay 2001a, 3–4). Some work on Middle Eastern women has reflected a Western emphasis on elite and literary figures (Jelinek 1980; Booth 2001a; Fay 2001b). Other writers have addressed the underrepresented, including middle-class, illiterate, and working-class women (Makdisi 2006; Atiya 1988; Mernissi 1988; Shaaban 1988). Recent work on contemporary Arab women's autobiographical writings has emphasized transnationalism, communal identity, and cultural hybridity. Writers of such works have deliberately addressed texts that challenge literary traditions, attest to gender oppression, share communities' struggles, and strengthen group identification (Golley 2007; Golley 2003, 69, 74; Gale and Gardner 2004, 4). Other life studies have explored Arab women's roles in cultural and political movements on both national and international scales (Clancy-Smith 1991; Victor 1994; Nelson 1996; al-Ali 2001).

Life studies of women artists in the region have similarly portrayed figures ranging from the ordinary to the iconic (van Nieuwkerk 1995; Danielson 1997; Zuhur 2000). Umm Kulthūm's iconic status provides a valuable means of bridging area studies and a growing body of star studies (Dyer 1998; Baty 1995; Maland 1991). For much of her career, Umm Kulthūm's celebrity was an achieved one, based on outstanding skill.[8] Yet within the taxonomy of celebrity, Umm Kulthūm transcended the status of artist, icon, and star to reach that of hero—a famous person who did something significant in an active sense (Monaco 1978, 8–9, discussed in Mäkelä 2004, 211). Her response to the 1967 defeat was cast by both the Arab media and herself as a profound and selfless act of sacrifice that aided both Egypt and the Arab nation in a time of crisis. Her posthumous reception reflects her ascendance to hero status, a status that has been accorded to a small number of stars—like John Lennon—and contrasts sharply with the tragic and self-destructive image of other women stars, such as Marilyn Monroe. As posthumous accounts of Lennon's life emphasized his suffering and messianic qualities (Hampton 1986, 6; Mäkelä 2004, 212), biographies of Umm Kulthūm stressed her willingness to sacrifice herself for Egypt and the Arab nation.

Posthumous mythologization of heroes like Lennon and Umm Kulthūm imposes the ideals of the collective society (Hampton 1986, 6). This imposition was noted decades ago by *Rolling Stone*'s Jon Landau, who characterized the star system as the "crudest and most primitive form of escape, in which we express our dissatisfaction with ourselves by endowing another with superhuman qualities" (Anson 1981, 81). Posthumous accounts in particular are inclined to ignore or rewrite content that does not fit neatly into a collective mythology (Hampton 1986, 6; Elliot 1999, 4). As a result, Umm Kulthūm has been remembered and memorialized as an ideal citizen—and specifically an ideal woman—in ways that sometimes contradict the events and choices of her life.

Looking beneath this layer of mythologized knowledge, one can discern in Umm Kulthūm a remarkable degree of individual agency, a topic that has attracted the attention of several ethnomusicologists (Rice 1987; Qureshi 2006; Barney 2007; Monson 2007; Dudley 2001, 2008). A close rereading of Danielson's study in a graduate seminar devoted primarily to women in jazz prompted me to refocus my earlier interest in Arabic music around the strengths of Umm Kulthūm's personality and their impact on her career. Having felt disturbed by recurring representations of women blues and jazz singers as troubled figures controlled by powerful men and prone to self-destruction through drugs, alcohol, and violent relationships, I was struck by the self-determination of the singer portrayed by Danielson. While Billie Holiday, for example, "was introduced" to other musicians and "was booked" for gigs by the men foregrounded in Nicholson's 1995 biography, the Umm Kulthūm in Danielson's account made her own artistic decisions, chose the musicians she wanted to work with, and handled financial matters shrewdly. She emerged as neither victim nor object of others' control and decisions. Rather, she emerged as a calculating subject.

Comparison with M. S. Subbulakshmi—India's "voice of the century," and a closer parallel—further highlights Umm Kulthūm's value for exploring women's agency. Seeking greater opportunities for success, both Umm Kulthūm and M. S. Subbulakshmi moved with their families to larger cities. Both benefited from the advent of the microphone, which allowed them to develop nuanced performance styles. Both were known for their careful pronunciation and the emotional intensity of their performances. Both came to dominate their respective markets for female singers in the 1940s. Audiences left both singers' concerts with feelings of ecstasy. Yet after M. S. married in her mid-twenties, her husband acted as her manager and cultivated her public persona (Weidman 2006, 124–27). Umm Kulthūm, in contrast, disentangled her performance career from that of her family, delayed marriage until her fifties, and maintained a remarkable degree of control over her career and her public persona. Her focused approach to her work, the high standards she set for herself and those around her, and her refusal to be deterred by challenges only enhance her appeal as a subject for examining the agency of women artists.

While some scholars, such as Ingrid Monson, have addressed an aesthetic agency focused on the shaping of a musical voice (2007, 318)—whether instrumental or vocal—I explore a broader agency that encompasses the shaping of both an artist's public image and her art. For this I use the term "artistic agency." In contrast to the compressed, accelerated process of image formation broadcast on a host of *American Idol*–type shows, image formation historically has been a protracted process requiring the ongoing construction, renewal, readjustment, and reconstruction of an image over several decades (Fairchild 2007; Mäkelä 2004, 219). In the case of Umm Kulthūm, such a process entailed the careful navigation of several national and international crises, several changes of national leadership, and several generations of listeners.

Acquiring and maintaining a sense of agency is valuable for stars, as a perceived lack of agency or voice can expose them to criticism (Lowe 2003, 138; Hawkins and Richardson 2007, 607). The comparison with M. S. Subbulakshmi reveals that Umm Kulthūm's control over her public image was quite strong, particularly in the second half of her career. As Richard Dyer has demonstrated, a star's image is constructed across a variety of media texts, and Umm Kulthūm played a major role in shaping many of these texts in the course of her career (Dyer 1998, 60–63).[9] To begin with, she shaped promotional texts—the materials consciously constructed to sell her and shape her image. For example, she displayed a consistent concern with her physical appearance in posed photographs, wearing conservative attire and placing a scarf over her skirt hem at her knees when seated. She also carefully shaped publicity texts—the seemingly more "authentic" information that the press "finds out." She orchestrated the release of information on a wide range of her activities, information that was often published as front-page news. And she played an important role in shaping her repertory and films—another type of media text—even changing the words of the poetry she sang (Danielson 1997, 89, 178). Her control spilled over into texts normally classified as criticism and commentary, as journalists and biographers testified after her death. Her agency and her active role in shaping her image and art stood in stark contrast to her contemporary Fayrūz, who was publicly ridiculed for her reticence and was seen as embodying an image and giving voice to a sound designed by ʿĀṣī and Manṣūr al-Raḥbānī rather than herself (Stone 2008, 156–59).[10]

While Umm Kulthūm's star image was shaped by traditional autobiographical texts, such as memoirs first published in the late 1930s (Danielson 1997, 165), it can also be understood to have been shaped by a wider range of autobiographical acts. I read much of her later career as a performance of "self" in the public eye, a "performed autobiography" encompassing a vast collection of carefully rendered autobiographical acts that were perceived as self-representations (Gale and Gardner 2004, 3; Bruss 1976, 4–7, 163; Hawkins and Richardson 2007, 607). Such a reading is supported by recent understandings of personal narratives as performative and autobiographies as hybrids of fiction and truth (Fay 2001a, 4; Nelson 2002, 211; Hawkins and Richardson 2007, 607; Golley 2003, 58). Samar Attar, reflecting on her experiments with autobiography, memoir, documentary, and fiction, discussed what has rarely been acknowledged by creators of autobiographies: "The self recalls the past, arranges the events, presents its history as something verifiable, claims responsibility for the creation and arrangement of the text, and is not sure whether it is itself an essence or a socially created construction" (Attar 2002, 221).

While these recent interpretations of personal narratives may seem to bridge the gap between written life stories and broader approaches to image formation, they do not evince clear boundaries between the public, the private, and the self. Longstanding distinctions between private and public selves no longer hold up. Thomas Postlewait explained that "theatre historians exploring theatre autobiographies 'may well find not only no separation can be established between face and mask, presence and absence, private and public personality, life and art, but also that even these dualisms are too neat because they split identity, documents, and historical conditions in ways that are reductive'" (1989, 259, quoted in Gale and Gardner 2004, 3).

In the absence of such neat distinctions, an artist's presentation of self to the public is constructed and consumed through a complex set of references to the private. Consumption of the star image—"all that is publicly known about the star"—often stimulates a desire to penetrate what has been withheld (Gledhill 1991, 214–17, quoted in Mäkelä 2004, 19). Amid growing awareness of the constructed nature of star images, audiences readily dissect the star image in an effort to understand the star as person (Rojek 2001, 19). In this pursuit, the public places great value on the perceived private, evidenced by stars' claims that they desperately wish to preserve their privacy and the fact that it cannot be purchased easily (Cowen 2000, 131). The perceived private is often exposed when the gap between the person and the star image is decipherable in promotional texts (Dyer 1998, 61). Once evidence of the star as person becomes public knowledge, it forms part of the star image and the excavation process must begin again. As a result, whether they wish to or not, stars must constantly maintain the border between public knowledge and what remains private.

While people who lead largely private lives often have no choice but to make the private the subject of autobiography and therefore transform it into the public,[11] stars often decide to use a mixture of the public and the perceived private as a means of crafting their star image. Umm Kulthūm divulged this "private" knowledge on her own terms. She often withheld information when questioned about love and her family life, topics that were well known to be off-limits to journalists. Nevertheless, on certain occasions and in certain texts she deliberately disclosed information that she wanted known in order to construct a public image founded on ideals of piety and motherhood. She followed the path of actors, who "have used, and use, autobiography and performance as a means of expression and 'control' of their public selves, of both the 'face and the mask'" (Gale and Gardner 2004, 3).

What makes Umm Kulthūm's agency in shaping her public image especially noteworthy is the high degree of influence that she ultimately wielded over her posthumous reception. Artists' image-shaping efforts—particularly midcareer adjustments—may be devalued, misconstrued, ignored, or neutralized after their deaths. Josephine Baker's transformation from sex symbol to maternal figure in the late 1930s was forgotten, Elvis Presley's overhaul of his rebellious image in the early 1960s has been devalued, and the househusband image that John Lennon cultivated in the late 1970s was largely overshadowed by the mythology of heroic martyrdom that took hold after his death.[12] In Umm Kulthūm's case, however, the patriotic role that she cultivated so prominently during her later career is foregrounded in posthumous accounts. Her influence over her posthumous reception marks an extension of the high degree of musical control and image control that she exerted during her lifetime (Danielson 1997, 183–84).

A significant part of Umm Kulthūm's influence over her posthumous reception can be traced to her alignment of herself with powerful national symbols. As S. Paige Baty explained, "It is possible to approach specific cultural subjects as they have been and continue to be made, and in doing so to approach the narrations of nation, the rememberings of political culture, as companion pieces to articulations of single and collective selves" (1995, 36). Umm Kulthūm facilitated such readings in the final years of her career, when she ensconced herself in a host of national symbols and cast herself as one of them. As written life narratives have the ability "to construct or affirm the identity of an individual, of a group . . . or of a community . . . or the modern nation-state" (Fay 2001a, 2), Umm Kulthūm's star image, both in her lifetime and after her death, has come to represent and affirm the identity of individuals in the Arab diaspora, generations of Egyptians in relation to a series of polarizing political figures, and the state itself. This may explain why her posthumous reception has not matched the progression common for other cultural heroes: initial idealized accounts born of grief give way to criticism, and then to reconciliation (Mäkelä 2004, 221). Biased accounts of artists' lives—whether glowing or critical—often emerge in an attempt to "keep at bay the ambivalence and ambiguity of individual subjectivity" (Elliot 1999, 33). Absent from Umm Kulthūm's reception have been the boldly critical accounts, like Albert Goldman's *The Lives of John Lennon* (1988), which claimed to reveal shocking truths about Lennon's private life. Negative accounts of Umm Kulthūm have largely been excluded from print and confined to oral tradition even after her death. Once she shaped herself into a national symbol, criticizing her became tantamount to slandering the nation itself.

In addition to examining the formation of the star image, with an emphasis on individual agency, this study contributes to a growing body of literature on music's relationships to politics. Scholars have increasingly turned their attention to the role of music and musicians in negotiating state politics and bolstering regimes. Focusing on China and Zaire, respectively, Nimrod Baranovitch (2003) and Bob White (2008) have addressed state attempts to control a popular music scene and the value of music in disseminating state ideology and consolidating its hegemony. Articulating substantive and symbolic links between popular dance music and political culture in Mobutu's Zaire, White explored the ways in which the political system rewarded musicians' public displays of loyalty and used money and violence to control them. His study of how musicians' responsive strategies of public praise, self-censorship, and showmanship became integral parts of the aesthetics and performance of popular dance music counters a musicological tendency to dismiss explicitly political music as less sophisticated artistically and less worthy of study than music with multiple, implicit meanings. White's study points to the importance of closely examining Umm Kulthūm's patriotic songs and other public acts of support for ʿAbd al-Nāṣir.

Scholars have also addressed the role of music and musicians in defining nations and national subjects. Within the Middle East, Chris Stone explored the role of the Baalbek festival in disseminating a particular vision of the Lebanese nation (2008). Monson investigated the roles that jazz played in shaping and responding to African nationalist movements in the 1950s and 1960s (2007). In Asia, J. Lawrence Witzleben examined the role of music in the Hong Kong handover ceremonies of 1997, the purpose of which was "teaching the community to re-imagine itself" (2002, 130). Music enabled the events to articulate selected political ideals—including internationalization, multiculturalism, patriotism, nationalism, and a reunited motherland—while ignoring specific political realities, such as the history of dictatorship, racial discrimination, economic suffering, and political repression. From a musicological perspective, Marcus Rathey (2007) addressed music's role in fostering patriotism within a smaller community. Focusing on C. P. E. Bach in Hamburg, Rathey demonstrated how Bach's oratorios and serenades staged an idealized patriotism and contributed to contemporary literature stressing the importance of law, industriousness, modesty, virtue, and the communal fight against internal and external threats to the law of the land.

My study of Umm Kulthūm's later career and posthumous reception contributes not only to this examination of music's role in defining nations and national subjects but also to a growing cross-disciplinary literature addressing the political significance of music and musicians during times of crisis. As Christina Gier has explained, "The social role of music in violent conflicts is multifaceted. Both a vehicle for propaganda and an agent of comfort, music in wartime produces a complex web of pleasure, power, and identity" (2008, 4). Music shapes the identity of those on and off the battlefield in times of conflict. Thus, Gier finds that the masculinity of the World War I soldier was manipulated through song, musical affect, and representations of women (19). Singing was used as a tool to promote unit cohesion, mental discipline, physical strength, and, as a consequence, greater efficacy on the battlefield (5). Music is also often used to influence those manning the home front. During World War II, Tin Pan Alley songs promoted national unity, moral and spiritual support for soldiers, and morale and active national involvement at home, showcasing specific projects such as women's work, bond drives, rationing, and salvage efforts (Jones 2006, 180–214). Many of Umm Kulthūm's efforts following the 1967 defeat were similarly devoted to promoting thrift, public donations, and women's charitable work, as well as public cohesion after the traumatic resignation of ʿAbd al-Nāṣir.

What is remarkable about Umm Kulthūm's reception is the durability of the political significance of her music and image. Despite the power of music during times of crisis, its political meaning can erode over time. After uncovering the significance of Aaron Copland's music in relation to Progressivism, Communism, and the Popular Front during the Great Depression and World War II, Elizabeth Crist concluded that his music has endured because it has been largely emptied of such political significance (2005, 200–201). In contrast, Umm Kulthūm's political relevance was not forgotten or erased, but both reinforced and enriched. Members of subsequent generations have invoked her name, music, and image to address an array of contemporary political challenges. Within Egypt, the changing needs of the al-Sādāt and Mubārak regimes prompted starkly contrasting treatments of her image and legacy. Outside Egypt, those troubled by the Palestinian-Israeli conflict, misguided foreign policy, and political incompetence have harnessed her image and music to promote peace, raise the profile of oppressed communities, and challenge unresponsive leaders.

Umm Kulthūm's posthumous mythologization and the political significance resonating from her postwar career have intersected in complex ways in the decades since her death. Through careful fashioning of her later career, she established the foundation for her reception as a nation's hero in its time of crisis. She emerged as a powerful embodiment of a nostalgic fantasy of Arab will, unity, and strength in the face of imperialist powers and a redeemer of national honor. Her posthumous idealization as the mother of the nation went beyond this, not only encapsulating her patriotism and self-sacrifice but also reconciling her unconventional life choices with her gendered location as an Egyptian woman. Her long life and posthumous reception overlapped with important shifts in the perception of marriage and sexuality in the Middle East, and biographers and filmmakers have worked to gloss the ways in which this icon's life seemed to deviate from cultural norms. As marriage shifted from being seen as a procreative relationship to a romantic one, and as understanding sexuality through the lens of identity came into increasing conflict with understanding it through the lens of acts, key facets of Umm Kulthūm's life may well have rendered her an imperfect icon (Najmabadi 2005; Massad 2007). Her elevation to the status of a nation's figurative mother resulted from a strategy to cast her as fulfilling cultural expectations such as romantic marriage, maternalism, and normative heterosexuality.

In addition to exploring intersections between music and politics, a study of Umm Kulthūm's later career and reception history can extend recent testing of the disciplinary boundaries that have traditionally separated musicological and ethnomusicological inquiry. As illustrated by the work of Danielson and Veal (2000), the study of the individual artist, with its noticeable reliance on archival research, can further the cross-disciplinary efforts of scholars like Kingsbury (1988) and Shelemay (2001). The biographical study of musicians outside the Western classical canon can help demonstrate alternatives to traditional methods and lines of inquiry. As a performer rather than a composer, Umm Kulthūm offers us an opportunity to develop and demonstrate a different approach to the problem of relating an artist's life and artistic production. To do so, I adopt a broad conception of performance that encompasses both Umm Kulthūm's musical performance and her public presentation of self (Crane 2002; Royce 1982). I avoid both the disconnection of artist and art, seen in "life and works" studies (Osborne 2007; Tarasti 1995; Kenton 1967), and the treatment of artistic production as a direct expression of self, seen in psychoanalytic studies (Chipman 2000, 2004; Downes 1996; Brophy 1988).

This study also facilitates further questioning of the categories of "classical" and "popular" music that continue to shape much research. As an individual artist, Umm Kulthūm resisted this division by making lastingly popular among several social strata highly sophisticated artistic forms that were distant from colloquial expression. Ali Jihad Racy argued that music in Cairo and other large cities in the Levant eluded simple division into classical and popular categories (1981)—a view extended by Ruth Davis to Tunisia (2003, 125–29). Instead, Racy saw the music of Cairo as "a group of overlapping and interconnected musical domains" (1981, 11). Intersecting a central domain were peripheral ones of folk music, religious music, Western art music, Western popular music, and music predating 1919, with individual compositions often drawing on several of these styles. Racy cautioned that paradigmatic approaches rooted in distinctions between classical music and popular music offered "limited utility" for research on world music (22). Even as Umm Kulthūm's career illustrates the inapplicability of these categories, her music has been judged through them, with art music values fueling a tendency to dismiss her patriotic songs, which may be seen to fall short in their musical complexity. An examination of her later career and reception history offers a valuable opportunity to revisit Racy's caution about urban music scenes in the Levant nearly three decades later.

As a largely historical study, this book draws on extensive research using written sources available in the United States and Egypt. These sources include dozens of newspapers and magazines published in Egypt and the Arab world. During my fourteen months in Cairo beginning in early 2003, I also spoke with many Egyptians and Arab visitors about the singer, including leading journalists who covered her later career, media figures, and ordinary Egyptians of several generations. In addition, I viewed and collected a large number of audio-visual materials, including original recordings housed in the archives of the Egyptian Radio and Television Union. Although it has not been possible to include these audio and video recordings along with this text, I encourage readers to explore online resources such as YouTube, where footage of the singer's concerts abroad and recordings of her late songs can often be found.

The first three chapters of this book examine Umm Kulthūm's final years. Chapter 1 articulates 1967 as a turning point in her career. With her multifaceted response to the Six-Day War, she sustained her career through an extraordinary fifth decade. Her high-profile charitable efforts and production of new patriotic songs redefined her relevance for Egyptian society and lent vital support to the Egyptian regime. Her efforts foregrounded the patriotism that remains one of the most conspicuous elements of her legend today.

Chapter 2 examines the personal, local, and pan-Arab significance of her Arab world concerts of 1968. Her concerts across North Africa and the Middle East intensified her relationships with listeners outside Egypt and brought her numerous international honors. At the same time, she reinforced the Egyptian regime's efforts to address both domestic and international challenges. She used her trips to cultivate a powerful demonstration of pan-Arab cultural unity intended to ease the psychological blow delivered by the war of June 1967. While abandoning her regular series of concerts within Egypt, she continued to build her image as a selfless patriot devoted to her country.

Chapter 3 articulates her final years of public activity as a vital time of survival and legacy-building through speech, action, song, image, and print. Following ʿAbd al-Nāṣir's death, she strived to continue her career through the ascendancy of Anwar al-Sādāt and a first lady intent on marking the transfer of political leadership through artistic change. Umm Kulthūm portrayed herself as mother, believer, humanitarian, and patriot through detailed autobiographical accounts, a carefully crafted return to the religious repertory of her youth, proliferating charitable initiatives, and conspicuous stances on the Palestinian issue. At the same time, she promoted an expansion of her international status, spurred her own entry into the *turāth* (heritage), and laid the foundation for her memorialization through physical monuments.

Chapters 4 through 6 examine Umm Kulthūm's reception after her death, revealing the processes and agendas that have transformed her public persona into an internationally relevant legend. In particular, chapters 4 and 5 evaluate dozens of print and film accounts of her life that have emerged since 1975. While Danielson rightly raised and addressed the question of "why she became so important" (1997, 195), chapter 4 looks into "why and how she has remained so important" as a revered icon after her death. In chapter 5, I analyze a variety of strategies that authors and filmmakers have used to reconcile her unconventional life choices as an Egyptian woman with cultural expectations and perceptions of gender and sexuality. The singer emerges in these chapters as an important site for defining the values and ideals of the nation and for defining womanhood.

In chapter 6, I examine Umm Kulthūm's role as part of an evolving heritage with international reach. I consider both physical memorials, such as the Umm Kulthūm museum and cafés, as well as sonic memorialization achieved through radio programming practices, cover songs, and remixes. As part of the *turāth*, she has become an attractive subject of reconstruction efforts by artists and cultural producers across the Middle East and the Arab diaspora. Artists from the United States and Israel have also explored the "enhanced use value" of her image and art, imbuing them with a host of contemporary political and social meanings (Buxton 1990, 429). As efforts to memorialize Umm Kulthūm have been motivated by remarkably diverse agendas, including several political ones, they exemplify Barbara Kirshenblatt-Gimblett's characterization of heritage as "a new mode of cultural production in the present that has recourse to the past" (1995, 369–70). These representations have both sustained and challenged key aspects of Umm Kulthūm's public persona and have targeted a variety of audiences. In doing so, they have effectively articulated her relevance for an expanding international audience during the three and a half decades since her death.

CHAPTER I

"A New Umm Kulthūm"

To understand the particular reverence that Umm Kulthūm has been accorded in the decades after her death, one must first explore the details and context of her public life in 1967. The landmark event of that year was the defeat of Egypt—along with Syria and Jordan—in the Six-Day War, a rapid defeat that precipitated a lasting psychological, economic, and military crisis. Amid this crisis, Umm Kulthūm was unable to continue giving three-hour concerts of romantic songs as she had done before the war. Retirement offered one alternative. Yet once she had actually been blamed by some for the defeat (Danielson 1997, 185), the implications of retirement would have cast a pall over her otherwise illustrious career and damaged her image. She rejected both retirement and the continuation of her career as before, instead constructing a new role for herself in the years ahead. She used press statements, charitable efforts, and propaganda work to refashion herself as an artist of new, vital importance to Egypt in its time of need. Remarkably, she not only sustained her career but also developed a strategy to fulfill previously made commitments abroad that had been designed to advance her career and expand her international fame.

Umm Kulthūm, like other artists, demonstrated the political value of music in times of crisis. Examples abound from the perspective of mid-twentieth-century America. The U.S. State Department dispatched jazz and rhythm and blues musicians overseas in tours designed to counteract the country's racist image, which was poised to push newly independent states abroad into alliance with the Soviet Union. Though placed in horrid conditions and largely ignored by embassy officials, these artists helped achieve the State Department's goal of changing attitudes about the United States: of the various tours held between 1956 and 1969, audiences abroad were particularly impressed to see Dizzy Gillespie leading an interracial band (Monson 2007, 107–108, 117, 119). While these U.S. efforts were aimed at achieving political goals abroad, Umm Kulthūm's addressed political problems at home. She performed songs expressing varied sentiments for different purposes. This was not all that different from the use of country songs in the United States during World War II and the Korean War. Artists on the NBC Radio Network's *National Barn Dance* presented songs designed to "inspire, motivate, and console a nation at war" (Daniel 2005, 92). Likewise, Umm Kulthūm's performances celebrated a victory that never would be achieved, supported a troubled leader, and reaffirmed religious faith, as many Korean War–era country songs did (Tribe 2005, 128–30, 137–38). Ultimately, following the defeat, her songs shifted in tone, much like country songs shifted from "smug self-confidence" to somber self-reflection once the American public realized that World War II would be a long haul (Wolfe 2005, 31).

As Umm Kulthūm went on to develop her public role as a fundraiser and leader of social and welfare campaigns in 1967, she adopted a stance like that of many U.S. musicians during World War II. Radio singer Kate Smith and the hillbilly and western entertainers in the *National Barn Dance* used their renown to spur public participation in nationwide war bond and stamp drives (Merton 1946). Admission to the cross-country *National Barn Dance* shows was granted through the purchase of a war bond or donation of materials that were in short supply. *National Barn Dance* entertainers themselves toured the United States on behalf of the USO to provide social, welfare, and recreational service for members of the armed forces and their families. They also demonstrated practical ways of dealing with difficult wartime conditions. In traveling by bicycle and using carpools, *National Barn Dance* artists showed members of the public how to cope with the ban on the production of civilian vehicles (Daniel 2005, 87–92, 97).

While such efforts served government agendas, they also shaped artists' images. In a striking case of this phenomenon, Elvis Presley's charitable activities in 1961 reinforced careful media coverage of his military service to transform his rebellious image (Inglis 1996, 62–63). A closer parallel to Umm Kulthūm is offered by Kate Smith, who led several all-day war bond drives during World War II. Public perception of Smith's sincerity, benevolence, and patriotism led Americans to respond in astonishing numbers to her marathon appeals, while her participation demonstrated that a public entertainer could acquire the traits of a moral leader (Merton 1946, 76, 82). Intensive interviews conducted shortly after Smith's bond drive on September 21, 1943, offered Robert Merton unusually specific insights into public perceptions of an artist engaged in a public campaign. While no similar study was conducted following Umm Kulthūm's postwar campaign, the Smith study suggests several parallels. The physical demands of Smith's eighteen-hour marathon of appeals, her efforts to cast herself as one of the "plain folk," and her humility underscored perceptions of sincerity. Guided by these cues, listeners interpreted Smith's efforts as acts of selflessness rather than attempts to gain publicity and enhance her own reputation (Merton 1946, 86, 90, 98–99, 155). Umm Kulthūm's campaign would be framed in a similar way, as the media stressed her extraordinary work ethic and her status as an ordinary citizen. As a result, despite initially having been blamed by some for the 1967 defeat, by year's end she emerged as the shining example of a patriotic artist willing to sacrifice herself for the sake of her country.

The defeat that stunned Egypt and the Arab world in 1967 was the product of decades of international turmoil.[1] In 1917, Britain pledged to facilitate the creation of a Jewish national home in Palestine, and the Jewish community swelled through waves of immigration. In 1947, a United Nations resolution outlined the establishment of two states, one Arab and one Jewish, but such a partition was foiled by ensuing Palestinian-Jewish violence. After alternative solutions had been rejected, the Jewish leadership declared independence in 1948, and the Arab-Israeli war of that year led to a Palestinian exodus, a solid Jewish majority, and an Israeli gain of 30 percent more territory than specified in the UN resolution. Territories intended to be part of the Arab Palestinian state were annexed by Jordan and occupied by Egypt. The General Armistice Agreements of 1949, which opened the door to Arabs to renew hostilities at will, only perpetuated the conflict.

Within Egypt, President Jamāl 'Abd al-Nāṣir kept the Palestinian issue "in the icebox" in the early 1950s, downplaying the conflict with Israel while supporting a moderate level of Palestinian guerilla activity. He intensified his support for the guerillas beginning in the mid-1950s. In 1956, 'Abd al-Nāṣir nationalized the Suez Canal, spurring the Tripartite Aggression, during which Israeli forces—supported by the French and British—gained control of the Sinai Peninsula, Gaza, and the Straits of Tiran. Replacing them in the next year was the United Nations Emergency Force, stationed along the Egypt-Israel border in Sinai, in Gaza, and in Sharm al-Shaykh. Turbulent inter-Arab relations in subsequent years swung from divisiveness toward cooperation in 1964. The Cairo summit of that year established the United Arab Command, which was aimed at strengthening Arab military efforts and redeeming Palestine.

Tensions along Israel's borders increased in the mid-1960s. In November 1966, Israel attacked Palestinian villages near Hebron in retaliation for aiding the Palestinian nationalist movement Fatah. Although Israel's move had been intended as a warning to its neighbors, Syrian tanks responded by shelling a kibbutz over the border in January 1967. As border incidents escalated and relations among Egyptian, Jordanian, and Syrian leaders deteriorated, the Soviet Union repeatedly warned that Israeli troops were massing on the northern border with Syria. In early spring, Syrian sponsorship of Palestinian guerilla attacks on Israel prompted a miniwar. Soviet leaders reasserted their warnings, advising former vice president Anwar al-Sādāt that Israel intended to invade Syria between May 16 and 22 to topple the Baʿth Party leadership.

ʿAbd al-Nāṣir, criticized by Arab leaders for his inaction during Israel's previous reprisals following guerilla attacks, could not sit idly by this time. Although the Egyptian army and air force were stretched thin due to a protracted conflict in Yemen and spending constraints, Egyptian troops were directed to cross the Sinai Peninsula in mid-May. Their conspicuous movements simultaneously suggested a lack of aggressive Egyptian intent and an intolerance for Israeli aggression against Syria. Independence Day celebrations diverted the attention of ordinary Israelis and their leaders from the impending crisis. Egyptian troop buildup continued, rousing fears that Egypt had designs on the Dimona nuclear reactor, and Israel turned to the long-planned Operation Focus as it prepared to take preemptive action.

Meanwhile, ʿAbd al-Nāṣir ignored evidence that Israeli troops had, in fact, *not* gathered near the Syrian border, knowing that withdrawal of his Egyptian troops from Sinai would bring untenable humiliation whereas continued buildup would enhance his standing. The growing crisis provided Egypt with the opportunity to satisfy a long-standing desire to expel the United Nations Emergency Force. As national and international tensions mounted, ʿAbd al-Nāṣir closed the Straits of Tiran to Israeli shipping, providing Israel with a *casus belli*. Military maneuvers shifted from political to strategic in nature. Arab armies were activated in Lebanon, Kuwait, Saudi Arabia, and Iraq. Egyptian field marshal ʿAbd al-Ḥakīm ʿĀmir implemented an offensive operation, code-named Dawn, which was quickly canceled upon its discovery by the Israelis. At the same time, U.S. appeals halted Israel's own preemptive attack.

Although both Israel and Egypt had momentarily decided not to make the first strike, a series of portentous, rapidly unfolding events brought war ever closer. On the Arab side, military contingents from Morocco, Libya, Saudi Arabia, and Tunisia were sent to the Sinai Peninsula. Amid repeated American pleas for restraint, leaders of the Israel Defense Forces continued to call up reserves. Jordan's King Ḥussayn hurried to align himself with ʿAbd al-Nāṣir, ordering tanks across the Jordan River near Jericho and signing a mutual defense treaty with Egypt that paralleled one signed by Syria and Egypt in 1966. The Jordanian king's moves increased pressure on Israel to fight. An impending sense of catastrophe pervaded Israel, and international public support swelled as the country faced a multifront attack from Egypt, Syria, and Jordan.

As Egypt moved closer to war during the last week in May, Umm Kulthūm provided financial and moral support. She promised special benefit concerts for the armed forces and donated £E 5,000 to the war effort ("Umm Kulthūm tatabarra'" 1967). She increasingly exercised the political approach she had adopted in the early 1960s (Danielson 1997, 165). Her low, determined voice resonated through the radio airwaves, assuring soldiers in Sinai, "I am with you, with the millions, in the appointment with victory," followed by one of seven spoken appeals that she had cowritten ("Nidā'āt" 1967; 'Aṭīyah 1967). In one such appeal, she predicted an Arab liberation of Palestine, achieved under Egyptian leadership:

> Our fearless soldiers, when you were on the way to the borders, the past fortified me. I saw her—a young girl trembling with fear and terror under the bullets of the enemy. I saw him say, "Tomorrow, that could be my daughter." You know the girl. The girl is Palestine. And you know the man—our man, Jamāl 'Abd al-Nāṣir. Where is this girl today, to hear his voice calling you to her? God will help you as long as you help her ("Sab'a nidā'āt" 1967).

Umm Kulthūm fed an overconfidence common among the Egyptian public and military leadership.[2] She stressed 'Abd al-Nāṣir's past victories and predicted another, declaring in one interview: "I myself will sing in Tel Aviv this year!" ("Rajul al-shāri'" 1967; al-Bandārī 1967). Just four days before the outbreak of the war, she opened her regular monthly concert with a new patriotic song that boosted confidence and enthusiasm across the region. During the live broadcast, radio announcer Jalāl Mu'awwud framed the concert by stressing the coordinated participation of multinational forces under Egyptian leadership. In his portrayal, "The Arabs stand as one to face the one enemy, to confront Israel and those who stand behind Israel. . . . The Arab armies stand under a united leadership . . . to return with armed force the claim of the Arab Palestinian people to the land of Arab Palestine" ("Allāh Ma'ak" 1967). Though marred by uncharacteristic errors in performance because the song had been arranged quickly, the premiere of "Allāh Ma'ak" ("God Is with You") stirred listeners enough to be described as "an atomic bomb that unleashed the feelings of the masses in the region from the gulf to the ocean" ("Ughnīyat Umm Kulthūm" 1967).[3] Opening with driving eighth notes in the timpani and a rapid ascent and descent through the bright *jahārkāh* mode (similar to the major mode), the song quickly captured the audience's attention. The male chorus intensified the energy of the performance with aggressive upward leaps and crisp dotted rhythms. With triplets that were lyrical by contrast, Umm Kulthūm assured the joined forces, "Army of Arabness, God is with you." Proceeding by rising melodic sequence, her declamation accentuated

Beginning of "Allāh Maʿak." Music by Riyāḍ al-Sunbāṭī, lyrics by Ṣalāḥ Jāhīn. Composed and recorded in 1967. *Aghānī waṭanīyah li Sayyidat al-Ghināʾ al-ʿArabī Umm Kulthūm*, vol. 1. Ṣawt al-Qāhirah 00/031/401, D00/1015. Audiocassette.

the superlative description of the armed forces, and built tension as she invoked the anticipated liberation of Palestine. The verse drew strong cheers from those in the hall, as did nearly every other verse of the song ("Allāh Ma'ak" 1967).

Umm Kulthūm nourished this feverish atmosphere by programming two religious songs, rather than two romantic songs, as the second and third selections. The "surprise" song she had promised turned out to be "Salū Qalbī," which had fallen out of her repertory after its premiere two decades earlier. Aḥmad Shawqī's text commemorating the Prophet's birth contained the potent lines "Demands are not met by wishing; the world can only be taken by struggle." In the 1940s, these lines had been heard as a nationalist motto expressing dissatisfaction with the British presence in Egypt and with King Farūq (Danielson 1997, 113–14). Now they were reframed by Jalāl Mu'awwud's introductory comments as a call for immediate action to reclaim Palestinian land, and Umm Kulthūm's audience demanded numerous repetitions of this climactic line ("Salū Qalbī" 1967). She ended the concert with a recent song, "Ḥadīth al-Rūḥ," and its lines intensified faith in the outcome of the impending war: "Who began to shout your name before us? Who invoked the One, the Subduer? . . . We declare publicly, there is no God except He who created existence and the fate of fates." The enthusiastic response from the audience underscored the importance of faith and fate that Umm Kulthūm had articulated through "Allāh Ma'ak" ("Ḥadīth al-Rūḥ" 1967).[4] Her unusual but timely program prompted the invigorated audience to denounce imperialism and urge the nation's armed forces to victory (Farghalá 1967). Their response resonated throughout Egypt as the concert was broadcast on television (Darwīsh 1967).

As Umm Kulthūm stoked popular expectations of victory, plans for a military offensive military were canceled just days after being implemented. Assurances of victory and invincibility masked the chaos that would soon unfold in Sinai (Oren 2002, 93, 159). Unwilling to draw international rebuke for striking first, Egypt ultimately fell victim to an Israeli air offensive honed through several years of planning. Within just three hours on the morning of June 5, Israeli jets destroyed the Egyptian air force by targeting both runways and parked aircraft. Lacking air cover and saddled by inefficient communication, the Egyptian army suffered a crushing defeat during the next four days.

Aftermath

The public mood was subjected to dramatic shifts after the cease-fire was declared. Initially boosted by false reports of military successes, Arabs were shocked and dismayed by the regime's surrender. Egyptians secretly called 'Abd al-Nāṣir *al-waḥsh* (the beast), Algerians shouted "Traitor!" and attacked the Egyptian embassy, and protestors in Tunis set fire to the Egyptian cultural center. Yet the next day, June 9, brought an entirely different response. When 'Abd al-Nāṣir announced his resignation in a live television broadcast, hundreds of thousands of Egyptians swept into the street shouting, "Don't leave us!"[5] Demonstrators also filled Beirut's streets, while a hospital in the Libyan capital admitted dozens of people with "their bodies rigid in a hypnotic trauma."[6] Across the region, Arabs suffered pronounced physical and psychological symptoms as a result of the defeat, and many Egyptians in particular remained dazed for weeks (Farid 1994, 103; Hussein 1977, 25).

Although Westerners have long doubted that the massive public about-face in Cairo could have occurred without orchestration by government entities, a catalyst for the response can be found in 'Abd al-Nāṣir's June 9 speech itself.[7] 'Abd al-Nāṣir cast Egypt as the victim of international manipulation, citing foreign pressure on the nation not to fire first and "imperialist collusion" behind Israel's victory.[8] He also assured listeners that the war would continue, while expressing his willingness to take responsibility for the immediate outcome. Thereafter, he asked the public to help him in his decision to "give up every official post and political role." Having invoked a continued fight against colluding international forces, however, 'Abd al-Nāṣir chose a successor, Zakariyā Muḥī al-Dīn, who seemed incapable of fulfilling the task ahead. 'Abd al-Nāṣir then stoked listeners' feelings of abandonment as he recited all the country's accomplishments under his leadership. He left his distraught audience with the directive "This is an hour for action" ('Abd al-Nāṣir 1992a).[9] In inviting fellow Egyptians to join him in keeping up the fight against humiliation by "imperialist" powers, 'Abd al-Nāṣir gave them the opportunity to reject his abdication. Egyptians filled the streets demanding that honor and dignity be restored and that he stay in power (Oren 2002, 288). In Beirut, listeners attacked symbols of a foreign presence by smashing and burning American and British businesses, and a Libyan mob stormed the British embassy in Tripoli (Morris 1967; Fawaz 1998; Munro 2000, 67). Buoyed by public support, 'Abd al-Nāṣir rescinded his resignation on June 10. He accepted the resignations of key regime and staff members and consolidated his power by assuming the roles of prime minister and secretary general of the Arab Socialist Union (founded in 1962 as the nation's sole political party) while continuing to lead as supreme commander.

Although bedridden by illness for a week during the war, Umm Kulthūm took multifaceted action in support of 'Abd al-Nāṣir at its close (Jawdat 1967). She was the first of a group of artists to write a letter supporting him after his resignation. She commended him as a successful leader, expressed faith in his ability to continue the battle, and carefully recharacterized the war as one initiated by Egyptian action rather than a response to a surprise attack:

> Life without respect and honor has no value. And it will only have value with the liberation of the stolen homeland. The battle that we plunged into boldly is the decisive battle. The battle of respect. The battle of honor. (Umm Kulthūm 1967)

She then began work on a musical expression of this support in the song "Ḥabīb al-Sha'b," or "The People's Beloved" ("Umm Kulthūm taghannā taḥīyat" 1967). She also donated a £20,000 (sterling) payment received from Kuwaiti radio to help rebuild the Egyptian military (al-Malākh 1967c).

By the end of June, Umm Kulthūm's swift response to the country's needs drew accolades. The press chastised other artists for their relative inactivity and stinginess. This contrast was demonstrated strikingly on the cover of the popular magazine *al-Kawākib*, which asked, "Where Are 'Abd al-Wahhāb and Farīd al-Aṭrash in the Battle?" while announcing one of Umm Kulthūm's new patriotic songs on June 27, 1967. Inside the issue, Fūmīl Labīb wondered why the famously efficient composer Farīd al-Aṭrash had not yet written songs for the war effort (1967b). Contributor Ṣāliḥ Jawdat launched a scathing attack on other artists:

> One of them donated £E 10 to the battle. Another donated £E 20. I learn that the former drives a car that costs no less than £E 3,000. These £E 10 do not even amount to the cost of the benzene that it burns each month. The latter earns more than £E 3,000 in one film and her £E 20 do not amount to the cost of the cheapest of her dresses. The family of art, these—do they not sense that the country is in a severe trial and that their sacrifice for the battle, with other citizens in different spheres, is the means of escaping the trial, and that if they do not sacrifice for the battle, they will be in the vanguard of its victims? (1967).

While other artists elicited journalists' attacks, Umm Kulthūm was held up as a model. Citing her as an "impressive and unrivaled example of the Arabs' profound love for their good land," Muḥammad Jalāl called artists to follow her lead and donate to the cause (1967).[10] Fūmīl Labīb placed her "at the head of this artistic battle" and praised her for confirming "that the great artist who sits on the throne of art also sits on the throne of sacrifice" (1967b).

To Work

While 'Abd al-Nāṣir's resignation speech had quickly roused the support of a shocked public, different tactics were needed to sustain that support once the challenges of daily existence came to the fore. A severe shortage of hard currency made life difficult throughout Egypt. Yet the Egyptian press took steps to set these troubles in context, cultivating cross-class support for the leader and the regime with strong visual images, such as a drawing of a resolute peasant standing next to a soldier behind ʿAbd al-Nāṣir. The caption reminded readers of the fifteen years the people had spent "under the leadership of Jamāl ʿAbd al-Nāṣir, rushing into battles, realizing victories, transcending challenges, and surmounting difficulties" ("al-Niḍāl" 1967). Magazine pages showcased stacks of letters from Westerners supporting ʿAbd al-Nāṣir (ʿAbd al-Laṭīf 1967). In her new song "Ḥabīb al-Shaʿb," Umm Kulthūm reminded the public of its earlier demand that ʿAbd al-Nāṣir stay in power. While she echoed their shouts, singing "Stay, for you are the people's remaining hope," she also voiced what the regime wanted people to feel and think. Singing lyrics by the poet-journalist Ṣāliḥ Jawdat, she directed listeners' attention to the "continuing" war and referred to ʿAbd al-Nāṣir as the people's beloved and protector, the leader needed to "Push us beyond the Naksah and raise the head of the nation." Broadcast almost daily in July, the song was aimed at consolidating support for ʿAbd al-Nāṣir by repeating the demonstrators' notion that he was their only hope.[11]

The public was called upon not only to support ʿAbd al-Nāṣir but also to help the country cope with its grave financial problems. Egypt was set to lose nearly $450 million in annual revenues from tourism, Suez Canal shipping, and oil reserves in Sinai, which Israel now controlled. These losses resulted in a sudden shortage of hard currency just as funds were most needed to rebuild the military. On this front, Soviet arms shipments began arriving immediately after the war and Arab countries quickly offered $58 million in government aid (Oren 2002, 286; Feiler 2003, 6). A leading journalist called for the financial equivalent of a blood bank in late June, and throughout July, the public was urged to make cash, gold, and material donations (al-Tābiʿī 1967).

Umm Kulthūm played a visible role by coordinating people's contributions. She first asked those working in her villa to donate their gold to the burgeoning war effort and then worked with a youth organization to aid the injured (al-Bahī 2000; al-Malākh 1967d). She also sought to create a broader organizational structure to mount a multifaceted response to the war. A month after the cease-fire, she called a comprehensive meeting of national women's organizations. More than one hundred representatives of twenty-five different groups formed an umbrella organization, the National Assembly of Egyptian Women (NAEW). Members met daily in Umm Kulthūm's home to organize their work and established committees to direct their efforts on four fronts: thrift, hospital work, communication, and the collection of donations ('Abd al-Ḥayy 1967b; al-Bīlī 1967). Citizens came to donate cash and gold jewelry at the assembly's initial meetings ("Umm Kulthūm tuqarrir" 1967).[12]

Umm Kulthūm characterized the collection campaign as one that spanned generations, regions, and classes, and the public responded accordingly (al-Bīlī 1967). In Giza, a couple and their three children presented forty-one grams of gold jewelry, while a peasant woman donated a small bracelet ("Umm Kulthūm sallamat" 1967). By the end of one week, Umm Kulthūm presented to the Bank of Cairo sixteen kilograms of gold collected through the NAEW. She also urged citizens to donate ordinary clothes, which supported the assembly's goal of aiding the hundreds of thousands of refugees streaming west from the canal area that was still rocked by clashes between Egyptian and Israeli forces ("Umm Kulthūm tusāfir" 1967; al-Malākh 1967g). By creating this larger organizational apparatus, Umm Kulthūm helped people participate in a productive and cathartic response to the war rather than feel like powerless and passive victims in the face of national crisis.

Not content to run the assembly as a figurehead, Umm Kulthūm participated in every facet of its work, and she was soon likened to a train running on more than one track (Sa'd 1967). The hospital committee selected her to deliver radio and television appeals to families of the wounded. On two other radio programs, she addressed working women and housewives and called for them to donate jewelry to support the military. To aid in international communications, she helped distribute images of the wounded and propaganda letters describing the plight of a young Palestinian girl who had been disfigured by Israeli napalm bombs. Named Amal (Hope), she symbolized the fate and future of Palestine.[13]

Umm Kulthūm's work with the NAEW helped change public perceptions at a crucial turning point in her career and the nation's history. Previously criticized for distracting people from active involvement in current issues (Danielson 1997, 185), Umm Kulthūm was now praised for directing citizens to coordinate their efforts in addressing urgent economic, social, and political challenges. Her work in collecting donations and leading the NAEW was recognized as unprecedented. Less than two months earlier, she had helped produce propaganda that deluded people into believing that victory would occur. Now a factory worker in the industrial center of Helwan applauded her efforts to raise morale in a different way (Maṭar 1967). While in March a fan had suggested, out of concern for her advancing age and weakening health, that she shorten her concerts to two songs, now she was called a dynamo (Jādū 1967; Sa'd 1967).[14] Afternoons formerly spent resting were now divided among meetings, broadcasting obligations, speech-writing, and propaganda distribution ("Umm Kulthūm tusāfir" 1967). Seeing these efforts as a significant change, one writer declared, "The Umm Kulthūm of today is other than the Umm Kulthūm of previous days" (Sa'd 1967). In the six weeks following the cease-fire, she had redefined herself as newly relevant to Egyptian society in its time of financial and psychological crisis. Her new nickname, "Fannānat al-Sha'b" (Artist of the People), encapsulated her responsiveness to the nation's crisis ("Umm Kulthūm tuqarrir" 1967; "Umm Kulthūm fannānat al-sha'b fī al-ma'arakah" 1967, 44).

Umm Kulthūm's efforts were particularly valuable to the government as it tried to contain and divert desires for popular participation in the continuing battle. While Egyptian special forces repelled Israeli strikes in the canal zone in July, movements propagating a people's war or organized sabotage of the enemy in Sinai were repressed. The regime stressed that the battle required traditional warfare waged by a regular, qualified army and that it involved a larger international political context that was too complex for the people to understand. With the help of the press, it sought to focus the public's attention on productivity rather than participation in a popular war (Aboul-Enein 2002; Hussein 1977, 288–91). Accordingly, the peasant next to the soldier behind 'Abd al-Nāṣir was outfitted for a workday on the land rather than the battlefield. To forestall popular initiative and demonstrations, one writer explained that while "there is no doubt that all of us are prepared to sacrifice our life . . . the one path to victory is confidence in ourselves. This confidence bestows upon us the strength for quiet organized work, equally in the field of production or in the field of war. It is upon us to let the leadership choose for us the appropriate sphere." When the writer characterized productivity as the foundation of the coming military battle, he implied that abandoning one's duty as a worker would spell certain defeat (M. Sālim 1967). Such articles directed the public to support the regime without protest and to refrain from making political or military demands counter to its goals.

While playwrights began penning works criticizing the regime (Aboul-Enein 2002), Umm Kulthūm bolstered it by echoing a message of productivity.[15] She recorded radio appeals likening idleness and waste to espionage (al-Sādāt 1967). She stressed that productivity in one's ordinary work was commensurate with military participation. As she explained, "All of us are soldiers: Whoever carries a hoe. Whoever carries a pen. Whoever carries a cup of water, and whoever carries a child at her breast nursing him with love of the homeland" ("Umm Kulthūm tusāfir" 1967). Her new song "Ḥaqq Bilādak" conveyed this message more infectiously than any spoken or written text when it was broadcast almost daily in August (*Ughnīyāt Waṭanīyah*).

Excerpts from "Ḥaqq Bilādak." Music by Riyāḍ al-Sunbāṭī, lyrics by ʿAbd al-Wahhāb Muḥammad. Composed and recorded in 1967. *Ughniyāt Waṭanīyah* Ṣawt al-Qāhirah. 82025/602 D1454 1981. Audiocassette.

While officials had asked ʿAbd al-Wahhāb Muḥammad to write lyrics that would "lighten the gravity of the Naksah on the people and diminish their sadnesses" (Nūr al-Dīn 2003), melodically and rhythmically, the song represented the regime's desired transformation of citizens' preoccupation into productivity. Against the clockwork motion of the drums, the delayed entrances of the strings resemble a sluggish, maladjusted machine, but they are soon replaced by the precise dotted rhythms of the male chorus. A pair of ascending declamatory sequences gives the chorus added motivating intensity as listeners are exhorted to work. Later, Umm Kulthūm takes over the message, abbreviating a previously introduced string motive into a series of compelling directives: "Farm! Produce!" She explicitly identifies such work as tantamount to taking up arms, singing, "Each of us is a soldier in every field."

To the Governorates

Shortly after recording "Ḥaqq Bilādak," Umm Kulthūm developed the artistic and charitable program for which she would be remembered a quarter century after her death. In late July, she presented a plan to extend the collection of donations outside Cairo. A full-page story in the magazine *Ākhir sāʿah* explained her meeting with the first citizens who donated gold—two brothers from the agricultural and trade center of al-Qalyūb (Ṭanṭāwī 1967). Despite the high symbolic and monetary value placed on women's jewelry in the countryside and the pressures of feeding seventeen children as food staples doubled in price, this "combatant Egyptian family" made repeated journeys to donate in person.[16] The family not only went to great lengths to give away their own possessions but also to collect items from other villagers. Having asked to meet the family, Umm Kulthūm used their story to highlight the need for a larger organized effort to collect donations in the countryside and to portray herself as the focal point of the collection effort. Journalists abetted her self-portrayal by crediting her with starting the collection of cash and jewelry donations among artists and placing her atop an "honor roll" of charitable Egyptian artists ("al-Akhbār" 1967; Labīb 1967a; "Ughnīyah jadīdah" 1967). Although the family cited the prominent journalist Muḥammad al-Tābiʿī's call to donate wedding rings as the initial catalyst for their contributions, the culminating and photographed visit with Umm Kulthūm showed that she had now become the symbol of the collection effort (Ṭanṭāwī 1967). She announced her readiness to visit any city or village that collected at least ten kilograms of gold and to sing in any governorate that could generate at least £E 30,000 in proceeds ("Umm Kulthūm tusāfir" 1967; "30 alf ginīh" 1967).

In August, Umm Kulthūm began to enact this plan, which appeared to unite the work of the NAEW with her own tradition of giving monthly concerts. She started with concerts in Damanhūr and Alexandria on August 17 and August 31, respectively. She donated concert proceeds to the war effort, while merchants, farmers, and contractors purchased tickets at exorbitant prices just to boost revenues (ʿAbd al-Ḥayy 1967a). She framed these concerts as occasions for citizens to make additional contributions like those collected by the NAEW in Cairo. In the weeks and days leading up to her concerts, adults and children alike donated money, jewelry, and gold, ranging from small trinkets to massive ingots. Umm Kulthūm fashioned her concerts, like the NAEW's collection work, as events at which everyone could contribute something, regardless of age or class (al-Bīlī 1967; "Umm Kulthūm tusāfir" 1967). In Damanhūr, hospital workers and vocational students donated cash according to their means. Peasants and textile workers joined forces to donate thirty kilograms of gold. At Umm Kulthūm's Alexandria concert, gold donations amounted to quadruple her expectations. Building on this success, she announced her plan to collect £E 1 million by presenting a single fundraising concert in each of the twenty-four governorates (ʿAbd al-Ḥayy 1967a; al-ʿAbbāsī 1967; "Ākhir sāʿah" 1967).

Umm Kulthūm's provincial concerts helped the regime manage popular enthusiasm for continuing the war. As the public desired to resume the war and to take part in it, her concerts provided a safe, cathartic mechanism that encouraged people to lend money, rather than ideas and opinions, to the war effort. Although the press construed popular participation in the performances as a form of combat, the concerts focused attention on arming the regular military, rather than arming ordinary civilians ("Maʿa fannānat al-shaʿb" 1967).[17] Although large crowds gathered for her concerts, each was a controlled, highly ritualized event adhering to a well-known format with which the public had been familiar for decades. While displaying a public commitment to the regime and the military, individuals engaged in a ritualized negation of their underlying personal dissatisfaction with the government as they made contributions. For those who did not participate directly, the publication of anecdotes, financial figures, and photographs from the fundraising concerts showed evidence of widespread, cross-class support for the regime and the military. The cultivation of such support became all the more important for the regime's survival as military and civilian officials plotted to overthrow ʿAbd al-Nāṣir. Held in giant tents in provincial sports stadiums, Umm Kulthūm's concerts showcased both the magnitude of public support and its breadth within both rural and urban communities.

Following her first two provincial concerts, Umm Kulthūm continued to participate in the NAEW. When she explained the organization's goals in the press, she stressed its initial phase of collecting donations, selling donated and handmade goods in the duty-free shops and tourist areas of Egypt, exporting them to obtain hard currency for the war effort, and aiding the families of those killed and wounded in action. The second, more gradual phase of action entailed a battle against wastefulness ('Abd al-Majīd 1967). Umm Kulthūm joined in the sale of NAEW products and gold donations from the public in the Cairo airport and practiced thrift when serving guests in her home (al-Malākh 1967f).[18] Soon, she took the NAEW's work abroad.

Paris

In the fall, Umm Kulthūm turned her attention from her provincial concerts to Paris, where she would give two concerts. Initially scheduled for early October, the concerts eventually took place on November 13 and 15. In conjunction with the press, she framed her trip to Paris as an extension of the NAEW's propaganda work. The head of the Olympia theater in Paris characterized her trip as a "golden opportunity" for propaganda, while an Egyptian journalist wondered, "What will she do to disseminate the truths in countries like France?" ('Awnī 1967a; Sa'd 1967). Umm Kulthūm described the concerts beforehand as a battle of propaganda. To counter the "destructive propaganda describing the Arabs as the instigator of the war and the aggressors," she vowed, "I will say to each European I meet that every centime, penny, or cent he gives to Israel is turned into a bullet that kills an Arab" ("Umm Kulthūm fī Faransā" 1967). Such language, coupled with the arrival of hundreds of Arab fans from places as diverse as Morocco, Saudi Arabia, and England, prompted world news agencies to describe her concerts as an Arab political-artistic rally in Paris ("Umm Kulthūm taftatiḥ mawsimahā" 1967; "Wa 'ādat Umm Kulthūm" 1967; Tanner 1967). Members of the Egyptian and French press interpreted her presence as a political event designed to gain public support in Europe ("Ṣawt Umm Kulthūm" 1967). After returning to Egypt, Umm Kulthūm hailed the success of her trip, confirming that the opinion of the French had changed after their discovery of Israel's "deceptive propaganda" predicting the Arab slaughter of Israeli children (S. Fu'ād 1967).

Media coverage also cast the trip as a vital display of cultural and political Arab unity. Egyptian television featured interviews with enthusiastic Arab audience members from Europe and North Africa, many of whom were seeing Umm Kulthūm perform in person for the first time. One interviewee simply proclaimed that all Arabs love Umm Kulthūm's songs, an assessment that might seem to be confirmed by extended scenes of thunderous rhythmic applause and repeated standing ovations ("Riḥlat . . . ilá Bārīs"). The singer herself cited both Arab and Muslim unity to explain her satisfaction with her trip: "Members of the Arab emigrant communities visited me . . . and told me about Egypt, the love that they harbor for Egypt, and the trial that it undergoes. How many sons of Morocco, Tunisia, and Algeria, even the sons of black Africa, and many non-Arab Muslims came to visit me, and most of their discussion was about their love for Egypt and the great place that it occupies in their hearts" ('Awnī 1967b). In both domestic and international media, her trip showcased a human counterpart to the governmental financial support that, in the previous weeks, had flowed to Egypt from Saudi Arabia, Kuwait, and Libya ("Paris" 1967; "Mu'tamar ṣaḥafī" 1967; Feiler 2003, 6–8).

At the same time, Umm Kulthūm and the Egyptian media suggested that her Paris trip could be an occasion to win European hearts through cultural appreciation. In interviews, Umm Kulthūm stressed the richness of Egyptian history, art, and culture, as well as the fundamental fact that "we are human beings" ("Kull bins" 1967). Egyptian media featured an enthusiastic response among the French to her concerts. On Egyptian television, one girl who was interviewed confessed to loving Umm Kulthūm despite not understanding the Arabic language, and the press explained that hundreds of others like her were in attendance ("Riḥlat . . . ilá Bārīs"; "Umm Kulthūm taftatiḥ 1967). This reception extended far beyond the theater where she sang. Newspapers detailed the television and radio broadcast of her performances in Europe and Canada ("Mu'tamar ṣaḥafī" 1967). The Egyptian press reported that all of Europe was talking about Egypt because of Umm Kulthūm's trip to Paris and proved it by reproducing French press coverage (Khalīl 1967; Tawfīq and Ibrāhīm 1967; "Umm Kulthūm a'ṭham ḥadath" 1967).

Yet the framing of the trip as an ideal opportunity to propagate Egyptian cultural and political values obscured the fact that it had been conceived long before the war. As set by contract in September 1966, Umm Kulthūm's compensation would be £14,000—more than double that of Maria Callas for the same venue ("Tataghannā Umm Kulthūm" 1966; 'Awnī 1967b). Supporting her generous compensation were admission prices up to four times that for a Sammy Davis, Jr., concert ("Umm Kulthūm fī al-Fījārū" 1967; Tanner 1967). If carried out as originally conceived, her Paris trip would have shown her to be a self-interested member of the Egyptian elite who was disconnected from the postwar reality of the masses. Yet she fulfilled her personal mission to sing in Paris—a landmark in her career—by redefining herself after the war and creating a new context for the concerts.

One of the many youths who rushed to kiss Umm Kulthūm onstage in Paris. *Photo courtesy of Farūq Ibrāhīm*

Umm Kulthūm had taken several steps throughout the summer and fall of 1967 to refine her image and articulate the purpose of her Paris trip. She made the case that her actions were selfless, declaring, "I do not have any desire for any profit. . . . All my revenues from my art are for the war effort until the traces of aggression are eliminated" ('Abd al-Ḥayy 1967a). She cast herself as belonging to the people rather than the elite, characterizing her efforts simply as a "citizen's duty" ('Abd al-Majīd 1967).[19]

Through careful press statements, charitable efforts, and propaganda during the summer, she had reshaped herself as a powerful artist of new relevance for Egyptian society in its time of crisis (Aḥmad 1967). Although one observer noted that "after the attack of June 5, 1967, there is not much for Umm Kulthūm, the authentic artist, in the front line of peace," the singer's many contributions to the war effort led Egyptians to recognize a new Umm Kulthūm who operated at "the front line of war" (Maṭar 1967). By summer's end, the crossword puzzles of the weekly magazine *al-Kawākib* reflected her new relevance. Black squares, which in previous weeks had formed the phrases "God is greatest," "Arab unity," and "God is for Egypt," spelled "Umm Kulthūm" on August 29.

The singer sustained her new image during her Paris trip. Obscuring the fact that she had signed the contract for the concerts long before the war, she cast the trip as the product of her devotion to her country rather than her own career. She described it not as a personal success but rather "a success for Egypt" (ʻAwnī 1967b). She skillfully invoked her patriotism and selflessness at a Paris press conference, saying, "I am a patriotic woman and I love my country. I am ready to make any sacrifice for the sake of the freedom of my country—the concern of all Egyptians" ("Mu'tamar ṣaḥafī" 1967).

Umm Kulthūm took additional steps to portray her Paris trip as an extension of her provincial concerts and her work with the NAEW. She donated her sizable compensation to the war effort and raised thousands of additional pounds by selling photographs of herself in the Olympia theater (Khalīl 1967). In the name of the NAEW, she gathered gold donations from Arabs living in France, thereby "completing what she started in Cairo" (Labīb 1967c, 6). While in Paris, her persuasive case for the NAEW's goals appeared in the Egyptian press, intimating that, despite the tenuous connection between singing on a famed Paris stage and donating small sums of money to the national treasury, her two endeavors might be linked by a unity of purpose. As she explained in an Egyptian magazine that the NAEW sought support in Europe and America through letters expounding the Egyptian point of view, her Paris sojourn seemed to illustrate her personal contributions to the assembly's goal (Qandīl 1967). Finally, she claimed success in her concerts, reporting that she had "felt the love of people from all corners of the world for Egypt" ("Akbar ḥadath" 1967).[20]

Public Frustration

Following her November stay in Paris, Umm Kulthum resumed her provincial fundraising concerts in al-Manṣūrah on February 1, 1968. Thousands gathered under a huge tent in the local sports stadium; many purchased tickets for the quoted price only to return them immediately for resale in order to double the proceeds (Qandīl 1968e). Some donated valuable personal items, such as wedding rings. Others presented items with little inherent monetary value but of special use for fundraising, including a symbolic handful of local soil that was auctioned for £E 3,000 ($6,900) (M. ʻAwaḍ 1969b, 156–57). During the concert, the on-stage presentation of a check for £E 100,000 in ticket sales to be donated to the war effort attested to local support for the war's continuation (al-ʻAbbāsī 1968c).

Shortly after this third provincial concert, Umm Kulthūm was honored with a prestigious state award in the arts. After decades of artistic success at the highest level, she was granted the award at this particular hour in acknowledgment of the financial, psychological, and emotional support she had generated at home and abroad for both the regime and the "battle of the future." Officials explained that she had "offered the state, on every national occasion, an illustration of how art and the experience of art react to great events" ("Manḥ" 1968). While this explanation reflected a superficial truth—she had recorded patriotic songs celebrating events like the evacuation of the British, the rejection of the Tripartite Aggression, the union of Syria and Egypt as the United Arab Republic, and construction of the High Dam near Aswan—it failed to express the deeper reasoning behind the award's timing: to give credit for her efforts to focus the public's attention on productivity and donations. Though she was being lauded as a "new Umm Kulthūm," at a deeper level she was merely continuing to aid the government as she had for years (Danielson 1997, 166). Sustaining her career required that she adapt to both the emotional needs of the public and the regime's imperative to contain and direct those emotions away from military and political channels.

Achieving such a redirection of the people's energy would become as urgent as ever in February 1968. Even Umm Kulthūm's continued calls for productivity could not prevent public outrage over the acquittals and lenient sentences for military officers involved in the June defeat (F. Ibrāhīm 1967). Demonstrations spread across metropolitan Cairo and Alexandria as factory workers and university students rejected the terms of the sentences and the deeper government hypocrisy that they represented. Proclaiming "It is not about pilots but about freedom!" and "End the rule of internal security," protestors decried the regime's repression and their own inability to participate in the government.[21] While the police and army exacerbated public outrage by injuring demonstrators with gunfire, 'Abd al-Nāṣir responded in his so-called March 30 Statement with pledges to support political liberalization, supremacy of law, and the reorganization of the Arab Socialist Union (Hussein 1977, 293; Erlich 1989, 193; Ansari 1986, 145; 'Abd al-Nāṣir 1992b). Umm Kulthūm's "Ḥaqq Bilādak" once again found an increasing presence on radio airwaves as part of an effort to stem public outrage.

After the June 1967 war, Umm Kulthūm could no longer take the stage with her romantic repertory in her regular monthly concerts. As a result, she established a new context for herself and her work. Through a program of artistic and charitable efforts, she redefined herself as newly relevant to Egyptian society in the aftermath of the war. She positioned herself to fulfill her long-standing personal goals, such as performing in Paris, while addressing the needs of both the people and the government. Yet when challenged by the frustrations of the Egyptian public in early 1968, she removed herself from the sphere of turmoil. Abandoning her plan to sing in each of the twenty-four governorates, she launched a new international phase of her fundraising campaign that would take her to three countries in the next three months.

CHAPTER 2

For Country or Self?

Following her concert in al-Manṣūrah in February 1968, Umm Kulthūm began a remarkable series of trips that would extend her fundraising campaign across the Arab world during the remainder of the year. She gave concerts in venues from Morocco to Kuwait and generated both financial and moral support for Egypt. Praised abroad and at home, she enjoyed a stateswoman's reception and was deemed an expert on artists' responsibilities in wartime. Although she took care to demonstrate respect for local traditions, she also worked with Arab media to showcase the region's cultural and emotional unity. She used her public appearances on and off the concert stage to highlight traditions, values, feelings, and experiences shared across the region and to prompt displays of Arab unity in support of Egypt.

While her trips prompted enthusiastic responses that were portrayed as being "for Egypt," they also generated great personal gains. Her concerts manifested her determination not simply to sustain her career through her country's crisis but also to enhance it, and to play a major role in shaping the way she would be perceived from then on. Throughout 1968, she intensified her relationships with listeners abroad and expanded her international profile. She received concert invitations from across the Arab world and media attention from the farthest corners of the globe.

As she pursued these goals, she demonstrated an acute sensitivity to the needs of the Egyptian regime. In the weeks leading up to the Six-Day War, Egypt had forged valuable ties with onetime rivals, signing defense pacts with Jordan and Syria, and Umm Kulthūm's performances in the Arab world continued to showcase such ties. The concerts also helped direct the public's attention toward international challenges, such as the ever-promised "coming war," and away from internal ones, like the growing demands for greater political participation. Her appearances not only enhanced her international standing, they also reinforced the regime's efforts to deal with military and political challenges at home and abroad.

To the Arab World

At the end of her Paris trip, Umm Kulthūm had declared, "I will sing for the sake of Egypt in all of the Arab countries" (Tawfīq 1967).[1] Invitations soon poured in. When Sudan's minister of information and social affairs wrote his invitation, he summarized the singer's accomplishments and appeal: "With art you created a message anchoring the concepts of Arabism, patriotism, and the reclamation of the stolen part of the Arab homeland" (al-Naqqāsh 2000, 79). She visited five countries in ten months, performing to great acclaim and donating her compensation to the war effort. By the end of 1968, she had sung in Morocco, Kuwait, Tunisia, Lebanon, and Sudan, and her concerts had yielded half a million Egyptian pounds for the war effort (al-ʿAbbāsī 1968e).

Umm Kulthūm's expanded fundraising program also drew great acclaim at home. While she described her efforts as simply a citizen's duty, others praised her initiative and sacrifice (Bahjat 1968; Jalāl 1968). Nabīl ʿIṣmat and Samīr Tawfīq commended her for dedicating "all of her art and effort since the hostility of June 5 for the sake of the Arabs, for the sake of the war effort, and for the sake of victory" (1968b). Another writer explained what distinguished her efforts: "The difference between Umm Kulthūm and some artists is that Umm Kulthūm works without stopping, giving concerts in Arab countries from the ocean to the gulf and returning with thousands of Egyptian pounds for the war effort. Some artists give concerts on the pages of newspapers and are satisfied by aspirations without work" ("Laqaṭāt" 1968).

The press underscored the singer's extension of her domestic fundraising campaign to an international stage, obscuring the fact that concerts in the Arab world had been proposed in the months *before* the war. Such concerts, including two in Kuwait, were being planned as early as February 1967 in conjunction with the Egyptian Ministry of Tourism. They were intended as a means of reaching her large audience outside Egypt, most of whom could not afford to travel to attend her regular monthly concerts in Egypt (al-Bīṭār 1967). The concerts also promised to enhance her international career. Umm Kulthūm had sung abroad both early in her career and again in the 1950s and early 1960s, giving performances in Lebanon, Kuwait, and Syria, scheduling concerts in Tunisia (but not giving them), and expressing an interest in visiting Morocco in the early 1960s ("Hiya tughannī" 1964; al-Rāmī 1968, 186). In the days leading up to the war, the

Media, security forces, and officials front the large crowd of fans who assembled at the Khartoum airport to welcome Umm Kulthūm. *Photo courtesy of Farūq Ibrāhīm*

press raised the possibility of her giving concerts outside Egypt, a proposal that would have continued to build her international presence while celebrating Arab victory (Darwīsh 1967). As with her Paris concerts, Umm Kulthūm remained silent about these prewar plans when asked about them after the defeat. Instead, she maintained that the idea of performing across the Arab world had been generated after the war ("Qālat" 1969), and through her public statements and appearances she effectively framed the trips as an extension of her domestic fundraising campaign.

On all her trips, Umm Kulthūm was treated like a stateswoman (Danielson 1997, 186). Already dubbed "Egypt's miraculous ambassador" (Tawfīq and Shafīq 1967a), she received a diplomatic passport in April 1968. Presidents, kings, first ladies, and ministers not only attended her concerts and receptions in her honor but also gave her official tours and hosted folkloric concerts for her pleasure. A Kuwaiti princess renovated her coastal home at the cost of £300,000 (250,000 Kuwaiti dinars) to ensure Umm Kulthūm's satisfaction during her stay (al-Bandārī 1968a). She received numerous state honors, including awards from Tunisia, Lebanon, and Pakistan.[2] As one

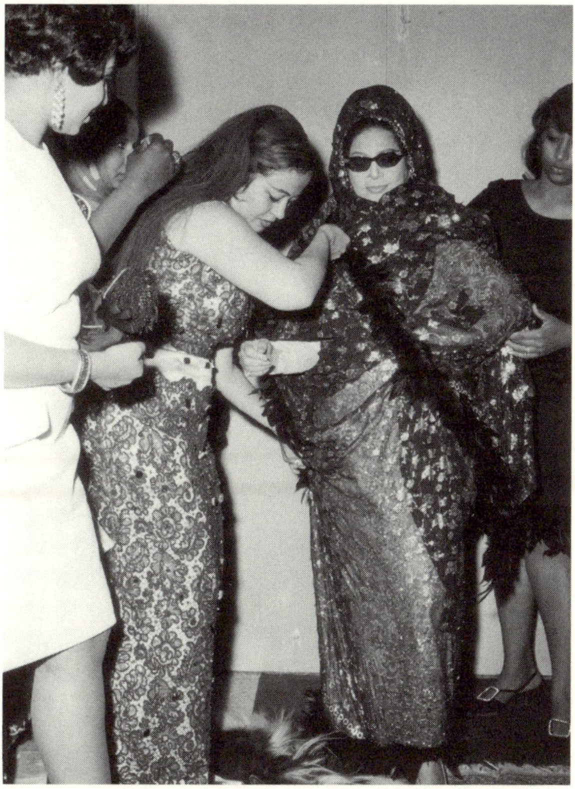

Umm Kulthūm prepares to appear onstage before one of her concerts in Khartoum. Assistants wrap a Sudanese-style dress made of black chiffon and embellished with gold embroidery, ostrich feathers, and crystals over the concert dress in which she would subsequently perform. *Photo courtesy of Farūq Ibrāhīm*

journalist explained, these awards—normally reserved for heads of state—celebrated her support of "the Arab right and Arab unity" (Nāṣif 1968a). To honor her further, officials bestowed her name on a street in Tunis and a school in Khartoum.

Popular response to her visits matched these official accolades. Throngs of fans blocked her descent from airplanes and held up her car in the streets. Sudanese fans purchased a year's worth of television sets in a single week once they learned that her concerts would be televised. Additional seats were added to theaters when possible, and overflow crowds stood during her marathon performances (Tabārak 1968; al-Naqqāsh 2000, 84–85). Thousands sent telegrams requesting particular songs and additional concerts. While ticket prices soared on the black market, people deliberately purchased tickets from official outlets for many times their face value, sometimes in excess of £E 1,000 (about $2,300) (Nāṣif 1969; al-Bandārī 1968b, Darwīsh 1969f). Parents in Morocco and Sudan named their newborn girls "Umm Kulthūm" in commemoration of her visits (Tawfīq 1968b; Darwīsh 1968; Yaḥyá 1968a).

Umm Kulthūm greets some of the hundreds of Moroccan folk dancers gathered in Marrakesh by King Ḥasan II to display the country's regional folk arts for the singer. She participated with some of the women in their dance performances.
Photo courtesy of Farūq Ibrāhīm

Arab Cultural Unity

Enthusiastic popular reception of Umm Kulthūm across the region was rooted in shared linguistic and musical idioms. Many of her songs featured lyrics in *fuṣḥā*, the elevated form of Arabic used in newspapers, literature, and news broadcasts in North Africa and the Middle East. And many of her lyrics were written in the classical poetic form known as the *qaṣīdah*, which could be traced to pre-Islamic times and was used by writers across the region. Other songs written in Egyptian conversational Arabic were also readily understood abroad, thanks to the country's historical dominance in the production and regional distribution of films and audio recordings. For similar reasons, the musical elements of Umm Kulthūm's songs were familiar to audiences across the Arab world. Even in Morocco and Tunisia, where local repertories of Andalusian music relied on different modes and rhythmic patterns, the prominence of the Egyptian media ensured listeners' familiarity with the *maqāmāt* (modes) and *iqāʿāt* (rhythmic patterns) of Egyptian music. Tunisian radio was modeled after Egyptian radio in the makeup of its resident performing ensemble and its programming practices

Umm Kulthūm performed in a sports stadium in Tunisia that held thousands of people. *Photo courtesy of Farūq Ibrāhīm*

from the late 1950s, and little native Tunisian music was available on tape even into the 1980s. As a consequence, Egyptian music long outranked local traditions among Tunisian listeners (Davis 2003, 133–36). These shared linguistic, poetic, and musical idioms enabled Umm Kulthūm, when asked about audiences abroad, to state simply that "the Arab listener is one" (Nāṣif 1968c, 60).

Umm Kulthūm used and developed her repertory to affirm this cultural unity. When she performed in Sudan in December 1968, she chose to sing "Hādhihī Laylatī." With lyrics by the Lebanese poet George Jardāq, music by the Egyptian composer Muḥammad 'Abd al-Wahhāb, and numerous repetitions of sections demanded by the enthusiastic Sudanese listeners in the crowd, the performance perfectly illustrated a cultural heritage that was shared and sustained across the region. On a broader scale, she announced her intention to sing a *qaṣīdah* by a poet from each Arab nation and reviewed the collections of leading Arab poets (Jawdat 1968; Qandīl 1968d). She explained that her goal was "to realize the unity of Arab thought and to shorten the region's distances through word and melody" (Qandīl 1968c, 32). Projects initiated earlier, like "Hādhihī Laylatī," the composition of which began in summer 1967, seemed to embody her rapid realization of this program (Qandīl 1968c; Tabārak 1971b). Later projects included the setting to music of Saudi poet Prince 'Abd Allāh al-Fayṣal's "Min Ajli

'Aynayk" and Sudanese school principal al-Hādī Ādam's "Aghadan Alqāk." In November 1971, Umm Kulthūm heightened the pan-Arab nature of her art by singing the Sudanese poet's lyrics, set to music composed by an Egyptian, for listeners in Abu Dhabi.

She also encouraged Arab cultural unity by performing in a way that invited audience members to collaborate with the musicians on stage to create a shared ecstasy, or *ṭarab*. Listeners across the Arab world understood not only the language, modes, rhythms, and forms of her songs but also how to contribute to this heightened musical experience. They recognized appropriate moments to show their pleasure in order to spur an artist's creativity.[3] Audiences in Morocco, Tunisia, and Sudan responded vigorously to her use of ornamentation, her emotive manipulation of varied vocal timbres such as hoarseness and nasality, and her vocalizations during instrumental interludes. Listeners abroad exhibited a wide range of behaviors in response to the music, as they had in Egypt.[4] In Sudan, certain listeners waved, danced, conducted, and even prayed along with her performances (al-Naqqāsh 2000, 78; "Hādhihī Laylatī"). Yet as a whole, the audience in Sudan helped create an environment familiar enough for the Egyptian journalist Rajā' al-Naqqāsh to experience "a state of Sufi intoxication" when Umm Kulthūm performed "Hādhihī Laylatī" (al-Naqqāsh 2000, 87). While some listeners outside of Egypt displayed their enchantment in excessive ways, Umm Kulthūm noted that, from one country to the next, audience members used similar language to express their approval (Yaḥyá 1969a). By doing so, they contributed to a feedback cycle and prompted the singer to offer improvisatory repetitions of melodic lines, as well as extended passages of improvisation. The ecstasy experienced by members of the audience was an integral part of her reception abroad. A Moroccan observer noted that each listener became completely mixed with Umm Kulthūm and that all listeners became one (al-Khatābī 1968, 163). When asked to describe the relationship between Arab listeners in Sudan, other Arab countries, and Egypt, Umm Kulthūm responded, "I confirm that there is no difference." Likewise, she described the feelings and sensitivities of listeners across the Arab world as "almost one," and cited "the same habits of listening" as "evidence that affirms the unity of the Arab people and its cohesiveness from the most ancient times" ("Qālat" 1969, 38).

Umm Kulthūm's emphasis on these shared listening habits diverted attention from actual differences in the quality of her reception. She remarked that when she sang in the National Theater in Umm Durman, Sudan, she felt just as though she were singing at the Nile Palace in Cairo (Yaḥyá 1969a). Yet her performances of songs like "Fakkarūnī" and "Amal Ḥayātī" often generated more enthusiastic response and, therefore, more substantial displays of her improvisatory skill outside Egypt than within it. When she sang "Ba'īd 'Anak" in Tunisia in early June 1968, she began improvising in the middle of the first line of text. Enthusiastic response from sensitive listeners prompted further improvisations over the rest of the song. One extended passage of improvisation featured modulations through several *maqāmat*, intricate motivic development, and complex rhythmic interplay in a metrical context.

Umm Kulthūm shaped each performance to allow her to connect with her respective audiences. In Sudan, she appeared onstage at the beginning of each concert wearing a Sudanese-style wrap over her concert dress. The wraps had been inspired by her March appearance in Rabat, where she had donned a black and gold Moroccan caftan. One Moroccan observer noted that her wearing of the caftan reflected "mental preparation to enter the public's emotional atmosphere so that the spirits of the artist and the people [were] exchanged as if they became one and the same" (Bin 'Abūd 1968, 157). Despite this preparation, when she began performing "al-Aṭlāl," her Moroccan audience seemed less than fully engaged, presenting her with the implicit challenge of finding ways to move them. She tapped into her well-known reserve of vocal timbres, cadences, and techniques for melodic variation to do so (Danielson 1997, 146–53). As a result, the audience response grew from polite in the opening three sections to enthusiastic as she punctuated the lyrics' meaning through hoarseness, melodic ornamentation, and strong cadences.

In the song's seventh section, she offered an unusually wide variety of rhythmic, melodic, and timbral variations to further draw her audience in to her performance. She added ornamentation to the composed melody with a number of rapid turns and introduced accents, heavy pulsations, and a nasal timbre that drew cheers. Over the fans' rhythmic clapping, she immediately repeated lines, adding rhythmic variations and anticipatory accents that dissected the final syllable of "sukārā" into a series of *ha*'s. When singing this section for the second time, she reprised some of her particularly effective variations, including the anticipatory *ha*'s, and introduced new ones, such as a portamento on "sukārā." The approving audience response prompted her to join her ensemble by singing the instrumental interlude on vocables. Singing the seventh section for the third time, she offered additional variants on accented *ha*'s, but when these proved less effective than her other techniques, she returned to the nasal timbre that had worked before. She added further rhythmic variations and rapid turns and elicited a strong audience response when she emphasized the nasal linkage of the *m* and *b* of "kam banaynā," following principles of Qur'ānic recitation. Returning to this section for the fourth time, she offered a highly

"Ba'īd 'Anak," line 1 and ametrical improvisation. Music by Balīgh Ḥamdī, lyrics by Ma'mūn al-Shināwī. Premiered in 1965 and recorded in Tunis in 1968. "Ba'īd 'Anak: Ḥaflat Tūnis." Ṣawt al-Qāhirah. SC81115/901. Audiocassette.

effective exaggerated, or "drunken," rendition of the first phrase and continued to employ this variation when she performed the section for the fifth, sixth, and seventh times. The rising response that she invoked during the course of this performance illustrated not only the *ṭarab* feedback cycle but also its powerful impact in a once-in-a-lifetime setting. This creative effort

"Ba'īd 'Anak," *ghuṣn* 2, metrical improvisation. Music by Balīgh Ḥamdī, lyrics by Ma'mūn al-Shināwī. Premiered in 1965 and recorded in Tunis in 1968. "Ba'īd 'Anak: Ḥaflat Tūnis." Ṣawt al-Qāhirah. SC8III5/90I. Audiocassette.

“Baʿīd ʿAnak,” *ghuṣn* 2 (*continued*).

"Baʿīd ʿAnak," *ghuṣn* 2 (*continued*).

and its reception stood in stark contrast to the less glowing appreciation she received at some of her Cairo performances.[5]

Umm Kulthūm's concerts embodied not just a shared art but also shared feelings, experiences, and values. The singer herself emphasized the performances' demonstration of cultural unity. "These concerts in the Arab homeland—in its entirety—have the power," she said, "to display the shared feelings that tie together the Arab people everywhere . . . and confirm that all

"Baʿīd ʿAnak," *ghuṣn* 2 (*continued*).

of the Arabs are of one heart and one pulse" (Qandīl 1969b, 40). Broadcasting practices furthered this goal, as several concerts were played over radio and television in host countries and reached audiences in neighboring ones as well (F. 1968; ʿIṣmat and Tawfīq 1968b). A traveling exhibit of photographs taken from her fundraising concerts outside Egypt, with stops in Kuwait, Tunisia, and Sudan, also showcased Arab cultural unity. While local press coverage sometimes highlighted the local holidays and charities honored by her performances, the photo exhibits demonstrated the continuing vitality of shared cultural traditions and modes of popular participation

Umm Kulthūm performs in a Moroccan caftan made of black velvet with gold trim. *Photo courtesy of Farūq Ibrāhīm*

across the Arab world ('Iṣmat and Tawfīq 1968a, 1968b; Yaḥyá 1968c; "Riḥlat . . . ilá al-Maghrib").

Umm Kulthūm reinforced this display of Arab unity off the concert stage. She greeted Tunisians publicly as her "siblings" and referred to Arab countries as her "homeland" to invoke the idea of a larger Arab nation ("Telegram" 1968; al-Khalīsī 1968, 20). She also spoke of the common faith uniting Arabs and demonstrated it by celebrating 'Īd al-Aḍḥá—a holiday commemorating Abraham's willingness to sacrifice his son—with a needy Moroccan family (Nāṣif 1968c). Moroccan citizens underscored this shared faith onstage during one concert by giving her a green candle representing Moses' staff ("Oum Kalthoum" 1968; Tawfīq 1968b). While the singer demonstrated respect for and interest in local artistic and culinary traditions, she frequently used them to highlight the underlying similarities of Arab culture. She likened Moroccan folk singing to the songs of Upper Egypt, Kuwaiti folk songs to those of the Egyptian coast, and a Sudanese wedding to counterparts in the Egyptian countryside (Qandīl 1968a; "Qālat" 1969).

"al-Aṭlāl," section VII. Music by Riyāḍ al-Sunbāṭī, lyrics by Ibrāhīm al-Nājī. Premiered in 1966 and recorded in Morocco in 1968. "al-Aṭlāl." Egyptian State Radio library. Reels 50386N, 50387N, and 50388N.

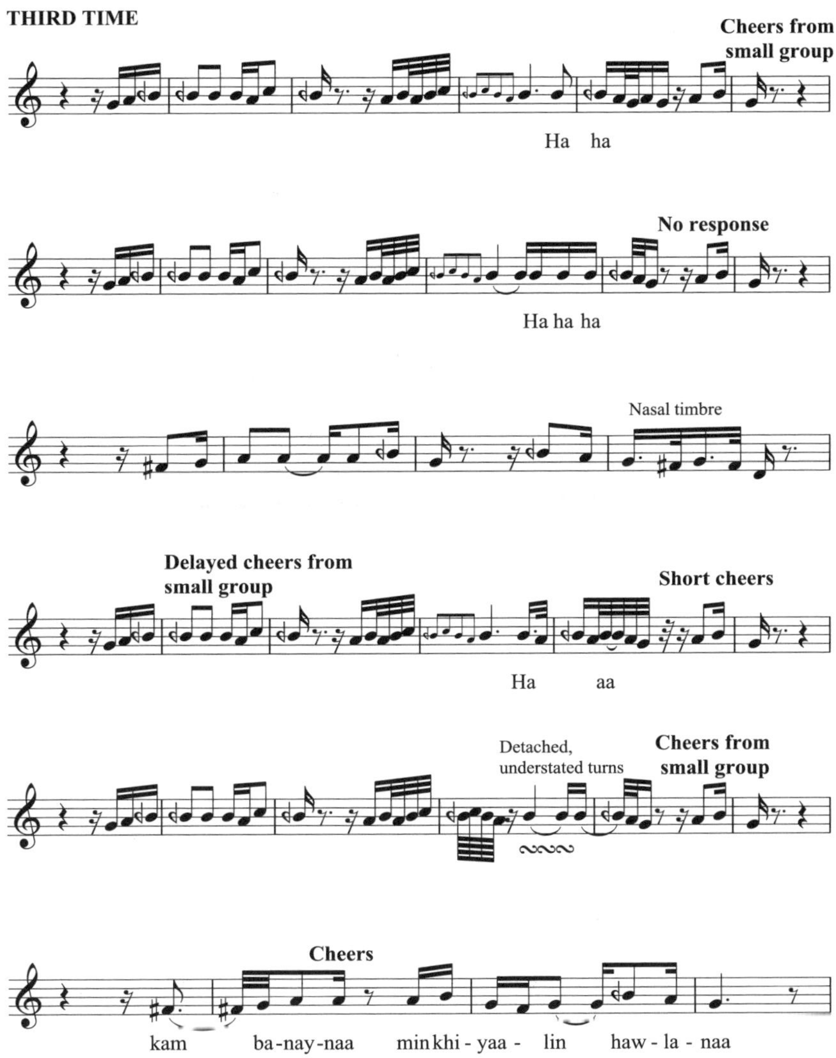

"al-Aṭlāl," section VII (*continued*).

For Egypt

Umm Kulthūm and the Egyptian press portrayed the response to her trips as support for Egypt and not just adulation for an individual artist (S. Fu'ād 1968, 9). Although concert proceeds were sometimes directed to local causes, including Tunisian first lady Wasīlah Būrqībah's charitable projects, the Egyptian press repeatedly quantified listeners' financial contributions to the war effort (al-ʿAbbāsī 1968e). Umm Kulthūm and the Egyptian press stressed

FOURTH TIME

“al-Aṭlāl,” section VII (*continued*).

that Arabs were united in backing the war effort. One reporter paraphrased the singer’s primary aim in giving concerts abroad: “Umm Kulthūm performs her important, powerful role in this decisive journey of the Arab nation by uniting the hearts and gathering feelings toward one goal—victory. And this is the hope that Umm Kulthūm lives for the sake of, as she told me many times” (Tawfīq 1968b). Another writer portrayed the Sudanese as professing their love for Egypt to the singer herself (Karīm 1969a).

In planning her concerts, Umm Kulthūm used careful strategies to prompt displays of Arab emotional unity in support of Egypt. To do so, she avoided songs of specific political and local significance. Although her trips were often scheduled to coincide with local national holidays, she consistently refrained from performing songs associated through subject matter, authorship, or commissioning with the country in which she was singing.[6] Instead, she regularly included the staple romantic songs that fostered *ṭarab* and were best positioned to generate strong ticket sales. In avoiding patriotic songs with explicitly political messages, the singer prompted debate. On the one hand, a Jordanian fan praised her choice, effusing that “she participated in the purchase of tanks and airplanes with the sweetest songs of love!” He asked, “What is more magnificent than love, when it turns into a means of strength?” (Ṣalāḥ 1969; ʻAbd al-Ṣamad 1969). Others, however, deemed romantic songs to be inappropriate for wartime (“Hujūm”; Labīb 1967a, 11; al-Naqqāsh 2000, 98).

Amid this debate, Umm Kulthūm included a romantic song that admitted numerous political interpretations and prompted displays of Arab emotional unity. In every country she visited, she sang the *qaṣīdah* "al-Aṭlāl" ("The Ruins"). The song could be understood as a purely romantic expression, but the line "Give me my freedom, set free my hands" allowed for a range of alternative political readings. As the song mentioned no specific oppressor, oppressed people, or occupied land, this climactic line could be heard as a critique of repressive local regimes—whether colonial or otherwise—or of the occupation of local or distant lands, such as Sinai or Palestine. The line prompted cries of emotional solidarity in Tunisia, Morocco, Libya, and Sudan. In the broad patriotic framework of her concerts as expressions of both Egyptian and Arab pride, the words of "al-Aṭlāl" provided an ideal vehicle for reflecting on what was widely perceived to be a shared legacy of imperialism (Nāṣif 1968c). The song prompted a Tunisian in Paris to contemplate her "Arab brothers," including Palestinians, and led a listener in Tunisia to confess in both general and personal terms, while crying uncontrollably, "Her romantic words remind me of the tragedy of our homeland with imperialism and my tragedy with imperialism" (S. Fu'ād 1968, 9; Sāmīyah Ṣādiq n.d.). The calls and cheers of her audience members, following this line, coalesced in one regional voice of resistance, even as listeners likely imagined their own interpretations. Using the shared conventions of the *ṭarab* feedback cycle, these listeners demonstrated the vitality of Arab cultural unity even though political pan-Arabism was deemed to have failed.

The fluid significance of "al-Aṭlāl" helped the Egyptian press portray Umm Kulthūm's concerts as a healing force that forged together a strong transnational community through feeling and culture. Egyptian journalists demonstrated her success in marshaling emotional support for the war effort by presenting evidence from each country: Moroccans chanted the name "Egypt" in the middle of her first concert in March; Kuwaitis testified that "Umm Kulthūm was able to strengthen the Arab nation and help unite the ranks" in April; and a Tunisian declared in July, "She confirms our Arabness, our brotherhood, and our one destiny" (S. Fu'ād 1968, 8; 'Iṣmat and Tawfīq 1968b; "Umm Kulthūm 'wishsh al-khayr'" 1968). As one reporter summarized, "There was one pulsation throughout the one Arab nation around her" (al-'Abbāsī 1968b). Her concerts created a temporary, ritualized realization of Arab unity that was thought to have been destroyed with the breakup of the United Arab Republic (Egypt and Syria) in 1961 and the disastrous outcome of the 1967 war. Reflecting on this feat, one writer credited her singing with making "the geographic boundaries between the Arab countries dissolve" ("15 alf dīnār" 1968). Meanwhile, her concerts helped showcase regional support for Egypt, which still cast itself as the leader of an Arab battle to reclaim land from an enemy seen to be engaging in brutal hostilities against Arabs ("Umm Kulthūm 'wishsh al-khayr'" 1968; al-'Abbāsī 1968b).

Umm Kulthūm's public performances offstage reinforced this portrayal of Arab emotional unity. When speaking with the Egyptian press, she cited victory as the aspiration of every Arab, praised the solidarity displayed by other Arab soldiers fighting alongside the Egyptians, and testified to the unanimous Arab desire for victory in this "shared cause" (Nāṣif 1968c; "al-Fannānah" 1968; Darwīsh and Nudānī 1968; "Qālat" 1969). One particularly powerful example underscored such unity while displaying deference to local culture. During her tour of Tunis in early June, she prayed in the historic al-Zaytūnah mosque while wearing a *burnūs*, a long hooded cloak traditionally worn in Tunisia. While local commentators noted her respect for their own culture, the Egyptian press stressed the occasion on which she was praying—the one-year anniversary of the June War—and the tears shed by the first lady of Tunisia as she and the singer remembered those killed in action. In this perfect photo opportunity, high-profile escorts and the shared ritual of prayer enabled Umm Kulthūm and the press to demonstrate that Tunisians were united emotionally with Egyptians. The scene was reported as follows:

> The anniversary of June 5 occurred when Umm Kulthūm was in Tunis. That day was filled with various emotions and hopes. Umm Kulthūm spent it in the mosques of Tunis performing prayers and listening to the religious *tawāshīḥ* and prayers in support of Arabism and Arab unity. With Umm Kulthūm, emotion reached its limit. She began crying and with her cried all of the Tunisian people. . . . Everyone cried that day for the martyrs' souls and prayed for the sake of victory. (Nāṣif 1968a)

Offering reassurance that such shared feelings extended beyond the host country's leadership, the Egyptian press told readers of the financial contributions and "cries of Arab support" from thousands of ordinary Tunisians (Nāṣif 1968d).

Before Umm Kulthūm began her trips of 1968, an Egyptian journalist had warned that the "imperialist" powers would try to "strike the united Arab effort" and engender divisions within the Arab nation ("Aḍwā'" 1968). As portrayed by the Egyptian media and Umm Kulthūm herself, her trips furnished proof that the "Arab nation" was indeed united in its support for the continued war, foiling this perceived imperialist plan. To bolster these claims, Egyptian television showcased enthusiastic reception in Morocco, Sudan, and Tunisia ("Riḥlat . . . ilá al-Maghrib; Dāwud 1968). The complementary nature of broadcasting and print media created a powerful representation of her campaign: the temporal unfolding of her performances and her audiences' response, colored by the layers of interpretation in the print

Umm Kulthūm prays in the al-Zaytūnah mosque alongside Tunisia's first lady Wasīlah Būrqībah on the first anniversary of the June War. *Photo courtesy of Dār al-Hilāl.*

media, offered listeners and viewers a vicarious experience of her reception more powerful than prose descriptions and still snapshots could have achieved alone. Such portrayals furthered the singer's stated goal for the trips—"the renewal of cooperation among all Arabs and its conversion to something tangible." She explained her purpose at length:

> I wanted to prove that we are together in Israel's view and that we are together in facing the enemy. The destiny is one and the significance is one. Therefore I did not think in terms of money and was not striving to collect donations when I sang from Kuwait to Morocco to Sudan. There was something else that I intended to say through these concerts with an elevated voice and a resounding cry: This is Egypt, and I am one of its people. Her voice is still raised and louder, her battle still continues and is greater, her staying power is still unshakable and stronger (Qandīl 1969b, 40).

Egyptian Politics

While promoting an uplifting image of Arab unity, Umm Kulthūm also sought through her work to continue reinforcing the regime's efforts to address numerous domestic and international military challenges. The domestic demonstrations of February 1968, in which protestors rejected repressive measures and limited opportunities to participate in government, presented just such a challenge (Erlich 1989, 193). To show that he was receptive to the people's calls, 'Abd al-Nāṣir increased the role of nonmilitary professionals in the government and pledged to enact political reforms, uphold the supremacy of the law, and reorganize the Arab Socialist Union (ASU). True to her role, Umm Kulthūm wasted no time in praising the rebuilding of the ASU in a democratic manner and urged the public to participate by thoughtfully voting to select its members ("Umm Kulthūm taqūl ṣawtunā" 1968). Popular elections were also slated for the National Assembly, which would be granted a greater role in the government.

'Abd al-Nāṣir's proposals, designed to address the problems created by "centers of power," factions, and loyalty-based promotion, were encapsulated in his March 30 Program (Ansari 1986, 144–45). As Mahmud Hussein has argued, the program was also designed in the post-February scene "to divert the popular democratic aspirations from this field of action, to distract them, and to channel them back into the regime's framework." (Hussein 1977, 299). This task was made somewhat easier by the highly celebrated battle of al-Karāmah, during which *fidā'iyīn* claimed to have repelled Israeli forces from the Jordanian village of al-Karāmah. Touting the accomplishment, the Egyptian press portrayed abandoned Israeli tanks and transmitted odes to the *fidā'iyīn* (Abū Dhikrá 1968; Gharībah 1968).[7] 'Abd al-Nāṣir, aided by headlines like "In the Path of Victory with the March 30 Program," couched the program and the coming May referendum as part of the ongoing battle (Ṣalāḥ Ṣādiq 1968; "Ghadan" 1968). In her own promotion of the program, Umm Kulthūm equated rejection and failure to participate in the referendum with abandoning 'Abd al-Nāṣir and surrender ("Umm Kulthūm taqūl ṣawtunā" 1968). Presidential rallies provided ideal photo opportunities demonstrating the enthusiastic support of peasants, workers, intellectuals, and military members alike, with the program itself described as both a choice of the people and a confirmation of their steadfastness in the battle (al-Sibāʿī 1968a).

While people were enticed by opportunities to participate in the political system, they were still urged to view their ordinary work as a meaningful form of participation in the battle. They learned that their "Yes" votes on the referendum had committed them to work and productivity (Qandīl 1968b). To control tendencies toward popular resistance, the press continued to stress that everyone's work was an essential part of the battle. Leading journalists made the case that work gives the voice of the people its strength and "makes the domestic front line a strong support for the battle front" (al-Sibāʿī 1968b). Umm Kulthūm modeled the value of work through her trips and called on others to join her, saying that "those who love Egypt are demanded today to present to Egypt two things: work and hope" (Bahjat 1968). Journalist Maḥmūd Sālim explained that "there is no difference between the soldier and the worker, or between the soldier and the peasant, or the civil servant, or the intellectual." An accompanying drawing portrayed the peasant's self-confidence as a powerful weapon against the United States and Israel (M. Sālim 1968).

Umm Kulthūm also furthered the regime's goals by helping divert attention from its reluctance to make necessary changes in the country's economic, political, and social systems.[8] Naming what she viewed as the most important event of 1968, she stressed the victories achieved by the armed forces along the canal and their impact on the people and Israel ("Ahamm aḥdāth" 1968).[9] Likewise, through their highly publicized displays of Arab unity, her trips directed attention to regional support for the continually promised military action against Israel. By reinforcing, rather than challenging, government priorities and agendas, Umm Kulthūm's campaign and its representation in the domestic media allowed for her continued visible role.

Still, Umm Kulthūm's help was of limited utility when the government's own efforts to curtail public discontent backfired. The continual promise of war, which was intended in part to turn popular attention away from domestic problems, had not yet exceeded isolated artillery barrages, and by the fall it became clear that many of the government's domestic promises would go unfulfilled (Waterbury 1983, 331). The referendum on the March 30 Program was supposed to have yielded a "transfer of power to the people" (M. Sālim 1968), but elections for leadership positions in the ASU failed to break up faction-based centers of power and the organization's restructuring contradicted the principles of the March 30 Program (Ansari 1986, 145; Beattie 1994, 216). Increasing distrust of official policy, the National Assembly, the ASU, and the Ministry of the Interior and its police forces erupted in November, with demonstrators denouncing "bloody repression" across the country (Hussein 1977, 310–13).

To cope with public outrage, the ever-promised war was finally begun. Disgruntled students were shunted into the army, and the Egyptian media focused attention on what would become known as the war of attrition (Erlich 1989, 195). Umm Kulthūm's trip to Sudan in December 1968 helped portray the war as a regional effort with public support outside Egypt. In recordings intended for radio broadcast, Sudanese women praised her as a model for the combative Arab woman and recognized her efforts for what they described as "our battle" against Israel. Umm Kulthūm aided in this display of regional support by stressing the importance of cooperative work in "our collective cause" ("Istiqbāl"). A Sudanese author, quoted by the Egyptian press, described the singer as "a resistance fighter and combatant against imperialism and Zionism" in the Arab battle (Zarrūq 1969, 12). Such displays of regional support for the war effort cast Egyptian demonstrations of dissatisfaction as an unpatriotic, poorly timed distraction.

Personal Gains

Even against discontent in Egypt's domestic sphere, Umm Kulthūm's efforts in 1968 underscored the artistic change in her that others had detected in summer 1967. Observers noted that she had not debuted a romantic work for more than two years and that she did not give concerts in search of "profit, fame, or glory" ('Aṭīyah 1968; Nāṣif 1968a). Instead, she was recognized for her war effort project, which the media characterized as vast in scope. Print and television journalists proclaimed the singer's intent to "give concerts in every Arab country until victory is realized" and her dream "to sing for all Arabs on the day of victory" ("al-Fannānah" 1968; "Riḥlat . . . ilá al-Maghrib"). Through her fundraising concerts, she established herself as an authority on the artist's role in wartime and provided a model soon followed by other singers (Qandīl 1968d).[10] She sustained her war effort fundraising activities through the next several years, and observers recognized that the new stage in her career had continued. As the Egyptian journalist Aḥmad Ṣāliḥ saw it, "Umm Kulthūm rose with all perseverance . . . carrying a new message, collecting money and paying for the carrying of arms, spreading feeling with assurance, and returning a part of the lost honor. People were awakened by her fine sensitivity and new role—her new stance in the time of tribulation" (1970, 29).

Umm Kulthūm had effectively solidified her regional presence and legacy at the end of her career. As a Kuwaiti police officer explained to an Egyptian journalist, "It is not your [Egyptian] right to pride yourself on Umm Kulthūm alone—all of us take pride in her. You saw it yourself how we received her. We consider her an object of pride of the entire Arab nation" ('Iṣmat 1968b, 8). Invitations arrived from numerous Arab countries, including Iraq, Algeria, and Bahrain (Yūnis 1968; S. Fu'ād 1968, 9; Qandīl 1968a). The singer expanded her role from the "voice of Egypt" to the voice of the Arab world. Early in 1968, a journalist had declared, "In each step she took, Umm Kulthūm was the voice of Egypt responding, the Arab issue aroused, and the story of Egypt on every tongue" (S. Fu'ād 1968). Nicknames like "Uniter of the Arabs" were used with increasing frequency to describe her regional relevance (Nāṣif 1969, 55).

A Sudanese fan poses with the singer at a concert intermission. *Photo courtesy of Farūq Ibrāhīm*

While praised for devoting all her effort to her country's battle, she earned herself even wider acclaim internationally. Her performances across the Arab world laid the foundation to broaden her career even further. In the months to come, she continued to receive requests to perform in Europe, Asia, and the Western hemisphere from members of the Arab diaspora and cultural councils ("Daʿwat" 1967; "Umm Kulthum tughannī fī Kanadā" 1969; "Akhbār al-nās" 1968). She was the subject of reports on international radio and television broadcasts as far away as Japan and London ("Umm Kulthūm taqūl bi idhāʿat Lundun" 1968; ʿIṣmat 1968c).

In her travels, Umm Kulthūm also aroused the interest of a younger generation in every country she visited. Youths had rushed onstage to kiss her after each song in Paris, and adoring young Sudanese fans repeated the honor ("Riḥlat . . . ilá Bārīs"). The Egyptian press described the "frenzied" response of young listeners abroad (Tawfīq 1968b; Darwīsh 1969d). Images of enthusiastic young fans so eager to greet her both onstage and off helped portray her as still relevant in an Egyptian society whose younger members were increasingly interested in new fashions and cultural trends.

Umm Kulthūm's appearances across the Arab world in 1968 exemplified the tactical nature of her career development and image management. She took advantage of the postwar context she had created since June 1967 to give performances abroad that had been envisioned before the war. By realizing these trips as an extension of her domestic fundraising campaign, she marked them as selfless acts motivated by a sense of duty to country. Enhanced by her patriotic postwar mission and stateswoman status, she packed five Arab trips into a single year, elevating them to an altogether different status from her previous concerts in the Middle East as well as those of her musical peers.[11]

Framing her trips as selfless, patriotic acts did not prevent her from reaping personal gains. Ever the tactician, she managed to expand her international fame while addressing the needs of the Egyptian regime. She did so by reinforcing the leadership's efforts to deal with political and military challenges on domestic and international fronts, promoting work and hope rather than political participation, and diverting attention from internal problems. Her careful selection of songs and masterful improvisation intensified her connection with audiences abroad as they showcased the region's potential for unity and support of Egypt. While her comments and appearances offstage reinforced media portrayals of Arab cultural unity, these efforts were aided by the specter of imperialist attempts to "strike the united Arab effort." By channeling funds from across the region to finance the rebuilding of the military, and by helping create a moving display of emotional unity behind the war effort, she had elevated and magnified her voice into both the "the voice of hope" and "the voice of resistant Arabness" by the time the war of attrition began (Naṭhamī 1968, 38). She successfully realized the greater potential of her career in geographic and generational terms while remaining relevant to both the regime and the public at home. For a singer long past the age at which many others would have retired, it had been a carefully executed and highly productive year.

CHAPTER 3

Sustaining a Career, Shaping a Legacy

For all that was accomplished, Umm Kulthūm's whirlwind tour of the Arab world in 1968 left her audiences in Egypt feeling neglected. For eighteen months, she had all but abandoned her schedule of monthly Cairo concerts that were broadcast live throughout the country ('Iṣmat 1968a).[1] Her physical absence was compounded when efforts to broadcast her foreign concerts live in Egypt were thwarted by technical problems. In January 1969, after returning from Sudan, she finally resumed her regular schedule of first-Thursday concerts. Yet she was not fully prepared to continue another long-standing tradition by premiering a new song at her February concert. In less than three weeks, though, she and composer Balīgh Ḥamdī transformed a compositional fragment into a polished performance of a new romantic song, "Alf Laylah wa Laylah" ('Iṣmat 1969). Her highly publicized marathon of fundraising and ambassadorial efforts had allowed her to resume her performance of romantic songs at home, but bigger challenges awaited as she extended her career into the 1970s. One was that she had to contend with younger artists who had popularized more accessible and dance-oriented styles. As a result, she deliberately cultivated relationships with younger composers like Balīgh Ḥamdī and presented songs that were grounded more heavily in dance rhythms (Danielson 1997, 167, 182).

As Umm Kulthūm shaped her career trajectory, she accomplished two simultaneous goals: on the one hand, she remained an active, relevant artist, and on the other, she took steps to ensure and craft her posthumous legacy. Among the public appearances, photo-ops, and press statements that filled the last years of her career, she repeatedly seized opportunities to shape the way she would be remembered after her death. Her self-constructed portrait emphasized ideals of motherhood, piety, and charity. She allied herself with the nation's ancient monuments and helped transform herself into a reified part of its musical heritage. At the same time, to continue demonstrating political relevance through her music, she was compelled to navigate Egyptian and Arab political concerns that would shift in relative importance and diverge in intricate ways. She would also have to confront a change of leadership that would directly threaten her career.

Honing a Public Image

Umm Kulthūm did not begin to craft a consistent public image in her later career. She had been doing so since the late 1930s. Yet, in the late 1960s, as if anticipating the end, she took particularly intentional steps to craft a personal legacy. Virginia Danielson noted that the singer's "public self was clearly a construction but it was neither artificial nor false; Umm Kulthūm simply learned to present herself in the way she wanted to be thought of and remembered" (1997, 185, 191–92). Danielson's observation is especially true of those later years. The meticulousness with which Umm Kulthūm prepared her concert performances was matched by her care in constructing her public image offstage through interactions with the press. She was known for carefully choosing her words before the public and the press (S. Fu'ād 1968). She also maintained close relationships with members of the media and exerted unusual control over her representation. 'Alī Amīn (1975) noted her insistence on choosing every word and tearing up hundreds of pages when the two of them drafted a version of her memoirs in the early 1960s.

She applied this same level of care and control when issuing autobiographical statements in several venues during her later career. In 1969, she collaborated with journalist Maḥmūd 'Awaḍ to create a new biography and contributed to the production of a film about her artistic history (Maḥsab 1969a).[2] She made an agreement with the newspaper *al-Jumhūrīyah* to publish her memoirs in 1970 and recorded lengthy autobiographical interviews with radio broadcaster Wajdī al-Ḥakīm during the next two years. Her autobiographical interviews with other journalists and broadcasters appeared with increasing frequency both in newspapers and on the radio. Amid her growing international standing, set against advancing age and deteriorating health, these numerous statements reflected a concern with shaping both her current reception and the way she would be remembered after her death.

The singer's collaboration with 'Awaḍ epitomized the careful control she exerted over her public image and legacy at the end of her life. The book they produced, *Umm Kulthūm allatī lā ya'rifuhā aḥad* (The Umm Kulthūm No One Knows), was issued by the Akhbār al-Yawm Foundation in three annual editions from 1969 to 1971. Whereas the foundation normally chose

Umm Kulthūm places a brooch on her concert dress as she prepares to go onstage. The meticulousness with which she prepared her concert performances was matched by the care with which she constructed her public image off the stage through her interactions with the press. *Photo courtesy of Farūq Ibrāhīm*

the authors for its book series, Umm Kulthūm rejected its proposal for a book about her until she had selected the author. She collaborated with 'Awaḍ to produce a newspaper article and then the book. Her control extended beyond the choice of author into the actual content; she made him read aloud a draft of the article and raised objections to passages that were not to her liking (M. 'Awaḍ 1987, 8, 143). Her input further shaped his accounts through the reuse of portions of the memoirs she had previously dictated to Amīn.

Her collaboration with 'Awaḍ was designed to address a young generation of readers (and listeners). She had already used her Paris trip to cultivate younger fans back home in Egypt. She played a direct role in editing Egyptian television coverage of her Paris trip, which featured queues of young people waiting to enter the theater and interviews with enthusiastic young fans (R. Ṣāliḥ 1967). Now she and 'Awaḍ addressed skeptics from that younger generation in Egypt, whom they felt might ask "Why should we care" instead of greeting her singing with the automatic adoration of their parents. 'Awaḍ, a member of this younger generation, admitted, "I am a fan of Umm Kulthūm's voice, but I do not worship it. I belong to a new generation that does not worship anything" (Maḥsab 1969c). The singer

Umm Kulthūm, members of the Egyptian media, and the singer's ensemble travel together during her trip to Libya. *Bottom right,* radio announcer Jalāl Muʿawwad, whose enthusiastic commentary helped define the political and cultural significance of her concerts. *Photo courtesy of Farūq Ibrāhīm*

and her partnering writer seemed to be concerned not simply with the loss of fans to younger performers whose style was more accessible, like ʿAbd al-Ḥalīm Ḥāfiz (Ḥāfiṭh), but even more so with the loss of those who no longer revered artists at all. By working with ʿAwaḍ, Umm Kulthūm sought to win over a new generation of listeners who would support her art and avidly remember her after her death.[3] By emphasizing certain life events and downplaying others, the collaborators erected signposts that led readers to understand and appreciate her past as well as her future and legacy (Hawkins and Richardson 2007, 607).

Their narrative foregrounded certain aspects of her character with the aim of convincing skeptical readers that she was an artist worthy of their respect and attention. From early in her career, she had identified herself with the *fallāḥīn* (peasants) of Egypt (Danielson 1997, 187–92). Now at the end of her career, she once again stressed her upbringing as a *fallāḥah* to reveal her character for a younger audience. Umm Kulthūm and ʿAwaḍ characterized her humble beginnings by recounting the gifts of milk and eggs presented to her father—the imām of the village Tammāy al-Zahāyra—on her birth. They appealed to readers' compassion with descriptions of her father's struggle to build a mud house large enough for his growing family. They fostered admiration by stressing the basic values she internalized as a young peasant girl. One passage told of how she had confessed to stealing her mother's money to buy candy as a young girl, showing both her fallibility and her ultimate honesty. Another anecdote, from early in her career, explained how she fulfilled a contractual obligation to sing even though the house was empty, thereby testifying to her sense of duty (M. 'Awaḍ 1969b, 71–76).

Umm Kulthūm and 'Awaḍ preempted readers' possible skepticism of her talent by portraying singing as integral to her constitution. In their account, by age five she considered singing one of the essentials of life. During her precarious childhood, she wondered: "Will I find food? Will I find shelter? Will I sing?" (M. 'Awaḍ 1969a, 1969b, 74). Yet the writer and subject made clear that the latter not only possessed exceptional raw talent but also had refined taste even as a young girl. While her peers in the village were singing childish ditties, she was absorbed by the religious songs recorded by her idol Shaykh 'Abū al-'Ilā Muḥammad (1969b, 28).

Umm Kulthūm and 'Awaḍ cultivated further sympathy and admiration by demonstrating the singer's perseverance in overcoming the many obstacles she faced as a female performer. As a child, she seemed naively ignorant of the limitations imposed on her by society: after watching her brother carry his books to the *kuttāb* (school), she announced her desire to do the same, not recognizing that the education of girls was not the norm. Her initial ignorance, however quickly became transformed into an acute awareness of the measures required to preserve her reputation as a virtuous young woman. For instance, she learned not to leave her house alone in order to prevent rumored or illicit encounters with males from outside her family. Soon after she began singing between ages five and eight, her father insisted that she don boys' clothes during public performances to prevent her male listeners' gaze from falling on a young girl (M. 'Awaḍ 1969b, 11, 22, 24, 57). In the book, her negotiation of these challenges was represented so compellingly that one reviewer declared, "She passed through the gates of shame and *ḥarām* with purity" (Maḥsab 1969c).

The product of Umm Kulthūm's collaboration with 'Awaḍ, like the many other autobiographical accounts issued during her later career, was aimed at shaping the way she would be understood and remembered by her audience as a whole. It did not seek only to reach the younger generation. Through printed accounts, interviews, musical projects, and photo opportunities, she developed several facets of her persona for a broader audience, reaching beyond the patriotic image she had cultivated so effectively after the war of June 1967. Despite her vocal support of the Egyptian and Arab causes and her self-effacing assessments of her efforts as simply a citizen's duty, she was well aware of the significance of her fundraising concerts for her own career. During an interview in early 1969, she explained that she envisioned her international concerts remaining a regular part of her schedule even after the conflict with Israel reached a final resolution (al-Zarārī 1969). With an acute awareness of the impact of her actions and statements on her image and legacy, she also developed persistently several additional aspects of her public persona in the years following the war.

The Mother

As an adult, Umm Kulthūm cultivated the life and image of a highly independent woman. Only belatedly did she fulfill cultural expectations to marry. After marrying, she maintained her independence in her professional and personal life, sleeping in separate quarters from her husband and receiving separate social invitations. She displayed this independence to the public. When journalists used the axiom "there is a woman behind every great man" to prompt her to reveal the man behind *her* greatness, she used the opportunity to assert her independence. Rather than identifying her husband as that "behind the scenes" man, as most married women would have done, she named her father, who had passed away nearly four decades earlier (al-Zarārī 1969; Darwīsh 1969e). She underlined her continuing independence through accounts of her youth. While she acknowledged the important roles men had played during her early years, she was also quick to portray her younger self as a mature musician who took increasing control of her career. In her autobiographical accounts of her life as a young singer, she touted her own idea of replacing her accompanying vocalists with an instrumental ensemble, as well as her ability to compose her own repertory (M. 'Awaḍ 1969b, 79; al-Disūqī and Darwīsh 1970b). On a personal matter, she discussed her successful dealings with her father's friends in order to reverse his decision for the family to leave Cairo in response to the publication of slanderous magazine articles about her. Making the point that she was then outgrowing the controlling influence of her father, she recalled thinking, "Is it fair for my father to sacrifice my future because of false news?" (M. 'Awaḍ 1969b, 38).

Umm Kulthūm finessed the gap between her image as an independent career woman and her culture's archetypal female gender role by affecting a maternal sensibility. Childbirth was essential to a woman's ability to maintain her husband and her social and financial status. Without recourse to formal adoption, childless women often faced divorce, polygyny, financial crisis, community ostracism, and the resulting psychological problems (Inhorn 1996, 12–13).[4] Earlier in her life, Umm Kulthūm expressed the concern that she could not sustain an active performing career while having children (al-Muhāmī 1979, 38–39). With the resources to maintain her financial and social standing as a single woman, she successfully escaped public critique for being in a childless marriage: she delayed her marriage until after her childbearing years.[5] While defying cultural expectations by never having children, she took pains to present herself as the possessor of maternal feelings. She effused, "There is nothing in the whole world like a child's smile and a child's happiness. There is nothing worse than a child's misery and a child's tears" (M. 'Awaḍ 1969a, 1969b, 128). 'Awaḍ asked her if the lack of children created a weakness in her married life. When crafting her response, she avoided the terseness that she often used to dodge uncomfortable topics in interviews and instead seized the question as an opportunity to tout her "natural" maternal feelings. This "lack," she explained, "caused my feelings toward children and my love for them to grow and double" (1969a).

Public appearances supported her claim. She conspicuously presented herself as a maternal figure, in part by incorporating activities and photo opportunities with children on nearly all her fundraising trips. In June 1968, she visited orphaned children in Tunisia and held newborns in a Sudanese hospital in late December (Nāṣif 1968a; "Umm Kulthūm tuqabbil" 1969). Television viewers saw her talk at length with a young boy in Sudan and meet with schoolchildren during her March 1969 trip to Libya (Yaḥyá 1968b; "Riḥlat . . . ilá Lībiyā"). Newspaper and magazine readers saw her kiss a small Libyan child and affectionately offer another a soft drink (M. Sālim 1969). She performed a maternal role in front of cameras, just as she had performed a gender in her youth when she disguised herself as a boy. Children's responses bolstered the sincerity of her purported maternal feelings. Her "natural" affection was returned as another child in Libya fed her Coca-Cola (Shahātih 1969). And she set her love of children front and center by identifying a favorite photograph as one of herself kissing a young girl in Sudan (M. 'Awaḍ 1969a). These carefully staged photo opportunities, interpreted explicitly for readers by the press as "an expression of her love for children," solidified the singer's maternal image ("Umm Kulthūm tuqabbil" 1969).

Further bolstering this image, Umm Kulthūm gave the public an intimate look at her maternal role at home. She proudly identified the most important item that she purchased in Sudan as a monkey intended to amuse young children who visited and lived in her home (M. 'Awaḍ 1969a, 1969b, 128). In late 1969, she posed for photos playing with children in her ex-

Umm Kulthūm holds an infant in a Tunisian orphanage, with members of the media standing by to document the event. *Photo courtesy of Farūq Ibrāhīm*

tended family, including ʻĀdil—her cousin's son—whom she had raised for several years.[6] In return, the young ʻĀdil unknowingly boosted her maternal image—as the press reported, he called her "Mama" (Farghalá 1970). Labeling such manifestations of her maternal nature as "private" or "secret" enhanced the credibility of her public performances as a mother. A caption identified photos of the singer with children as "the most beloved pictures in her personal album. A secret that is the last of the secrets of her private life" (M. ʻAwaḍ 1969b, 123). Public glimpses of "private" maternal moments gained even greater value considering that so little was known about the singer's personal life in general.

Umm Kulthūm's displays of affection and affinity for children achieved two important goals. First, they softened her long-standing image as a powerful career woman who doggedly pursued her own professional success while exhibiting little concern for the needs of others.[7] Her publicized encounters with children seemed to reveal a compassionate inner life of "Umm Kulthūm the person, far from the lights, far from singing, far from fame, an affectionate mother to all the members of her family." Instead of perceiving

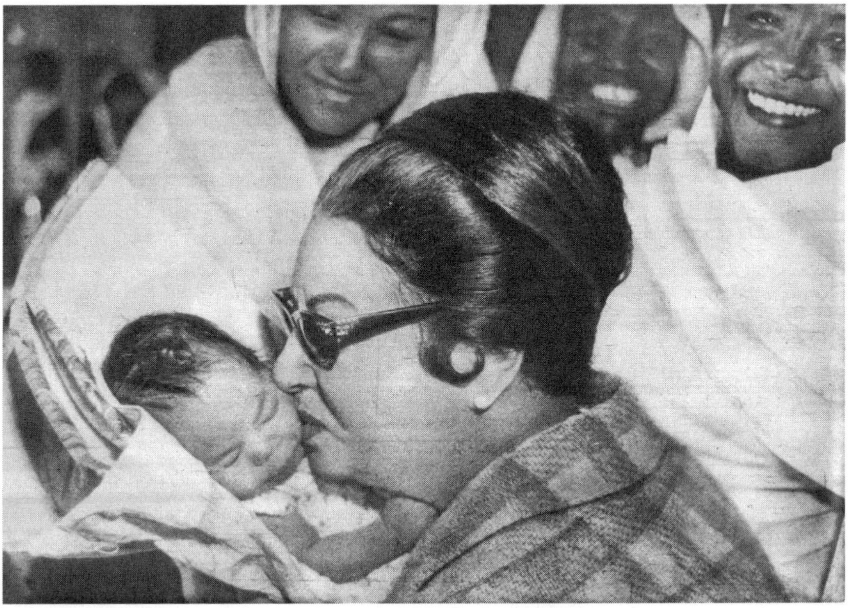

Umm Kulthūm kisses one of her namesakes in a Khartoum hospital. She held each child and recited the opening chapter of the Qur'ān. She also kissed each newborn's cheeks and asked God to give her happiness and health and fill both her and her family's life with goodness. In Sudan and Morocco, dozens of girls born on the occasion of the singer's trips were named after her. *Photo courtesy of Farūq Ibrāhīm.*

self-centered ambition, people could see how "she lives her life with all of life's emotion, love, and humanity ("Umm Kulthūm al-qalb" 1969). Second, these public demonstrations showed that she was not "aberrant" as a woman, lacking concern for children. They confirmed instead that she was a "normal" woman—one with "natural" maternal instincts and feelings. This "affectionate mother" and "normal" woman could be lauded as a model for Arab women (al-ʿAbbāsī 1968d; "Istiqbāl").

The Believer

Umm Kulthūm's status as a model for Arab women was reinforced by her public demonstrations of piety. When asked "Who is the exemplary person?" she did not select a contemporary figure, but rather chose the Prophet Muḥammad as the model for men and his wife, Khadījah, as the model for women (Ramaḍān n.d., 128). She portrayed herself as a devout Muslim through her words and actions (Danielson 1997, 190–91). Although known

Umm Kulthūm feeds the pet monkey that she purchased in Sudan for the amusement of the children in her extended family. *Photo courtesy of Farūq Ibrāhīm*

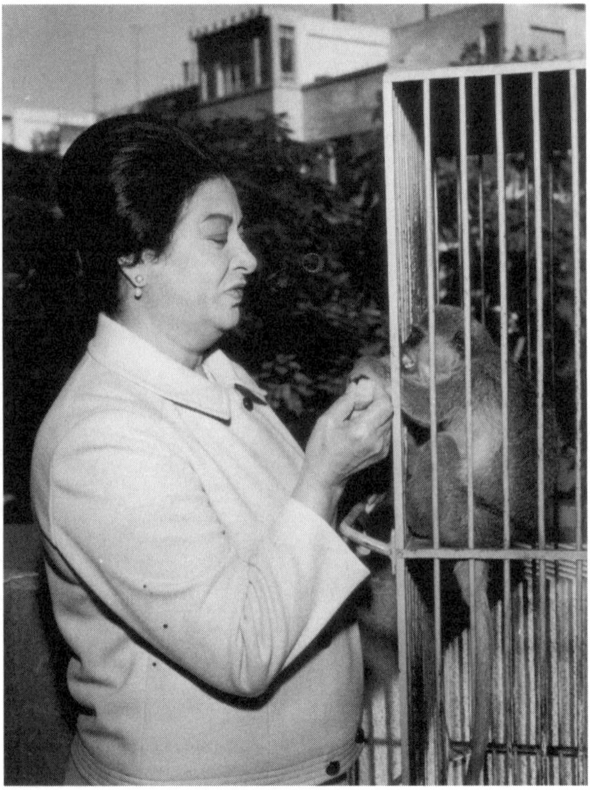

for giving curt responses to questions about private matters, she readily divulged intimate details about her religious life. She did not merely stress her religious upbringing but also explained the rituals of faith in her adult life. On several occasions, she related details of her observance of Ramaḍān and the role of the Qur'ān in her adult life, citing the specific chapters that she recited on particular occasions (Abū Sālim 1967c; Darwīsh 1969e; M. 'Awaḍ 1969b, 72). She depicted her faith as integral to her performances as a vocalist. She described her performance rituals in detail, including her practice of reciting the Qur'ān on her way to the concert hall, with her ensemble members before the curtain rose, and at the start of her recording sessions (Darwīsh 1969e; Tabārak 1969a; 'Aṭīyah 1968). She identified God as responsible for creating and preserving her voice as well as her artistic achievements (Nāṣif 1968c; Qandīl 1968c). In addition, she drew attention to the importance of faith outside her artistic life, publicizing her performance of the *'umrah* (minor pilgrimage) and her plans to build a mosque in her birth village (al-'Abbāsī 1969; al-Disūqī and Darwīsh 1970a). When she appeared as a guest host on the radio program *The Microphone with. . .* ,

Umm Kulthūm poses with a child in the garden of her villa. *Photo courtesy of Farūq Ibrāhīm*

she interviewed a prominent religious figure about the roles of women and *jihād* in Islam, portraying herself as a knowledgeable, committed, and conscientious believer (R. Ṣāliḥ 1968).

The singer's public demonstrations of piety in the postwar years strengthened her self-portrayal. Reporters noted that she insisted on praying and praising God soon after landing in another country (Darwīsh 1969e). When she visited Tunisia, she was treated to a local ensemble's performance of religious songs on the Prophet's birthday. Not content to listen, she joined along with the men, singing praises, as members of the media watched (S. Fu'ād 1968). Public response reinforced her self-presentation. As listeners offered her religious gifts, including a Qur'ān and a candle representing Moses' staff, they confirmed her public piety as a faithful representation and, in the process, helped generate powerful photo opportunities to showcase it (Darwīsh and al-'Abbāsī 1969; Tawfīq 1968b).

Along with Umm Kulthūm's public statements and actions, the artistic projects planned during her later career embodied a concerted effort to show off her piety. In this period, she returned to the religious genres of her

In Morocco, Umm Kulthūm receives a religious gift onstage from the people of Fez. The meter-long green candle, decorated with gold, represented Moses' staff. *Photo courtesy of Farūq Ibrāhīm*

childhood. Having continued to identify herself as a reciter, she began work on a recording of her own recitation of the Qur'ān (al-Malākh 1966). As difficulties arose with this project,[8] she became "content" with recording selected verses in a radio broadcast of *al-Sīrah al-Nabawīyah* (al-Zarārī 1969), the musical rendition of the Prophet's biography that she had performed with her family at *mūlid*s (saints' festivals) and during her early years in Cairo. She personally selected a poet for this project, which would feature choral anthems, *qaṣā'id*, and her recitation of several verses of the Qur'ān in the simple *murattal* style (Abū Sālim 1967a, 1967b). She amplified the importance of the project by marketing it as a gift to the entire Muslim community ("Umm Kulthūm amām" 1968; Qandīl 1968d). Initially she was set to participate in a radio broadcast of *al-Sīrah al-Nabawīyah* in 1965, but her participation in recording the Prophet's biography was delayed by both the June War and her subsequent fundraising trips ("Umm Kulthūm tuqaddim"; Abū Sālim 1969). Ultimately, neither project was realized; women's public recitation of the Qur'ān continued to be the subject of controversy and was considered by many to be *ḥarām* (al-Sa'īd 1968). She later showed her disappointment through curt responses when asked about the Qur'ān and its relation to music (Ramaḍān n.d., 143).

Following these aborted projects, Umm Kulthūm produced religious *qaṣā'id*, as she had in the mid-1940s. Two were inspired by current religious events. For the 1971 hajj season, she had lyrics that were written twelve years earlier by Bayram al-Tūnisī recomposed as "al-Qalb Ya'shaq Kull Jamīl" ('Iṣmat 1971). Al-Tūnisī's lyrics had been set to music by Zakariyā Aḥmad but could not be performed due to a legal conflict between Aḥmad and Umm Kulthūm; Riyāḍ al-Sunbāṭī created the new musical setting.[9] Al-Tūnisī's lyrics addressed themes seen in lyrics from the singer's childhood repertory:

O confused one, you were
        afraid of the pious.
Spend the darkness at night
        with the *dhikr* and the Qur'ān.
Give up your whole world
        and strive for the sanctuary of your lord
For he is the one who created you
        with grace and beneficence.
Make a dutiful repentance
        and cry over your sins
For God is the veil
        He accepts you with forgiveness. ('Abd Allāh 1995, 9)

"Al-Qalb Ya'shaq Kull Jamīl" similarly invoked the sinner's need to surrender to God after a period of godless living, an idea enhanced by the low string *lāzimah*s (melodic responses) in al-Sunbāṭī's setting. As in her childhood repertory, al-Tūnisī's lyrics stressed the transformational power of God's forgiveness, with transformation reflected later in the song when the metrical setting gives way to an ametrical one. String tremolos and contrasting major and minor thirds build drama, while the moment of transformation is enhanced by a modulation from *maqām nahawand* (similar to the minor mode) to *maqām rāst* (closer to the major mode).

Another religious song, "al-Thulāthīyah al-Muqaddasah," honored the three sacred mosques in Mecca, Medina, and Jerusalem. Cinematic passages combining a religious *īqā'* and a sweeping string melody to evoke a desert crossing pointed to the song's use in a television broadcast during the hajj and 'Īd al-Aḍhá (Māhir 1971b). Riyāḍ al-Sunbāṭī's setting of Ṣāliḥ Jawdat's lyrics brought to mind the longevity of Arab culture by using an early Islamic melody and words thought to have been sung by Medinans who welcomed the Prophet in the year of the Hijra. Al-Sunbāṭī's declamatory style of vocal writing, punctuated by low, static *lāzimah*s, casts Umm

Excerpts from "al-Qalb Ya'shaq Kull Jamīl." Music by Riyāḍ al-Sunbāṭī, lyrics by Bayram al-Tūnisī. Premiered in 1971. "al-Qalb Ya'shaq Kull Jamīl: Ḥaflat dawlat al-Imārāt al-'Arabiyyah." Ṣawt al-Qāhirah. 9910/401. Audiocassette.

Kulthūm's ametrical passages as prophetic utterances. After sections focusing on the mosques in Mecca and Medina, one such ametrical passage invokes the prospect of territorial expansion and unification and the reward of paradise for martyrs. Another in the final section has Mary distraught over the 1969 arson attack on the al-Aqṣá mosque in Jerusalem, an event that had struck Umm Kulthūm immediately as a worthy subject for song (Tabārak 1969b). The desert music returns with contemporary resonance as the lyrics predict territorial reclamation: "The land will be returned to its family surrounded by glory and power, the al-Aqṣá mosque will be returned to its lord, proud with prostrations."

Umm Kulthūm's autobiographical statements highlighted such religious songs as a full-circle return to the vocal performances of her childhood. Having grown up performing religious *tawāshīh* and *qaṣā'id* at *mūlids*, she resisted when listeners made aggressive demands to hear dissolute *taqtūqahs* (light songs) containing lines like "Close the curtains so we can enjoy ourselves." As she explained at the end of her career, she remained determined to continue singing praises of the Prophet and religious songs, even when men in the audience jumped onstage in anger and threatened her with violence because they wanted to hear secular songs (M. 'Awaḍ 1969b, 56–58, 60–61). Her commentary on such encounters pointed to a generative force behind the remainder of her career. In her assessment, "The lesson that came from this early on was not to give up. [It was] to persist in singing the type of song that I was singing . . . to develop what I sing for it to be well liked and not to sacrifice the level that I believe in singing" (62). Avoiding such "sacrifice," she used a tasteful romantic repertory to build her audience and attain powerful status in the music industry from which she could further develop her religious repertory in the mid-1940s. By demonstrating both competence and a willingness to conform by singing in these accepted, popular romantic genres, she amassed credibility in the form of "idiosyncrasy credit" that she would later exchange for the opportunity to break artistic boundaries and explore more challenging material, all the while maintaining and even accumulating status (Inglis 1996, 64–65).[10] Thus, Umm Kulthūm persevered in recording three religious *qaṣā'id*, despite her friends' warnings that audiences would not be ready for such serious and complex lyrics ('Abd al-Rasūl 1969c). And she performed them to great acclaim at home and abroad, taking enraptured listeners in Syria through a thirteen-minute improvisation on the climactic line of "Nahj al-Burdah" a decade later ("Nahj al-Burdah"). Having correctly read her audience and her ability to "sell" these songs, she expanded her religious repertory with *Rābi'ah al-'Adawīyah* in 1955 and "Ḥadīth al-Rūḥ" in 1967. As a result, the sole decade in which she did not perform religious music was the 1930s. In her telling of this return to her religious musical roots, she claimed to have developed the public's taste for the repertory to such an extent that when she returned to Alexandria many years after having been confronted by hostile listeners, she found that even a cabaret audience had been "converted" to hearing a religious *qaṣīdah* (M. ʿAwaḍ 1969b, 67).

Umm Kulthūm's narration of this trajectory was supported by other efforts during her later career. The incorporation of her religious performance in Tunisia in her autobiography broadcast on radio with Wajdī al-Ḥakīm reinforced this interpretation of her career. Her insistence on rerecording a passage of "al-Thulāthīyah al-Muqaddasah," even when the initial recording was set to be pressed, attested to the high value she placed on her religious performances. The decision gave weight to her assertions that religious performances were those closest to her heart (Tabārak 1971a; al-Zarārī 1969). Such artistic decisions not only helped cast her career as a full-circle return to the genres of her childhood but also backed up her efforts—through word and image—to have herself remembered as an admirably religious woman.

The Humanitarian

In her later career, Umm Kulthūm also sought to enshrine herself as a compassionate and charitable person. In the late 1960s, she increased her work for charitable causes, making them a more prominent part of her public image. The Egyptian war effort was just one of the causes to which she dedicated herself. When she resumed her provincial fundraising concerts in May 1969, she used her concert in Tanta, Egypt, to support a proliferation of other causes: the construction of housing along the Suez Canal, the Palestinian nationalist movement Fatah, Egyptian soldiers' families, and refugees from the canal zone (Maḥsab 1969b). In December of the same year, she used the ʿĪd al-Fiṭr holiday celebrating the end of Ramadan to launch an extended fundraising campaign for war victims and refugees and visited those who had fled from the canal zone during and after the 1967 war ("Umm Kulthūm sallamat 15,050 ginīhan" 1969). Having already met her earlier goal of raising £E 1 million through her fundraising concerts, she embarked on a new charitable project to benefit both refugees and soldiers (Darwīsh and al-ʿAbbāsī 1969). In Tanta, she raised funds to donate the first of thousands of sewing machines to refugee girls so that they could gain skills and earn money while clothing soldiers on the front line ("Mashrūʿ" 1970; al-Ḥīwān 1971; Labīb 1973). In taking part in this donation drive, she continued a long tradition of Egyptian women's humanitarianism. A similar workshop had been started in 1921 by Islamic activist Labībah Aḥmad, one of many women who established charities and started sewing schools to teach women profitable skills (Baron 1994, 149, 197; Badran 1995, 63).

At the same time, Umm Kulthūm took steps to expand her sewing machine–donation project into a charitable foundation in Cairo ("Umm Kulthūm wa ḥamalāt al-khayr" 1971). While she originally envisioned her foundation as a modest charitable organization of approximately £E 20,000 to provide displaced and orphaned girls with valuable skills and access to an honest source of income, her ambitious colleagues proposed running a lottery to fund construction of a £E 1 million complex carrying her name (M. 'Awaḍ 1987, 4–5; Labīb 1973). Umm Kulthūm was troubled by this radical suggestion, a sentiment that was explained by one of her more reasonable colleagues:

> When Umm Kulthūm goes to people and says, "I will establish a charitable project with £E 20,000 of my own money," people immediately understand the message that she sends to them. But when Umm Kulthūm goes to people and says, "I want to establish a large tower along the Nile carrying my name, but it will be completed with your money," this is a totally different thing. (M. 'Awaḍ 1987, 6)

Despite her initial concerns, she allowed this grand vision to proceed, presumably in the interest of solidifying her posthumous legacy. Plans for the Dār Umm Kulthūm lil-Khayr (Umm Kulthūm Foundation for Charity) ultimately entailed a twenty-story hotel with a pool and gardens, and a four-story building containing nine museum halls dedicated to Umm Kulthūm's works, along with both contemporary compositions and older Eastern music. While proceeds from the proposed hotel, cinema, and concert hall would cover the foundation's operating expenses, lottery tickets were sold in 1973 to finance the complex's construction. When ticket sales lagged during the difficult economic conditions of the October War of the same year, Umm Kulthūm herself bought the remaining £E 75,000 in tickets and donated her winnings to the organization. Although the foundation stone was laid, official paperwork concerning the project's land was reportedly buried in a bureaucratic maze, and the project was never completed ("al-Wajh al-khayrī" 1975; Tabārak 1974; Ḥāfiṭh 1973; "Qiṣṣat" 1982).

Even without a grand monument bearing her name, Umm Kulthūm still strengthened her legacy during her later career. She sculpted a well-rounded public image that added humanitarianism, maternal affection, and piety to the patriotism she displayed so prominently after the war. Through public performances on and off the concert stage, a host of autobiographical statements, carefully crafted photo opportunities, and press statements, she shaped her image and legacy so convincingly during this period that many posthumous biographical accounts have sustained and exaggerated these qualities. In addition to shaping several facets of her public image, she ensured her reception as a national symbol and an enduring part of the country's cultural heritage.

The National Symbol

During her later years, Umm Kulthūm was increasingly perceived as a national symbol and a part of Egyptian heritage. Even as she maintained an active career, she acquired the status of a living historical monument, much like Buffalo Bill did during his farewell tours in the early twentieth century (Kasson 2000, 7). As one writer remarked in 1970, "Umm Kulthūm became one of the symbols of Egypt through her stance after June [1967]" (A. Ṣāliḥ 1970, 29). The singer's activities reinforced this perception. As part of her expanding charitable campaign, she gave a fundraising concert in Giza to help the United Nations Educational, Scientific, and Cultural Organization (UNESCO) rescue the Philae Temple near Aswan (Farghalá 1969). This monument to Isis, a treasured example of ancient Egyptian architecture, was at risk of sustaining irreparable damage from Nile waters upon completion of the High Dam. The elaborate and costly process of dismantling and reassembling the temple on a nearby island would take several years. As Umm Kulthūm's concert helped fund the temple's reconstruction, it also shaped her image and legacy. In choosing the exact location of the stage—just seventy meters from the Sphinx and five hundred meters from the largest pyramid—she planted herself among the country's most famous and enduring monuments, as if she were one of them ("Laylat" 1969; Abū al-Majad 1969). One writer saw in her the solidity of the ancient monuments, while another described her as the fourth pyramid (M. Muḥammad 1969; "al-Aṭlāl fawq qimmat al-haram" 1969). The concert setting resurrected an association the singer had created a few years earlier through publicity photographs taken alongside the pyramids and the Sphinx for her concerts in Paris. Her arrangement of the visual concert scene portrayed her as both a national symbol and a durable part of the country's cultural heritage.

Umm Kulthūm's efforts to cast herself as an iconic, enduring symbol of the Egyptian cultural heritage were aided by other contemporary practices. Her work to establish an ensemble dedicated to live performances of music from the *turāth*—an expanding canon of old music deemed to be of high quality—ultimately did much to help her cause (el-Shawan 1980, 47–52, 185–87).[11] After the Firqat al-Mūsīqá al-'Arabīyah (Arabic Music Ensemble) was founded in fall 1967, her songs of the 1920s, 1930s, and 1940s gained a prominent place in its repertory. Her songs' absorption into the *turāth* gained additional momentum through programming on the radio show *From the Song Library* and inclusion in entrance auditions for the country's higher institutes of music (Ḥijāzī 1969; F. al-Shādhilī 1969). Other people precipitated her physical memorialization through sites normally reserved for the deceased. A fan maintained an Umm Kulthūm café devoted to her songs, while an Umm Kulthūm Studio was designated within the state radio and television building (Darwīsh 1969b). The Ministry of Culture prepared an archive of her songs, films, and world press coverage ("Wizārat" 1970). Near her birth village, the city of al-Sinbillawayn planned an Umm Kulthūm street and a museum including a theater, library, listening hall, and life-size statue (Darwīsh 1971b; Sa'd 1970, 8). Even absent Dār Umm Kulthūm lil-Khayr, a host of other musical tributes and physical sites established her place in the *turāth* and elevated her as a national symbol.

The Active Artist

Even as Umm Kulthūm began, in effect, to enter the archives of national culture in the late 1960s and early 1970s, she remained an active artist responding to the changing political and cultural needs of Egypt and the Arab world. She continued to raise funds for the Egyptian war effort as late as 1971, and she supported the Palestinian resistance to Israeli occupation, giving two concerts to benefit Fatah. The timing of the invitation to perform from a member of the Libyan royal family coincided with 'Abd al-Nāṣir's pledge, shortly before the fifth Palestinian National Council, to help Fatah and Yāsir 'Arafāt attain leadership positions in the Palestine Liberation Organization (PLO) (Shemesh 1996, 104). The Libyan invitation was extended by the king's cousin, Amīr 'Abd Allāh 'Ābid al-Sanūsī, who also paid the concert expenses, allowing ticket proceeds to benefit the Palestinian *fidā'iyīn* (Darwīsh 1969f). Just as al Sanūsī's efforts sustained previous Libyan financial support for the *fidā'iyīn*, Umm Kulthūm continued her earlier work in support of Fatah (Cobban 1984, 45; Blundy and Lycett 1987, 77). She had designated half of the proceeds from her Kuwait concert in April 1968 for the Palestinian resistance when 'Abd al-Nāṣir offered Egypt's support to the movement (Nāṣif 1968b; Shemesh 1996, 106–108). In the case of the Libyan invitation, Umm Kulthūm was—unusually—given just two days to decide whether to accept, which she did. Through this quick planning, her concerts coincided with the highly touted one-year anniversary of the proclaimed victory of the *fidā'iyīn* at al-Karāmah (Darwīsh 1969f). While echoing the Egyptian government's support for Fatah, the singer's carefully timed concerts simultaneously sanctioned the leadership of King Idrīs I, who would later be deposed in a military coup. The concerts coincided with the Libyan king's birthday and symbolically acknowledged his loan of £E 10 million ($23 million) to finance Soviet arms needed by Egypt in the war of attrition, which was then just beginning (Feiler 2003, 8).

While she had made a brief statement in support of the *fidā'iyīn* in 1968, her support became vociferous in early 1969 (Qandīl 1968d). Her rhetoric during the previous years had featured general terms such as "patriotic duty," "homeland," and "victory," drawing on widespread anti-Israel sentiment and admitting numerous interpretations. Now she mentioned Palestine in particular. She cited the *fidā'iyīn*'s work as the exemplary method of reclaiming Palestine (Darwīsh 1969a). Shortly after Arafat's election to the leadership of the PLO, she revealed the text of a new song lauding the *fidā'iyīn* (Yaḥyá 1969b). In an interview conducted shortly before she left for Libya, she praised the *fidā'iyīn*'s militant action as preferable to passivity. "I believe," she proclaimed, "that the beginning of the real work of liberating Palestine is the appearance of the Palestinian *fidā'ī* who carries the rifle, gun, and grenade, who crosses the wires and existing borders created by Israel . . . and is not content with the hope of freeing his country" (al-Naqqāsh 1969, 36). She promised to lend her credibility, effort, and money to aid the Palestinian resistance and singled out the Fatah organization as the primary inspiration behind her growing public support ('Abd al-Rasūl 1969a; Qandīl 1969b, 40). Identifying 'Arafāt as a model for others, she observed that "he could have become a millionaire but he chose to leave wealth and millions behind him and spend his days and youth for the sake of liberating his country" (al-Naqqāsh 1969, 36).

Through her numerous statements about the *fidā'iyīn*, Umm Kulthūm played up her political convictions. When asked to reveal one important goal that she had yet to achieve, she responded not with an artistic aim but with a political one: "liberating the dear occupied lands, cleansing Palestine of the stain of Zionism, and returning Arab Palestinians to their homeland" (al-Zarārī 1969). She not only met with Yāsir 'Arafāt but also touted her familiarity with his biography and said she had long desired that an armed uprising would liberate Palestine (Maḥmūd 2003; al-Naqqāsh 1969, 36). Portraying herself as a champion of liberation movements everywhere—not just in Palestine—she enumerated struggles taking place across the globe, spoke of the dignity of dying for the cause of liberation, and professed that she had considered "singing for the sake of Vietnam, its people, and its future" (Qandīl 1969b, 40).

Both on and off the stage, Umm Kulthūm portrayed herself as a spokesperson and even a member of the *fidā'iyīn*. Alluding to the title of her new patriotic song "Asbaḥa 'Indī al-Ān Bundūqīyah," she proclaimed, "I can say in their tongue with all of my heart . . . 'Now I have a rifle'" (al-Naqqāsh 1969, 37). In Muḥammad 'Abd al-Wahhāb's poignant musical setting of Nizār al-Qabbānī's lyrics, Umm Kulthūm sings in the voice of a youth joining the *fidā'iyīn*. Musically and poetically, the song expresses grief and nostalgia—sentiments often articulated through female figures of the widow and mother in wartime music—while lauding the masculine heroism of the soldier (Wolfe 2005, 32; Hatchett and McNeil 2005, 33). Following an introduction combining martial and lyrical elements, the pain of the youth's reflections is drawn out by strings, flute, and delicate pizzicati: "For twenty years, I have been searching for a land, an identity." Brass instruments enter gradually and lead into the song's first climax, as Umm Kulthūm sings, "Take me to Palestine with you, men, I want to live or die like men." After another poignant interlude, she continues, "Tell whoever asks about me that my gun became my cause." The brass instruments rise to a second climax with trumpet tattoos punctuating her declaration, "I am one of the revolutionaries." The most martial treatment is reserved for the final lines, "To Palestine there is one way—it passes from the mouth of a rifle." As the song concludes, this incisive vocal fanfare is split between the male chorus and Umm Kulthūm's overdubbed voice, which now represents the masses of mobilized youth.

Umm Kulthūm saw her *fidā'ī* role extending beyond her voicing of the resistance fighters' aspirations in this song. When four members of Fatah presented her with a storm badge representing the organization and its militant wing, she responded, "Does this mean that I have become one of you? One of the combatants? There is nothing greater than the day that I become one of you" (Qandīl 1969a, 60). During her performances in Libya, she was embedded in the visual symbols and mottos of the Palestinian resistance movement. The Fatah storm badge hung from the back wall of the stage, while around the stage, banners carried militant slogans, such as "Peaceful solutions will only continue over our dead bodies" (al-Naqqāsh 1969, 37; "Riḥlat . . . ilá Lībiyā"). While sporting her Fatah badge, she gave voice to the resistance as she sang "al-Aṭlāl," with its resonant words "Give me my freedom, set free my hands" ('Abd al-Rasūl 1969b).

By promoting the *fidā'iyīn* on Libyan rather than Egyptian soil, Umm Kulthūm served the needs of the Egyptian regime. Egypt's backing of the Palestinian resistance movement "allowed the regime to raise a new banner of 'support' for the kind of struggle toward which the sympathies of the Egyptian masses were drawn but which state power could not afford to let develop in Egypt itself" (Hussein 1977, 300; Cobban 1984, 45–46). As the government sought to control the notion of a people's war within Egypt against Israel by restricting it to civilian support of the regular army, Umm

Excerpts from “Asbaḥa ‘Andī al-Ān Bundūqīyah.” Music by Muḥammad ‘Abd al-Wahhāb, lyrics by Nizār al-Qabbānī. Composed and recorded in 1969. *Aghānī waṭanīyah li Sayyidat al-Ghinā’ al-‘Arabī Umm Kulthūm,* vol. 2. Ṣawt al-Qāhirah 00/032/401, D00/1016. Audiocassette.

Umm Kulthūm performs in front of the Fatah storm badge in Tripoli, Libya.
Photo courtesy of Farūq Ibrāhīm

Kulthūm and the press touted a popular movement located safely outside its borders (Hussein 1977, 290). While one journalist characterized her Libyan concerts to benefit Fatah as representative of "the Arab effort *in* Egypt for the sake of liberation," the concerts, in reality, manifested support for the resistance movement *outside* Egypt, away from the sites of the volatile demonstrations of February and November 1968, which had included calls to arm the people amid domestic protests ("Ṣuwar" 1969, emphasis mine; Hussein 1977, 299, 311, 313). The appeal of popular resistance was made plain by the 12,000 Egyptian youths who rushed to the Fatah office in Cairo to volunteer shortly after the al-Karamah success of March 1968 (Cobban 1984, 39). As the Egyptian government contained desires for the expression in Sinai of popular resistance against Israel, Umm Kulthūm helped direct Egyptians' energy through other, "safe" channels, such as economic boycotts against Israel's allies. Fatah sought to "condense the climate of hope"

through its own fighting and to buy ʿAbd al-Nāṣir time to rebuild his military power, so that the Egyptians could one day aid the Palestinians in their quest and also reclaim Sinai (Cobban 1984, 205). Entire magazine issues were devoted to the *fidāʾiyīn* (*Ākhir sāʿah* May 14, 1969). Meanwhile, Umm Kulthūm helped the Egyptian media showcase *fidāʾiyīn* achievements and quiet public impatience over the lack of major Egyptian advances against Israeli occupation of the Sinai Peninsula.

This was just one of several strategies employed by the regime and furthered by Umm Kulthūm, who also supported government and media efforts to dissociate the Egyptian liberation of Sinai from Palestinian liberation. When asked what she would write in a letter to the *fidāʾiyīn*, Umm Kulthūm offered advice that made their struggle sound remote and unrelated to the reclamation of Egyptian territory (Hussein 1977, 287, 290, 299; Qandīl 1969b, 40). When the June 1, 1968, cover of the magazine *al-Idhāʿah wa al-tilīfizyūn* asked, "What was accomplished from June 1967 to June 1968?" support for Fatah and the *fidāʾiyīn* was placed last, several positions after the rebuilding of the regular armed forces. The order reflected a desire on the part of government forces to subjugate the Palestinian resistance movement to the Egyptian army's reconstruction in the minds of Egyptians and the broader Arab public. The government maintained such a priority even as it agreed to support Fatah within the framework of the PLO, to the mutual benefit of Fatah and the regime.[12] In lending verbal and financial support to Fatah, Umm Kulthūm walked a fine line between these two seemingly unconnected goals. The challenge associated with walking this line likely explains why her Libyan concerts were not followed by similar performances, why her pro-Fatah statements ultimately tapered off, and why her Tanta concert in May 1969 yielded only a modest sum in support of the resistance.

During the first half of 1969, though, Umm Kulthūm succeeded in making herself a relevant voice for both Egyptian and Arab society. She was not deterred from taking stances at the multiple levels of allegiance and nationalism that proved so challenging for other Arab artists, such as Fayrūz. With her collaborators ʿĀṣī and Manṣūr al-Raḥbānī, Fayrūz struggled to navigate Lebanese, Syrian, Palestinian, and Arab allegiances (Stone 2008, 47). Umm Kulthūm's support of the Palestinian resistance showed that she was committed to a central issue facing the Arab world. Yet she remained conspicuously supportive of the Egyptian war effort. She recorded a new patriotic song for Egypt, "Miṣr," and donated her compensation for her Libyan performances to the war effort.

But by the time "Miṣr" was broadcast in August 1969, Egypt's conflict had declined in relative importance to the Palestinian conflict in the eyes of the Arab world. This was the case even as Umm Kulthūm still spoke of Egypt as the leader of the Arab battle (Qandīl 1969b, 40). The shift was captured at the beginning of her concert in Tripoli, Libya. Just three days before, Lt. Gen. ʿAbd al-Muʿnim Riyāḍ, chief of staff of the Egyptian armed forces, had been killed when an Israeli shell struck the bunker where he was observing the conflict at Ismailia along the Suez Canal. Though Umm Kulthūm stood onstage at the beginning of the concert crying over the general's death, she sang for several hours amid banners with the slogans and symbols of the *fidāʾiyīn*. She also devoted far more financial support from her two concerts to the Palestinian cause than to her own country's military accounts: ticket proceeds designated for Fatah totalled £E 150,000 ($345,000), nearly six times the personal compensation that she donated to the war effort (Qandīl 1969a, 59). Arab listeners supported such priorities. Just a few days after her first performance in Libya, a reader of Amman's newspaper *al-Dustūr* urged her to perform in Jordan—that is, in front of Palestinians and at the front line of Palestinian resistance (Ṣalāḥ 1969). When Egypt demanded increased aid from other Arab countries at the Rabat summit in late 1969, they did not comply; several Arab leaders stated that "priority should be given to the Palestinians over increasing aid to Egypt" (Feiler 2003, 8). As a result, Egypt relied more and more on Soviet assistance to wage the war of attrition (Khalidi 1973, 63–74, 80).

Final Years

While Egypt's status in the region declined, Umm Kulthūm's profile remained strong. She sang at Lebanon's Baalbek festival in July 1970 and in Abu Dhabi in November of the following year. Even though she was roughly seventy years old, her concerts generated enthusiastic public support: while critics occasionally knocked her outdated style, fans still sought tickets on the black market, men danced between the seats, and women raised their arms and swayed with the music (al-Khūrī 2000, 97). The Abu Dhabi theater overflowed with listeners, many of whom sat on the floor to hear her perform live ("Umm Kulthūm: 'Min Ajli ʿAynayk'"). Fans in Arab countries sent the singer thousands of letters requesting that she schedule more concerts ("Burqīyah" 1970). Invitations from Syria, Iraq, Bahrain, Algeria, and Morocco validated nicknames, such as the "Voice of Arabness," that captured the breadth of her art and her iconic status across the region (Darwīsh 1969g; "al-ʿIrāq" 1970; Māhir 1971c). Meanwhile, Egyptian print and television coverage of her performances abroad, such as those in Libya, showcased her political currency and cultural relevance across the region for listeners at home.[13]

In Umm Kulthūm's final years, she solidified her international status. Concert invitations and record sales confirmed her growing popularity in the Arab diaspora. Calls to perform in Paris, London, and Canada showed that her appeal stretched beyond Arab lands, with these invitations bolstered by the finding that her recording of Balīgh Ḥamdī's "Alf Laylah wa Laylah" outsold all other recordings of Arab music outside Egypt (Darwīsh 1969h; Darwīsh 1971a). As far afield as Malaysia, her songs were singled out as highly important works of emotional unity for Muslims (Dāwud 1969). Increasing attention from the international media included U.S. and Japanese press reports during the start of her season in late 1969, and French and German television recorded her performances (Darwīsh 1969c; Tabārak 1969a).[14] *Marie Claire* selected her as one of the fifty most famous women in the world, and a *Los Angeles Times* writer identified her as the wealthiest self-made woman in the Middle East ("Umm Kulthūm wa ashhar 50 sayyidah" 1971; Tuohy 1970).

In September 1970, amid this increasing international acclaim, Umm Kulthūm traveled to the Soviet Union, where she planned to give two concerts. Her performances were intended to benefit the war effort at home, while acknowledging Soviet aid in the form of electronic equipment, missiles, advisers, and pilots (Farghalá 1970). The Soviets also provided defensive capability for when Israeli air raids penetrated deep into the country, enabling Egyptian forces to concentrate their efforts on offensive measures in the canal zone (Khalidi 1973, 67–69). A landmark in her career, the trip prompted the publication of her life story and song lyrics in four languages (*Umm Kulthūm fī al-Ittiḥād al-Sūviyatī* 1970), and promised to supply valuable footage for a film on her life (al-Ḥiwān 1970). Yet before her first concert began, she learned of 'Abd al-Nāṣir's sudden death of a heart attack. Devastated, she did not eat or speak during the next twenty-four hours,[15] and she returned to Egypt without performing. Upon her return, she prayed with her fellow countrywomen and secluded herself for a week to mourn 'Abd al-Nāṣir's death (Goldman 1996; Darwīsh 1970). Despite her personal devastation, Umm Kulthūm put to rest a rumor that she would not sing in the upcoming season and recorded a new song honoring Egypt's fallen president, "Risālat Jamāl 'Abd al-Nāṣir" (Jawdat 1970). 'Abd al-Nāṣir was not only the leader for whom she acted as "muezzin" for fifteen years but also one of many friends and colleagues whom she had recently lost (Jawdat 1970; Danielson 1997, 166). Among such losses was her longtime *qānūn* player, Muḥammad 'Abd al-Ṣāliḥ, who had died on July 2. Also, she had only recently found a new *'ūd* player to take the place of Muḥammad al-Qaṣabjī, who had died in 1966. She began her musical season in January 1971 as promised, but the first concert was colored by her emotional response to 'Abd al-Nāṣir's death. She transformed the romantic "Wa Dārit al-Ayyām" into a lament, crying onstage during the song's final twenty minutes. Her tearful rendition of the passage "The days have passed, the days have slipped away" marked the end of an era and would evoke 'Abd al-Nāṣir's death for years to come ("Bakat" 1971; Danielson 1997, 168).

'Abd al-Nāṣir's death constituted a turning point in Umm Kulthūm's life not simply because she was devastated personally but because of the radical change of leadership it brought about. President Anwar al-Sādāt and his wife, Jīhān, would cultivate a younger female singer to replace Umm Kulthūm, who was seen as a symbol of the past regime (al-Maḥallāwī 1994, 176–207).[16] Yet her iconic status in Egyptian society proved difficult to suppress: her image even appeared on the front page of major newspapers to help sell television sets (*al-Akhbār,* February 17, 1971). Umm Kulthūm continued performing, preparing a new repertory and offering international concerts for the war effort, despite her deteriorating health. Performing in Abu Dhabi in 1971, she raised additional funds for the war as well as helping mark the formation of the United Arab Emirates. Asked in that year if she would stop singing, she rejected the possibility, even as she acknowledged her declining stamina (al-Khūrī 1971; 2000, 177). Her final concert came in 1972, when she faltered conspicuously on a high note, prompting pitying applause from the audience and, finally, precipitating her retreat from the stage (Guindi 1998).

During her later career, Umm Kulthūm's increasing attentiveness to her public image yielded several important results. She developed a many-sided persona designed to appeal to a broad public. Her public image only held more appeal once she was seen as a target of Anwar and Jīhān al-Sādāt. And her efforts at self-presentation, while solidifying her regional and international status in her later years, also prompted the type of hagiography that would dominate her posthumous reception. Seeing 'Abd al-Nāṣir's death as a turning point and possibly the end of her career, Ṣaliḥ Jawdat made a hyperbolic assessment in 1970 that sounded like an epitaph: "Umm Kulthūm's voice was the one voice that was able to carry consolation for us and awaken hope in us. After the Naksah we had no comfort or hope except Umm Kulthūm's voice" (1970). While premature, Jawdat's comments foreshadowed the ways in which the singer's later career would have an impact on her posthumous legacy.

CHAPTER 4

From Artist to Legend

In early 1975, Umm Kulthūm suffered kidney failure, which prompted a cerebral hemorrhage and the failure of other internal organs. Front pages of the region's newspapers detailed the progression of her illness, and after she died on February 3, biographical sketches and panegyrics filled the pages of Egyptian and other Arab periodicals, as well as publications across the globe ("Mātat al-shādīyah" 1975). While she was still alive, foreign leaders called the hospital for updates on her condition, and later they expressed their condolences to Anwar al-Sādāt and sent representatives to the singer's funeral ("al-Muḥāwalāt" 1975; "Wafūd" 1975; "Mātat Umm Kulthūm" 1975). Umm Kulthūm's funeral procession in Cairo rivaled 'Abd al-Nāṣir's in size, with millions attending. Across the region, radio and television stations broadcast her funeral and offered special programs in her honor.[1]

With her death, several shifts in the Egyptian music scene became more evident. The deaths of other artists who had been prominent for decades, including Farīd al-Aṭrash in 1974 and 'Abd al-Ḥalīm Ḥāfiz in 1977, along with the declining productivity of Muḥammad 'Abd al-Wahhāb, further heralded a changing of the guard. Despite efforts by younger singers like Wardah and Ḥānī Shākir to continue following the *ṭarab* approach, the loss of Umm Kulthūm and her peers led some observers to declare the age of *ṭarab* over (Frishkopf 2003, 159; Stokes 2000, 597; Gordon 2003, 77). Two alternative styles arose in Egypt in the 1970s. First popularized by Aḥmad 'Adawīyah, *sha'bī* (popular music) mixed rural with lower-class urban styles. Its brash, slang-filled, and often risqué lyrics addressed the harsh realities of urban life, as cities swelled with migrants fleeing rural areas and oppressive *infitāḥ* policies that opened the country to foreign investment but widened the gap between rich and poor. More broadly popular dance-pop—also called *jīl* and *mūsīqá shabābīyah,* meaning "youth music"—mixed Western pop rhythms and instrumentation with Arabic percussion and lyrics on traditional themes. Emerging through the work of artists like Muḥammad Munīr, dance-pop developed further in the 1980s, with important contributions from Libyan immigrants such as Hamid al-Shāʿirī. During the next two decades, key figures in dance-pop went on to compose and arrange songs for stars like ʿAmr Diyāb. *Shaʿbī* would find its continuation in singers like Shaʿbān ʿAbd al-Raḥīm, and elements of both styles would be fused by performers like Ḥakīm (Frishkopf 2003, 159–61).

With the help of a burgeoning cassette culture, popular and dance-pop styles came to dominate the Egyptian music scene. Yet, even so, writers and critics continued to honor Umm Kulthūm's artistic contributions. They commonly characterized her accomplishments using superlative terms, despite the ascendance of more contemporary and popular idioms. Kamāl al-Najmī identified her as "the greatest singer in the history of Arab singing" (1993, 212). Muhammad Saʿīd placed her atop his list of the one hundred most famous people in the field of Arab song (2002). Others stressed her influence on the vocalists who succeeded her (Ramaḍān n.d. 24–25, 186–87; Ilyās Saḥḥāb 1980, 17–19; Zakariyā 1983, 7). Many, including Tharwat Fahmī (1975), described her as a "school" or "professor" who trained generations of singers.

Other commentators offered more detailed assessments of the singer's historical contributions to the development of Arabic music, often singling out the quality of her song lyrics for praise (al-Naqqāsh 2000, 27, 32–33; al-Marīnī 1975, 184). Authors like Muḥammad ʿAdnān al-Khaṭīb credited her with a triumph over vulgar songs and for raising the level of Arabic song by choosing beautiful lyrics of value, quality, and moral substance (1975, 30). Some attributed to her a refinement and revolution of Arabic song through the elimination of "foreign blemishes" (al-Marīnī 1975, 184; ʿAbd al-Ḥamīd 1975). For others, she not only improved the quality of music but also the character of her audience. In Kamāl Raḍwān's view, "[S]he did not just sing—her voice taught and her performance elevated" (2000, 46). Several gave her credit for broadening the audience of religious songs (al-Marīnī 1975, 21; ʿAbd al-Fattāḥ 1992, 81).

In the decades following her death, the vast majority of observers refrained from offering critical accounts of her artistic contributions. Earlier claims that she stifled competition and actually stunted the development of Arabic song were largely omitted from the historical record (Tabārak 1969c). Writer Ilyās Saḥḥāb was unusual in recounting the view that Umm Kulthūm's voice "was one of the symbols of the retardation of, and obstacles to, artistic development in the Arab nation" (1980, 22). Few acknowledgements of the memory slips and negative public reaction that occurred during her final years tempered the paeans and hagiographic accounts most commonly used to recall her life (Mahfoudh 1975; Banjulūn 1975, 239; Qandīl 1999, 11).

Umm Kulthūm's outstanding artistic accomplishments clearly set the foundation for these accounts. Her exceptional talent, the quality of her artistic products, and her prolific output prompted glowing assessments. Her success in committing comparatively few artistic faux pas, and her unusual longevity as a performer—her career lasted into a sixth decade—underscored her extraordinary achievements. However, this hagiographic treatment has not been limited to Umm Kulthūm's art. It has been extended to, and has permeated, assessments of the singer as a human being, transforming her from a naturally flawed person to a faultless legend. The continued predominance of such reverent accounts prompts two questions: Why has she been worshipped so consistently since her death? And in what ways has this hagiography been constructed?

The latter question can be addressed initially through an examination of the writing practices of journalists and authors who portrayed and sometimes critiqued the singer. Those practices were often shaped by Umm Kulthūm herself during her lifetime. She cultivated friendships with powerful journalists and strived to keep close control over writers' work in Egypt. In addition to the direct control she exerted over journalists, as acknowledged by Maḥmūd ʿAwaḍ and ʿAlī Amīn, she exerted indirect control over content published about her. When a journalist began working on a biographical piece without her knowledge, Umm Kulthūm enlisted a friend to stop the project and ended her relationship with the writer, whom she viewed as overly independent (Raḍwān 2000, 50–51). By demonstrating that she would retaliate for unauthorized or negative accounts, she effectively trained Egyptian journalists to write adulatory articles and even submit documents for her preapproval. Her success was evidenced by the confinement of negative accounts to oral tradition and the foreign press. After the singer's death, authors' recycling of previous writing sustained these glowing portrayals, even in addition to the typically idealized assessments offered immediately after the death of a public figure. Publishing houses' clippings of old articles provided, and continue to provide, the basis for a surprising number of new articles, with previous stories being republished either verbatim or near verbatim, often with no indication of the piece's earlier publication or any new interpretive angle. This accepted practice has kept up the laudatory accounts that were published during her lifetime and quite possibly has hindered the development of new, perhaps critical, assessments. Similarly, Arabic-language books have recycled earlier work, particularly that of Niʿmāt Aḥmad Fuʾād, Muḥammad al-Sayyid Shūshah, and Rajāʾ al-Naqqāsh.[2] Arab authors have also turned to Western writing in creating new accounts. When *Life* magazine's Middle East correspondent Gordon Gaskill proclaimed, "In the Middle East there are two things that never change: Umm Kulthūm and the pyramids," he had unknowingly penned a nearly mandatory part of every posthumous Arabic account about the singer (Naṣrī 1975, 26; "Lamaḥāt" 1975).

Two additional factors have helped construct and fuel this one-sided portrayal of the late singer. First, the interactive nature of Umm Kulthūm's art form helped her forge strong connections with her audience. Enthusiastic public response to her music and image could serve to anchor glowing portrayals in the apparent reality of her life. Second, her careful crafting of a public persona provided writers with an attractive template for their own accounts. She presented herself not simply as an artist but as the embodiment of ideals held by Egyptian society and much of the Arab world. The efficacy of her self-portrayal was corroborated in works of Egyptian literature, in which characters' values could be measured according to their response to the singer. In one play, a father tests his prospective son-in-law's character by asking, "Do you listen to the Lady?" while in another, a police officer garners a woman's trust through his absorption in an Umm Kulthūm song on the radio.[3] As the singer herself spotlighted particular facets of her image, she offered writers carefully constructed statements and photo opportunities tailored for continued use. Consequently, unlike other artists, such as Asmahan, whose life stories have been filtered heavily through others' views (Zuhur 2000, 210), Umm Kulthūm was able maintain a hand in the shaping of biographical accounts after her death. By upholding rather than deconstructing her persona, authors have allowed her to contribute to a collaboratively built reception history.

The cumulative effect of these factors can be seen in the posthumous portrayal of the singer as devout. Accounts have relied extensively on her own statements and actions, the response of her public, and material from the Western press, with all these sources sustaining the image of a pious woman. ʿAbd Allāh Aḥmad ʿAbd Allāh established piety as an integral part of the singer's character when he portrayed the young Umm Kulthūm as a writer of religious lyrics, such as the following, in which God appeals to the believer:

> You will find me in your prostrations when you pray
> and when you stand, so search for me and you will find me
> You will find me merciful, devoted, and compassionate
> with all creation, so search for me and you will find me. (ʿAbd Allāh 1995, 10–11)

Photo opportunities facilitated by Umm Kulthūm informed numerous posthumous accounts. In biographical treatments, photographs were reprinted of her praying and kissing religious objects, including those given to her by members of the public, and were often grouped under explicit headings, such as "Faith in the Life of Umm Kulthūm" (Ḥassanayn 1998,

1; Abū al-Khayr 1975, n.p.). Authors were so determined to represent her piety that they transformed even nondescript photographs—such as of Umm Kulthūm reading a literary book—into evidence with captions like "Umm Kulthūm used to specialize in reciting the Qur'ān in quiet moments" (al-Marīnī 1975, 61). Captioned "With God and his book, her first teacher," a photograph of her kissing the Qur'ān sustained her emphasis on the significance of Qur'anic recitation for her development as a singer (Abū al-Khayr 1975, n.p.). An affectionate caricature of her as a singing bird captioned the "Blessing of God" echoed nicknames such as the "Lyre of God" and "Lyre of Heaven" (Ben Hammed 1997, 157; Muṣṭafá 1975, 17; Labīb 1975). These representations also supported her characterization of her voice as a divine gift ("Ṣawtī hibah" 1968). Complementing such visual evidence were extended statements from figures in the Western press and the singer herself. 'Izzat al-Amīr reported that the French press had referred to her as the "Nun of Islam" because she prayed after her concerts while other performers went out to celebrate and drink. As al-Amīr explained, "After her first concert in Paris, she went to her hotel, put her head on a pillow, and asked herself, 'What did I do to earn all of this success?'" She concluded, "Everything that I attained was thanks to God and I did not have any effort in it. It is a gift from God" (1975, 30). The writer used the singer's statements to turn her Paris concert, originally conceived before the war to fortify her growing fame, into the paradigmatic example of humility and faith in God.

Umm Kulthūm's maintenance of her own pristine image helped ensure that she would be portrayed in saintly fashion after her death. In this endeavor, she disclosed limited information about her personal life and took great care with photo opportunities and language in her interactions with the press. Particularly when coupled with the discretion and loyalty of family members and employees, these steps ensured that very few negative stories circulated. She cast herself as the embodiment of strong cultural ideals, including patriotism, piety, and the humanitarianism that was marked as an important value in the shaping of the Egyptian nation (Suleiman 1983, 99). Collectively, these practices helped set her up as a modern mythological figure, a real person readily accessible from recent cultural memory who has been glorified as a legend in order to ground the values seen to best characterize an evolving nation.

Processes of Idealization

Posthumous accounts have not simply upheld Umm Kulthūm's self-constructed persona—they have solidified her public qualities into enduring legacies of her character through processes of exaggeration, erasure, and simplification. Authors magnified her humanitarian image, dedicating articles and chapters to the role of "charity in Umm Kulthūm's life" and her "humanitarian stances" (Jumjūm 1983; 'Abd al-'Āl n.d., 18). Raḍwān dubbed her, simply, "Umm Kulthūm the Generous" (2000, 44). In Zakariyā Hāshim Zakariyā's exaggeration, she "inspired the Arab nation with the meaning of humanity" (1983, 5). Through her later musical career and public acts, Umm Kulthūm offered such writers ample material to support hyperbolic statements that established charity and compassion as integral parts of her character. One writer recounted the singer's personal meeting with the young man who had rushed her on the Olympia stage in Paris and her request that security forces release him ('Abd al-Rasūl 2000). To portray her as a generous person, rather than someone devoted to personal gain, a Sudanese newspaper cited the £E 1 million that she collected for the war effort in just one year and claimed that "she did not earn this much for herself in her lifetime" ("Riḥlātuhā" 1975). A Lebanese newspaper revealed "the depth of Umm Kulthūm's humanity" through a detailed description of her plans for her charitable foundation, Dār Umm Kulthūm ("al-Wajh al-khayrī" 1975). Authors also enhanced the portrait of her humanitarianism by presenting her as the victim of Jīhān al-Sādāt, who developed her own charitable project and launched a "war" against her rival's project by seeking her land, personnel, and public donations.[4] While authors characterized Umm Kulthūm's project as one designed to help others, they cast Jīhān's as a deliberately hurtful and self-serving attempt to gain social and political prominence. Such a composite demonstration of the singer's charitable and compassionate nature countered critical anecdotes circulating by word of mouth, such as those recalling her selfish treatment of 'Abd al-Ḥalīm Ḥāfiz and her withdrawal of her songs from a radio station following an unflattering broadcast.[5]

Authors mined Umm Kulthūm's image and career to defend her explicitly against criticisms found in foreign publications and the rumor mill. An article by 'Abd al-Jabbār al-Suhaymī in the Moroccan newspaper *al-'Alam* illustrates typical criticism offered during her lifetime. In 1969, al-Suhaymī complained that Umm Kulthūm had dominated Arabic music for too long, stifling other voices. Her omnipresence turned the public into "captives" of "the greatest tranquilizer of the Arab people" (N. Fu'ād 2000, 466). He described Umm Kulthūm as a drug of escapism from Arab political realities that "gave to us what we wanted, or to put it more exactly, what we could endure." He characterized the Arab community as one "oppressed by the defeats" of colonialism, continuing poverty, and feudal estates, which "Umm Kulthūm caused us to endure in the process of premeditated flight from our stubborn reality and [our] disappearance in the labyrinths of a dream that rescued us, for over an hour, from personal defeat and [our] powerlessness to change reality or rebel against it" (468). Upon the singer's death, an English-language Kuwaiti newspaper recounted accusations that her songs had helped the enemy "by sapping Arab energies." But most posthumous Arabic-language accounts omitted such criticisms or couched them in positive terms, such as her ability to "intoxicate people with her art" ("Umm Kalthoum" 1975; Raḍwān 2000, 55).

Some writers tackled these criticisms of the singer head on by citing her decision not to retire, and to continue singing for the benefit of the country after the war. The narrator of Sami Alkassim's experimental documentary *Far from You* proclaimed, "Blamed by some for the '67 defeat, for numbing the masses, she launched an international concert series. . . . She donated all proceeds to the Egyptian treasury, the families of war victims, and Palestinian refugees." Al-Naqqāsh responded to Libyans' complaint that she inappropriately sang about love during wartime (2000, 98) by turning to the interpretation of a foreign "Orientalist" with whom he spoke in Libya. The foreign scholar explained that while Arabs were often assumed to be a defeated people mired in hopelessness, he saw in Umm Kulthūm's concerts "another people, full of vitality, emotion, and zeal, completely removed from hopelessness and resignation." He reasoned, "If people sing of love when living in a time of battle, they cannot be weak, lacking power over life, but rather are a living people of open heart who can face their enemies with strength!" (99). Reminding readers that war did not require that doctors become pilots, nor that Umm Kulthūm abandon her art, al-Naqqāsh praised her for placing "her talents and all of her artistic history in service of the battle" (100).

The many writers who exaggerated the singer's patriotic image mounted a powerful defense against criticisms of her in the three-plus decades since her death. Many compiled lengthy lists of the occasions on which she offered patriotic musical and financial responses.[6] Others selected her postwar fundraising efforts for special emphasis ('Abd al-Ḥalīm 1987, 117). One proffered the exaggeration that "she did not let a national occasion go by without participating in it" (*Umm Kulthūm: Qiṣṣat ḥayātihā* 1977, 38). To attest to the depth of her patriotism, several attributed to her an obsession with ending the Israeli occupation of Arab land (Ramaḍān n.d., 222; Ṭirād 1999, 45–46).

Many commentators gave an inflated sense of Umm Kulthūm's patriotism by describing her response to the 1967 war as the product of a dramatic and profound personal transformation. Authors variously characterized her initial response as shock, stupor, extreme sadness, or numbness.[7]

According to her nephew and manager Muḥammad al-Disūqī, the singer "passed only in body" in 1975 because "she passed in spirit, vitality, and radiance the day that the defeat of 1967 happened" (al-Disūqī 1992). Ḥanafī al-Maḥallāwī depicted her initial devastation by inaccurately captioning a generic photograph of her wiping her face at a concert "Umm Kulthūm after hearing the news of the 1967 crisis" (1999b, 137). Many writers marked the war as so devastating an event for the singer that she was prompted to enter temporary retirement or self-imposed seclusion, an assertion that is contradicted by historical evidence.[8] Authors characterized this period of seclusion as a transformative one from which she emerged more productive and filled with renewed hope and resolve (Raḍwān 2000, 63–64; *Umm Kulthūm: Qīthārat al-ʿArab* 1978, 45–46). Muḥammad al-Disūqī offered a dramatic account of this transformation, in which he set her devotion to country and her willingness to place sacrifice above self in the foreground: "In the middle of the darkness of the bedroom flashed into her mind an idea like a lightning bolt. She left to do it immediately. She found that withdrawal was not the solution, but rather closeness to the people, to the millions, to ʿAbd al-Nāṣir. . . . She gave herself to Egypt, and her voice and songs to the war effort" (1992, 45–46). This notion of transformation was given even greater weight when one journalist situated Umm Kulthūm as the narrator of her own story: "I asked myself that day what I can offer my injured homeland, what I can do to wipe its tears or bandage wounds, to put a smile on the lips of the son of a martyr. I left with a plan for work, to sing everywhere and collect cash, gold, and enthusiasm for the battle" (Ḥ. ʿUthmān 1977, 26).

"Behind the scenes" moments suggested that such impassioned rhetoric was supported by the singer's deep feelings. Duriyah ʿAwnī shared with readers the singer's tearful reaction to the war during a private interview in Paris to demonstrate her sincerity (1998, 198). Muḥammad Wajdī Qandīl wrote of a private confrontation that testified to Umm Kulthūm's patriotism. At a celebratory dinner in a Kuwaiti prince's palace, one guest dwelled on the singer's collection of donations. Taking this as an attack against her country, Umm Kulthūm raised her voice in a vehement defense of Egypt and abruptly left the dinner (1999, 11). Many accounts suggested that her patriotism was so great that she was willing to endanger herself for her country. In the telling of several writers, the singer was under imminent attack in the Egyptian radio and television building during both the 1967 war and the Tripartite Aggression of 1956 and was willing to risk her life to record new patriotic songs (Jighām 1975b; al-Maḥallāwī 1994, 29). Another anecdote had her professing her readiness to die for her country outside the recording studio. During an extended period of severe turbulence on a plane bound for Benghazi, Libya, many passengers became hysterical in anticipation of their deaths, while Umm Kulthūm was said to react calmly, likening herself and her colleagues to martyrs through their "national service[,] like the combatant in the battlefield" ('Abd al-Rasūl 2000).

While such patriotic portrayals have certainly been effective in steeling Umm Kulthūm's image against criticism, the single most influential account, particularly among young Egyptians, was offered by the wildly popular Ramadan television series *Umm Kulthūm*. First broadcast in late 1999 and early 2000, the series contributed to the increase in Umm Kulthūm's record sales, particularly among consumers born after her death (Sabra 2000). It specifically boosted consumption of her songs from before the 1960s, such as "Shams al-Aṣīl" and "Raqq al-Ḥabīb" (Farag 2000b). The series also inspired young members of the diaspora to learn more about Umm Kulthūm's songs and the Arabic language (Atia 2000b).

The series *Umm Kulthūm* was particularly influential in shaping young Egyptians' perception of the singer as a patriot. The drama accentuated Umm Kulthūm's political sense by establishing a foil for her. In a scene from her childhood, Zaynab, a girl of similar age from a well-to-do family, insults Umm Kulthūm as a village singer who will never escape her peasant origins. Ultimately, Zaynab matures into a petulant wife whose incompetent attempts at political conversation with her husband and family are repeatedly rejected. In contrast, Umm Kulthūm becomes a sharp woman with whom the country's most esteemed journalists and artists are pleased, if not honored, to converse about the pressing political issues of the day. A strong parallel plot, centering on Zaynab's husband, portrays the growing nationalist movement and highlights the political ramifications of Umm Kulthūm's artistic endeavors, such as her recording of "Wulid al-Hudá." She sings the religious song well aware of the political significance of the line addressing Muḥammad: "You are the leader of the socialists. . . . You gave justice to the poor in front of the rich." When a representative of the royal family requests that the singer remove the line or alter the wording (which she never does), she emerges as a political threat capable of precipitating a popular revolution.

The final episode of the series seals the posthumous image of Umm Kulthūm as a devoted patriot. It portrays her as the mastermind of efforts to collect jewelry to benefit the war effort. At a concert intermission, she leads admiring women to join her in removing and donating their earrings, bracelets, and necklaces. Use of original film footage to portray her fundraising trips outside Egypt distinguishes them as real and important events in her career, rather than encounters colored through artistic license. Examples of the latter—scenes of Umm Kulthūm and her audiences singing patriotic songs of the 1950s together at her Egyptian fundraising concerts—also play an important role at the end of the series. These scenes magnify the impact of her war effort at home, condense the patriotism that she had actually displayed over several decades into the postwar period, and depict her campaign as the culmination of both a personal and a national effort.[9]

Considering the powerful portrayals of Umm Kulthūm's patriotism in the series, we might not be surprised to see that young Egyptians express similar feelings and ideas about the singer. When I lived in Egypt in 2003, teenage and twenty-something Egyptians regularly introduced the singer to me and other foreigners as a patriot, rather than an artist. They eagerly cited her fundraising concerts after the war as her most important accomplishments—an evaluation seconded by a government website ("Umm Kolthoum"). This stance of younger Egyptians gives credence to Lila Abu-Lughod's observation that the culture industry in Egypt is "in the business of producing not just art or entertainment but national pedagogy" (Abu-Lughod 2005, 159). Created by Egyptians raised in the 1950s and 1960s under a nationalist regime that aspired to revolutionary social reform, dramas like *Umm Kulthūm* play an important role in educating members of contemporary Egyptian society (136). Mamdūḥ al-Laythī, the former director of the Egyptian Radio and Television Union's film and serial production sector, outlined the sector's pedagogical goals to Abu-Lughod. "Our most important goal in relation to the citizens is to help individuals become cultured," he explained. "We must educate them, teach them the basics of morality and religious duty. The individual needs guidance. He needs information, and we need to inculcate the spirit of patriotism, morality, religion, courage, and enterprise. We have found that the best means to reach the individual is through drama. It works like magic" (11). The series *Umm Kulthūm* clearly did an effective job in instilling the spirit of patriotism, particularly among young Egyptians who, while relatively uninterested in the details of the 1967 war, are readily inspired by heroes of the past (Dawoud 1997). Still broadcast regularly on Egyptian television and satellite channels across the Middle East and the Arab diaspora, the series figures to continue playing a major role in shaping how young Egyptians, Arabs, and Arab-Americans view the singer.

In the years since her death, Umm Kulthūm's legacy has been guarded not only by convincing accounts of her patriotism but also by her portrayal as a national monument. This portrayal has rested on her close association with national historical sites, an association that has been cultivated in Egypt and elsewhere by other artists as well, though often with different outcomes. Fayrūz and ʿĀṣī and Manṣūr al-Raḥbānī, for example, developed close ties to the ruins of Baalbek, with their manifold historical-cultural valences. This connection contributed much to the shaping of modern Lebanon.[10] Aided by the artists' folkloric performances at the Baalbek ruins, the site became a powerful symbol of Lebanon—both within and beyond its borders—by the early 1960s (Stone 2008, 25).

In the case of Umm Kulthūm, her efforts to associate herself with Egypt's pharaonic monuments had a significant impact on her own legacy. Unlike the Baalbek ruins, the Egyptian pyramids and other pharaonic structures had already been tapped to carry out their nationalist work in the early twentieth century. Works like Maḥmūd Mukhtār's sculpture *The Awakening of Egypt* used the monuments to symbolize Egypt's ancient greatness and to make nationalist claims to territorial continuity (Baron 2005, 59–60, 65–68). The monuments had thus acquired a powerful set of established meanings that might be extended to Umm Kulthūm. Both Egyptian and other Arab authors cast the singer as one of the pyramids—a national symbol and an awe-inspiring, enduring presence. They rooted this characterization in her patriotic songs, her fundraising concerts, and the lyrical sophistication of her repertory (al-Makāwī 2003; Ṣāghīyah 1991, 119–20). Recalling her photographs with the Sphinx and her Philae concert, many, like Muḥammad Saʿīd, identified her as the fourth pyramid (2002, 12).[11] Others used the monuments to characterize her as an immovable, unchanging cultural presence. A drawing portrayed her as one of "the pyramids of Egypt, eternal through the passage of time," while her photographs with the Sphinx were captioned "Immortality on the sands and immortality in the hearts of millions" (Abū al-Khayr 1975, n.p.). Like the pyramids, many illustrations suggested, the singer and her art defied replication and even a comprehension of their creation. The former notion emerged in the biopic *Ḥalīm*, in which ʿAbd al-Ḥalīm Ḥāfiz characterizes Umm Kulthūm as one of the pyramids to demonstrate deference and minimize their previous conflict at a Revolution Day concert (ʿArafah 2006). The singer's status as a monument was sometimes cited as protecting her from criticism and reevaluation. As several publications proclaimed, Umm Kulthūm and the pyramids "are not subject to any change in their position, their value, or the people's interest in them" (al-Khaṭīb 1975, 8–10; al-Naqqāsh 2000, 12). Such "monumental" assessments ultimately pervaded popular discourse as fact. As an interviewee in Michal Goldman's documentary put it succinctly, "Umm Kulthūm is like the pyramids. Today, no one can do what she did."

The Enduring Value of a Hybrid Image

Umm Kulthūm's self-portrayal shaped her reception in other ways. Following the glorification of the Egyptian common man and the elevation of the peasant to the "culturally authentic" soul of Egypt,[12] Umm Kulthūm portrayed herself as faithful to this ideal. Even as she enjoyed lavish accommodations abroad and went so far as to use powerful connections to escape the legal ramifications when her dog bit a man, she assured her audience that she had not become "corrupted" by trappings of her success and elite status. She demonstrated her fidelity to her peasant roots through her statements and photo opportunities, even referring to herself explicitly as a *fallāḥah* (Danielson 1997, 190–91; Tawfīq 1968a). This self-fashioning made her an irresistible example of the strengths of indigenous art and character, and writers were eager to hold up her peasant image (Khalīl 1992, 151; al-Khaṭīb 1975, 21; al-Naqqāsh 2000, 20–21). A magazine editor set the following caption for a photograph of the singer eating with her hands: "A natural moment in which she eats figs. She never forgot that she was a peasant from the soil of Egypt" ("Min albūm" 1978, 17). Authors linked other aspects of her image, such as her charity and piety, to impoverished rural Egypt. Many enumerated the charitable projects in Tammāy al-Zahāyra in which she participated, including the construction of a school, a mosque, and a health services unit.[13] Al-Amīr explained, "Umm Kulthūm continued, despite all of the acclaim and praise that she received, to be the same pious girl of the village Tammāy al-Zahāyra" (1975, 30).

Writers strengthened Umm Kulthūm's peasant image and imbued her art with deeper value by portraying the singer and her music as organic products of the nation. Some, like Muḥammad ʿAdnān al-Khaṭīb, reiterated her carefully worded declaration that "I rubbed with my little feet all of Egypt, village by village, before moving to Cairo" (1975, 12–13). The statement stressed her physical connection to the land, like that of the peasants, and implied that contact with peasants—as opposed to the poet Rāmī's tutelage in poetic interpretation—was an integral element of her vocal development. Others offered their own formulations to depict both the singer and her art as being shaped by peasants, intimately connected to the land, and therefore "authentic" cultural products (ʿAbd al-Wahhāb 1981). Al-Amīr proclaimed with poetic affect, "Umm Kulthūm's voice sprang from the village with the voice of the call to prayer, the expression of the sublimity of God, with the good earth and the Nile, the gift of God" (1975, 30). Drawing on al-Naqqāsh's earlier work, al-Khaṭīb explained more prosaically, "Umm Kulthūm did not learn in a school or in a university, but in the alleys and barns where she learned the Arab Egyptian taste in the most simple and honest way. She learned the taste of the Egyptian peasants whom the days wore down and who faced the world with patience and limitless work" (al-Khaṭīb 1975, 13–14; al-Naqqāsh 2000, 14). Fashioned as the idealized products of the beleaguered backbone of the country, Umm Kulthūm and her art symbolized the longevity of indigenous culture and territorial continuity despite a long history of foreign occupation and rule.

Umm Kulthūm's idealization is all the more striking when contrasted with the treatment of Durīyah Shafīq, an Egyptian feminist and nationalist whose overly Western and modern image led to her punishment, both during her lifetime and after her death, for appearing to betray the revolution. Championing independence and women's rights with the tools of a French education, she represented the imposition of foreign culture and values. She was sentenced to house arrest and condemned, even after her death, as "an agent of Western colonialism and imperialism" (Nelson 1996, xiii, 275, 282–83). Against Shafīq, we reconsider Umm Kulthūm, whose being and work were seen to be formed of the soil of Egypt and who has yet to be thoroughly critiqued for encouraging her fellow citizens to accept a path of limited political participation and to refrain from openly criticizing the regime in the years following the 1967 war.

While some emphasized her "peasantness" to highlight the "authenticity" of her art and the longevity of indigenous culture, her public image was a hybrid constructed from disparate and sometimes contradictory elements. In sum, she was both an elegant, sophisticated international traveler and a self-proclaimed "peasant at heart." As Habib explained, her "elaborate and often contradictory construction of her public persona served to produce her as a quintessential Egyptian. Consequently, she came to signify an essence out of this hybridization" (Habib 1995, 31–32). Snapshots of this hybrid image can be pulled from her later career. For one example, she joined with elite Kuwaiti women to participate in folkloric dances, donning a *dishdashah* that made her resemble the folk dancers rather than the ministers' wives. Images from her trip to Sudan support Danielson's observation that "her public self was clearly a construction but it was neither artificial nor false; Umm Kulthūm simply learned to present herself in the way she wanted to be thought of and remembered" (1997, 185, 191–92). In photographs taken moments apart from each other during her trip to Sudan, she appears at first to be an elite woman learning about a local wedding custom and then is perfectly comfortable being adopted by the henna-wearing, toothless women around her. Synthesizing the elite and peasant aspects of her image, she had photographers capture her feeding farm animals in a jacket, skirt, and dress shoes in what became some of her most frequently reproduced images.[14] Upholding this picture, one sentence from a Lebanese biography referred to her as both "Umm Kulthūm the authentic, intelligent peasant" and "lady of ladies" (*Umm Kulthūm: Qīthārat al-ʿArab* 1975, 5). Even Sélim Nassib's novel sustained her hybrid image by chronologically linking her building of a mosque in the village of

Sudanese women surround the singer. *Photo courtesy of Farūq Ibrāhīm*

her birth with the construction of her villa in Zamalek (2006, 128). Conveniently, those who wished to continue to deify Umm Kulthūm into the 1990s—when an emphasis on education had rendered the peasants' stereotypical ignorance a weakness and the *ibn al-balad* (literally, "son of the country") stereotype could no longer represent "all that is good in Egypt" (Abu-Lughod 2005, 148–49)—could focus on the elegant, cosmopolitan parts of the hybrid.

Umm Kulthūm's sophisticate-peasant image, supported by the wide range of emotional needs and interpretations projected by listeners onto her songs, enabled her to be conceived and represented as an embodiment of national unity. During the singer's lifetime, observers noted her ability to encompass and appeal to all segments of Egyptian society. Salāmah al-'Abbāsī proclaimed, "The characteristics of Umm Kulthūm are the characteristics of all the people" (1968d). Such claims were rooted in the two opposing stereotypes that were fused in her image: *ibn al-zawwāt* and *ibn al-balad*. The former was understood to be a member of the upper class, fluent in European manners and languages but ignorant of Egyptian ones. The latter (defined earlier) was understood to be a traditional, less Westernized citizen who followed "truly Egyptian" behaviors—customs that were prevalent before the introduction of European ones. Typically a member of the lower classes, the son or daughter "of the country" uses proverbial

The rather formal exchange captured in the previous image is replaced with one of apparent familiarity, as the singer laughs heartily while being embraced by members of the same group of Sudanese women. *Photo courtesy of Farūq Ibrāhīm*

expressions and avoids foreign words (el-Hamamsy 1975, 297–99). Umm Kulthūm displayed traits of both stereotypes: she ascended dramatically in social status and could communicate in French but retained fluency in indigenous expressions and behaviors, which she took pains to display during her later career (Danielson 1997, 189).

As a result of Umm Kulthūm's efforts to synthesize elements from opposing stereotypes, listeners from all social groups could identify with her image and connect with her art. Both inside and outside of Egypt, listeners projected a wide range of emotionally driven interpretations onto her songs. A Moroccan writer imposed his mystical shading onto many of her songs, and ultimately onto her. He explained, "She was a Sufi when she sang religious songs, she was a Sufi when she sang songs of love, she was a Sufi during her patriotic anthems, and her Sufism comes out in profound feelings that she reached with her sweet, flexible voice" (al-ʿAzīz 1975, 233). Listeners' projections, however, sometimes could be disrupted by reality. When she performed in Libya, for example, her advanced age could not be overlooked by at least one audience member. In a frenzy of disappointment, an intoxicated man shouted in front of the entire audience, "Stop, woman! You are too old to be singing [about love] like this."[15] Some writers in the Libyan press similarly highlighted the dissonance they experienced in seeing a septuagenarian sing about love (ʿAbd al-Rasūl 2000). These isolated disconnects aside, listeners' attempts to project their readings onto songs were mainly satisfied, according to Zakariyā Hāshim Zakariyā: "In this effusive artistic spring each person found himself: the complainant found comfort, the bereaved found solace, the lover found his intoxication, the noble-minded found his generosity, and the Arab nation found its spirit and honor" (1983, 6).

As she fused elements of the *ibn al-zawwāt* and *ibn al-balad* stereotypes, Umm Kulthūm also bridged the traditional divide between rural and urban segments of Egyptian society (Habib 1995, 31; el-Hamamsy 1975, 297). From early in her career, she cultivated both a rural and an urban fan base. The rural Nile Delta audience that she had acquired through her early performances continued to consume her music through recordings after she had relocated to Cairo and gained urban listeners. In the late 1960s, her provincial concerts demonstrated her continued connection to rural Egypt after decades of performing in Cairo. Outside Egypt, her skill at blurring such social boundaries was appreciated as well; a Tunisian observer, for example, noted her unique ability to "make equality reign among the social strata" in the course of her concerts (Larbi 1968). One writer described her as "the singer of the village and the city, the intellectuals and the simple, the lovers and the Sufis" ("Umm Kulthūm fī kalimāt" 1970). Such a conception was maintained by many Egyptian and Arab authors after her death (Bakhīt 1975; Ramaḍān n.d., 136–37; al-Naqqāsh 1978, 33).

The singer's funeral itself provided a compelling visual demonstration of the unity attributed to her by so many. Between the delegation inside the large tent erected next to Cairo's ʿUmar Makram mosque, the downtown buildings, and the streets themselves, her funeral procession drew domestic leaders, old men from the countryside, urban working youths, and poor women to mourn her passing. The ritual prompted a renewed outpouring of emotion that testified to the public's attachment to the singer, and funeral footage, which has continued to be broadcast in the decades since her death, recorded a frenzy shared by those outside the mosque. Women wailed from the windows of downtown buildings, while men ran around the orderly columns of wreath-carriers and marching musicians to get a closer position. People filling the grassy center of Tahrir Square broke through police lines to storm across the lanes of the traffic circle. So violent was the public response that wreaths were defoliated to their skeletal frames by the time they arrived at the singer's final resting place. Footage of the intense and unguarded participation of so many individuals from different segments of Egyptian society has lent credibility to hyperbolic statements such as Zakariyā's.

Loss and Nostalgia

In seeking to understand public reverence for Umm Kulthūm, along with the national unity that she was understood to have helped create, we must explore the context of the politics and policies that followed 'Abd al-Nāṣir's death. As president, Anwar al-Sādāt strived to eradicate his predecessor in person and policy. Through al-Sādāt's "Corrective Revolution," members of 'Abd al-Nāṣir's regime were purged from the government in 1971 and Nasserist organizations were banned (Ryan 2001, 30–31). Old policies were reversed and new ones were constantly set in contrast with those of the previous regime (Meital 2003, 171). For example, al-Sādāt's *infitāḥ*—designed to open the door to foreign and domestic investment in the private sector—was presented as a marked shift from the country's previous economic domination by the public sector.

Sharp policy reversals under al-Sādāt entailed substantive, often painful, changes in the daily life of many Egyptians. The peasants and urban poor saw services and opportunities for political participation disappear. Under 'Abd al-Nāṣir, efforts were made—however imperfectly—to involve previously disenfranchised citizens, particularly the peasants. In this attempt, half of all elected seats on political, union, and cooperative activities at all levels were to be reserved for workers and peasants. Agrarian reforms also helped small peasants, prompting the rise of a wealthier peasant class and the weakening of the landed aristocracy (Aoude 1994). Low-income groups benefited from rent-control measures, improved access to medical care, and investment in public transportation. Yet under al-Sadat, these measures were reversed: services were pulled and peasants returned to a state of disenfranchisement, while the central government instituted controls to dictate the minutest aspects of farming (Hinnebusch, Jr., 1985, 249–53, 270–72).

Al-Sādāt's policies had negative repercussions for groups other than the peasants. Even his greatest supporters, Westernized members of the upper and upper-middle classes, expressed concerns over the widening economic gap between the rich and the poor. In 1974, inflation of 20 to 30 percent hurt small landowners, pensioners, white-collar workers in the government and public sectors, new university graduates, and the unemployed. Housing costs soon soared out of reach even for middle class workers. Following a period in which Nasserist policies had generated significant socioeconomic leveling, growing class inequality and rampant inflation sparked bitterness and resentment among industrial workers and the urban masses toward the wealthy, educated, and powerful.[16]

National unity was a substantial casualty of al-Sādāt's economic policies. In the 1960s, class identity had been subordinated to a sense of national unity (Shukrallah 1989, 69). One vehicle for reducing class conflict and dissolving class differences was the Arab Socialist Union (ASU), which defined itself as a "national alliance of working forces" that was intended to focus attention on social categories, such as intellectuals and national capitalists, and included members of various income-based social strata (Waterbury 314–15). While the ASU did not eliminate class tensions under ʿAbd al-Nāṣir, such tensions now intensified under al-Sādāt. In response to his public policies, which conspicuously favored the "haves" over the "have nots," workers, students, and the urban poor launched a "crisis from below," which surfaced in the early 1970s and peaked in the violence of early 1977. In January of that year, the reduction and elimination of commodity subsidies had sent prices soaring for basic foodstuffs, prompting workers' strikes, student demonstrations, and general confrontations with the police in urban centers across Egypt (Shukrallah 1989, 69–70; Hinnebusch, Jr., 1985, 243–49, 281).

National pride also suffered as a result of al-Sādāt's policies. After the 1952 revolution, Egyptians sought to redefine their identity through the nationalization of education, an emphasis on indigenous art forms, and the purchasing of local products. Under the new leadership, however, such priorities were eclipsed by the return of a "colonized consciousness," as foreign firms and employees were brought into the country to do jobs that could have been handled by Egyptians themselves (el-Hamamsy 1975, 295; Hinnebusch, Jr., 1985, 285–86). Al-Sādāt's *infitāḥ*—designed to open the Egyptian economy to trade and investment in the international capitalist market—did more than prompt an antiseptic set of financial transactions. Especially for those who had lived in Egypt prior to the 1967 defeat, the policy seemed to thrust the country into a state of dependence (al-Ali 2001, 165). Further, when money emerged as the leading measure of success, the prospect of a national sellout signaled to many the loss of an entire value system (Massad 2007, 348).

As al-Sādāt and his supporters attempted to erase ʿAbd al-Nāṣir's accomplishments, their narrative of the nation's recent history contradicted Egyptians' own experience and prompted nostalgia for earlier years (Guindy and Shukrallah 2000). Although Umm Kulthūm was not known for singing nostalgic songs, she emerged in the years after her death as a figure capable of prompting enormous nostalgia (Danielson 1997, 201; Souief 1992, 779–83).[17] For Egyptians, who "love to talk about something they lost," her idealized image provided a way to represent, remember, and honor the gains under ʿAbd al-Nāṣir that had fallen away after his death.[18] At the singer's funeral itself, mourners redirected the cortege in a three-hour meander through Cairo's streets, delaying her ultimate burial. We can view this act as more than an outpouring of emotion and reverence but also as a sign of public unwillingness to take the body to its final resting place—the mourners had to be urged to do so by a religious leader—and, by extension, an unwillingness to relinquish the ideals and achievements under ʿAbd al-Nāṣir that had already been erased and rejected by al-Sādāt (Danielson 1991, 74–75). The president and first lady's earlier efforts to simply replace Umm Kulthūm, rather than discredit or attack her, left her carefully constructed image intact and available for nostalgic invocation.[19] In a time of increasingly visible Westernization, Egyptian authors and filmmakers exalted the singer as the epitome of indigenous art. Their frequent characterization of her as a "pyramid" marked her as an "authentically" Egyptian artist who had reached the pinnacle of achievement in her field. The Egyptian journalist Muhammad Ouda, when interviewed in Goldman's documentary, revealed an important truth when he misspoke and then corrected himself. "Her voice touched not only the upper, the middle, and the lower classes," he explained. "It was a mass—She sang for the whole people." Although he began to characterize the singer's appeal as a "mass phenomenon," which would have stressed its scale, his final assertion emphasized instead her ability to unify a singular group, "the people," regardless of class. Coming after more than two decades of *infitāḥ* policies, with Egypt under its present leader, Ḥusni Mubārak, Ouda's comments reflected a tendency in the national media to emphasize images of local authenticity out of a "fear that Egyptian identity will dissipate" (Abu-Lughod 2005, 153, 159).

Through her personal generosity in helping those in need and her extraordinary success in elevating her own socioeconomic standing, Umm Kulthūm offered authors a high-profile example to address the social inequities that had emerged, in the three-plus decades since ʿAbd al-Nāṣir's death, under policies of economic liberalization and the erosion of government aid for the poor. One journalist used the singer's birth village to highlight the plight of the poor under Mubārak's continuation of al-Sādāt's economic policies. Fatemah Farag described the singer's village as "untouched by her glory," drawing attention to the garbage-strewn canal and lack of nearby employment. The villagers themselves used attacks on Umm Kulthūm to emphasize the current economic disparity affecting Tammāy al-Zahāyra. One villager expressed her frustrations by portraying the singer as a distant, elitist urbanite. She recalled, "We never saw Umm Kulthūm. She was never interested in coming to the village. If anyone wanted something from her, they would have to go to her in Cairo" (2000a).

The villager's comments provided an important alternative to the hagiography that has dominated Umm Kulthūm's reception. The journalists and critical residents of Tammāy al-Zahāyra used the singer's place of birth

Carefully coifed and wearing a jacket, short skirt, and dress shoes, Umm Kulthūm poses with farm animals. The often-reproduced photograph encapsulates her hybrid image. *Photo courtesy of Farūq Ibrāhīm*

not as a means of sustaining her hybrid image but rather as a wedge to isolate and probe its contradictory components. Claims that Umm Kulthūm was distant and absent from the village suggest that her pose as a faithful peasant was self-serving and hypocritical. Yet, for the most part, such an approach has rarely been used to dismantle the singer's image entirely. Still cognizant of the erasure of the past sought by al-Sādāt and his wife, many Egyptians have been reluctant to voice the type of public criticism that was offered of Fayrūz and ʿĀṣī and Manṣūr al-Raḥbānī's work in Lebanon. While Lebanese literary critic Khālida Saʿīd explicitly identified Fayrūz's Lebanon as utopian and even the singer's son had parodied her work in his own plays, such criticism of Umm Kulthūm was rare (Stone 2008, 13, 110–37).[20] This type of public criticism would require separating the image from the person and acknowledging her persona as a construction. This would open up to questioning and analysis her whole range of performative actions, including her music, her self-presentation, and their relationship to ʿAbd al-Nāṣir.

The far more common hagiographic image of Umm Kulthūm helps sustain a nostalgic view of ʿAbd al-Nāṣir. The singer's magnetic onstage presence provided an entrancing counterpart to the president's charisma, and the two figures were linked so inextricably that some dwelled on the break in her monthly concerts after his death and asserted that she had begun to die along with him (al-Maḥallāwī 1994, 241; Ṭirād 1999, 71).[21] Having been targeted for eradication, or at least replacement, during al-Sādāt's tenure, both the cultural and the national leader emerged as victims in the eyes of many. As was put forth in Sami Alkassim's documentary in a segment called "Acoustics of Memory," "The flame she ignited merged with ['Abd al-Nāṣir's]. From the war, from their deaths, and their funerals, the cinders smoldered for decades in spite of the changes of the seventies. Even al-Sādāt's ban on the pro-Nasserist songs she sang only served to reinscribe the memory."

In line with such responses, biographers and historians have refrained from exploring the ways in which Umm Kulthūm's "musical dominance," as Michael Frishkopf asserted, was "nearly a metaphor of state control" (2003, 157). Instead, glorification of the singer's patriotic responses to the war has, in its turn, helped sustain a reverent view of 'Abd al-Nāṣir. When she rejected retirement after the war, she avoided acting as a symbol of his failure. Her tenacious postwar activities, as portrayed so effectively since her death, have been seen to model duty rather than fear, action rather than defeat. She showed an ability to draw on qualities of perseverance and determination to overcome challenges. As 'Abd al-Nāṣir's "muezzin" displayed these values, the leader himself could still be seen to embody the glory of the nation and symbolize the expression of "independent national will" (Jawdat 1970; Guindy and Shukrallah 2000).

The reverent view of 'Abd al-Nāṣir is clearly a partial one, as is the idealized image of Umm Kulthūm presented in posthumous literature. Yet their mutually reinforcing images and the paucity of posthumous criticism need not obscure the direction of potential critiques in the future. During her lifetime, Umm Kulthūm was the target of pointed criticism, at times delivered in blunt terms. While she was often accused of "intoxicating the masses," one writer crassly described her performances of long romantic songs as the excrement of repressive regimes. He portrayed her songs about "love and its torment" as "the dross floating on the dung of Arab society under which miserable millions are awakening" ("Hujūm" 1967). The posthumous evaporation of such accusations reflects an unwillingness on the part of commentators to acknowledge the ways in which she helped to legitimize 'Abd al-Nāṣir when he was in power. She indeed provided an effective musical diversion from domestic and international problems in the years following the war. Yet because her art and her connection with her audience were based largely on a pleasurable form of interaction, her performances were dissociated from the repressive measures, such as police surveillance and arbitrary arrest, that were also important tools for sustaining the regime's legitimacy (Ryan 2001, 33; Shehata 1992, 80–82). When discussing her music, al-Maḥallāwī was unusual in acknowledging that

"'Abd al-Nāṣir himself was eager to push this type of art that stimulates the feelings and paralyzes thought, or at least delays it" (1999b, 120). A truly critical analysis of Umm Kulthūm's art and her self-presentation would entail the acknowledgement of the public's manipulation by 'Abd al-Nāṣir, the regime, and the press. Driven by a sense of shame to avoid criticizing the country's political and artistic leaders before an international audience and by a desire to defend 'Abd al-Nāṣir's image before a domestic one, most authors, filmmakers, and ordinary listeners have shied away from such interpretations (Shehata 1992, 80). Instead, by manipulating her posthumous image, they have preserved a space for an idealized version of the nation's political and social history.

CHAPTER 5

Mother of Egypt or Erotic Partner?

The many nicknames that Umm Kulthūm acquired during her career give insight into her value for Egyptian and Arab listeners. Monikers like "Qithārat al-'Arab" (Lyre of the Arabs), "Muwaḥḥidat al-'Arab" (Uniter of the Arabs), and "Fannānat al-Sha'b" (Artist of the People) leave no doubt as to her success in establishing a regional presence, symbolizing the ideal of Arab unity, and maintaining a strong connection with ordinary citizens. However, these nicknames say less about her value—and her vulnerabilities—as a female icon. Their tacitness about such issues has only increased since her death, as several explicitly feminine titles, including "Sitt al-Kull" (Lady of Them All) and "Fannānat al-Sha'b" (Artist of the People), have faded from common usage.

Visual representations, often stressing the physical aspect of her art, have offered richer interpretations of Umm Kulthūm's significance as a woman icon. Many illustrations capture her in the act of singing, scarf in hand. Flying doves often accentuate the physicality of her musical production. And, as discussed earlier, many images emphasize the timelessness of her art by placing her alongside a pyramid (M. 'Awaḍ 1987; al-Marīnī 1975, 53).

The visual artist Ḥijāzī cast a singing Umm Kulthūm as the fourth pyramid (Shūshah 1976, 110–11). In his rendering, she towers over the three other pyramids at more than twice their height. Her skirt flows widely as the fourth pyramid itself; the multicolored checks of fabric resemble the orange, red, pink, and black stones of the three pyramids around her. Her curvaceous figure is accentuated by a blue bodice ornamented with a heart-shaped flower and scalloped trim. Flying doves symbolize her melody. A tiny male figure sits under two palm trees at the base of her skirt-pyramid with a radio at his side. Tears flow down his face.

Comparison with a related image highlights the conceptualization of Umm Kulthūm's musical creation and reception, as well as the linkage of physical artistic production and emotive reception to the feminine. Whereas Ḥijāzī's inclusion of a listener foregrounds the interactive and emotional nature of the singer's art, with her voice as mediator, Abū Ṭālib's portrayal of her colleague Muḥammad 'Abd al-Wahhāb as a timeless symbol of Egypt captures the intellectual and solitary aspects of the latter's work as a composer. His motionless profiled head is superimposed on the uppermost section of a pyramid, with his wrinkles resembling the edges of the pyramid's blocks (al-Najmī 1992, 1). Ḥijāzī's image of Umm Kulthūm represents both the performer and the listener, reflecting their integral contributions to the shape of music under the conventions of the *ṭarab* feedback cycle. In contrast, the portrait of 'Abd al-Wahhāb exhibits the privileging, drawn from Western classical music, of creation through the act of composition. Returning to Ḥijāzī's image, Umm Kulthūm is depicted as "living" in the hearts of her listeners, including those of future generations. The notion is made explicit through the caption, "I preferred to live with the hearts of the people, and my heart is with every fan" (Shūshah 1976, 111).[1] In another contrast, the portrait of 'Abd al-Wahhāb extends Western notions of the composer as an isolated genius who is memorialized through tangible historical documents. Further, the portrait of 'Abd al-Wahhāb—both a singer and a composer—reproduces the Western emphasis on the composer as creator over the performer as re-creator and, especially when aligned with Ḥijāzī's image, marks the voice as an emotional, feminine instrument.[2] 'Abd al-Wahhāb's portrait also reinforces his appropriation of Western musical styles in an effort to modernize Egyptian song. Finally, Ḥijāzī's image reflects the fact that Umm Kulthūm's music was valued as it was experienced in performance, rather than as it existed on paper, a notion closer to Western popular music than Western art music.

Ḥijāzī's image invites further interpretation of the relationship between the woman singer and the listener. Although the image's context—it falls in the middle of a biography identifies the performer as Umm Kulthūm, Ḥijāzī's imaginative, ambiguous renderings of the singer and listener offer the viewer several ways to assess their relationship. The woman, with her buxom figure, may represent an unattainable object of his desire. This reading recognizes Umm Kulthūm's ability to function as an object of desire both during and after her lifetime, as seen in the distressed shouts of the Libyan fan and the criticism of the excessive weight of the lead actress in the Ramadan television series. Filmmaker Sami Alkassim's careful manipulation of Umm Kulthūm's voice and image—including the use of high-quality recordings of her singing to render ambiguous, visually degraded, and color-processed images of her body unsatisfyingly generic—similarly drew attention to Umm Kulthūm's potential as an object of desire.

Ḥijāzī's image admits other interpretations. The woman may serve as a mediator, rather than a direct object, of the man's desire, stoking his feelings and provoking his tears for an absent beloved. She may be a counselor in desire, not causing his tears, but leading him out of his suffering and furthering his emotional growth. This nurturing role is made possible by the listener's ambiguous age. He could easily be in his teens, twenties, or thirties. As a young man, he may respond to the singer as a maternal figure, rather than a peer standing in for his beloved.

This representation can also be understood as a response to decades-old rumors about the singer's sexual orientation. With knowledge of this back story, a viewer might see the overly busty rendering of the singer in the presence of a young man as an effort to assert her heterosexuality through an exaggerated representation of her as a sexualized object. While rarely addressed in print or film, rumors of her homosexuality were fed by her failure to fulfill cultural expectations that she marry as a young woman. They were passed on orally in the Arab world beginning in the middle of her career and continuing into the twenty-first century; those who acknowledged them in writing were most frequently individuals raised, educated, or employed in the West (Habib 1995, 57, 78–81; Giammusso 2004; Euroarabe).[3] The attempted outing of the singer, particularly by Westerners, has often caused Egyptians offense. Yet concerns also surfaced when an Egyptian journalist close to Umm Kulthūm indirectly approached the topic in a conversation with me and a young Egyptian woman. The journalist described the separate sleeping quarters used by the singer and her husband, a revelation that discomforted the young woman at our table even though the arrangement was explained as being designed to accommodate the spouses' different work and social schedules. For the young woman, the journalist's account likely conjured the common anecdotal characterization of the couple's relationship as a marriage of convenience designed to end the rumors about the singer's sexual orientation.[4]

The writer Kamāl Raḍwān offered a rare printed response to continued rumors of Umm Kulthūm's homosexuality. He attacked the disseminators as nonbelievers and enemies of Egypt for disgracing such a national symbol. He then argued that the singer's status as the fourth pyramid, as well as her closeness with leaders and first ladies, made her "off limits" from such accusations of "deviance" and "the disclosure of things that Egyptian society refuses." Raḍwān distanced the icon from the accusation by using the noun *shudhūdh* (deviance) rather than the descriptive adjective or noun *shādhdhah*, meaning "deviant" (2000, 57–59).[5]

While Raḍwān's charged language might be dismissed as crass, he does acknowledge in print an important, long-standing part of Umm Kulthūm's reception that has likely shaped accounts by many other authors, artists, and filmmakers. Raḍwān's use of the word "disclosure" suggests that his concern was not with any of the same-sex activities in which the singer might have engaged according to the circulated accounts, but rather was raised by the public flaunting of such activities, in this case the rumor form itself. Such an interpretation is supported by the responses of Egyptian graduate students studying in the United States who took offense to an American professor's public assertion that the singer was homosexual. The students objected specifically to his speaking without firsthand knowledge and to his revelation of an aspect of her life that she had kept private, "between herself and God."[6] A related attitude motivated the 2001 police raid on a Cairo club frequented by gay Egyptian men. The raid was an attack on the public nature of the men's activities and their public use of homosexuality as a group identification, not on their sexual inclination (Massad 2007, 183, 393). Such recent events extend views that have long held in Egyptian discourse: in the 1947 novel *Midaq Alley* by Naguib Mahfouz (Najīb Maḥfūth), it is not the café owner's same-sex practices to which his son objects but rather the scandals caused by his public flaunting of his proclivities (1989, 63).

Rumors of Umm Kulthūm's homosexuality have persisted for decades despite the absence of a factual basis for them. While these rumors may be seen to threaten a national icon, they also represent an attempt to come to terms with the ways in which Umm Kulthūm's life deviated from local cultural expectations for women. Under what Marcia C. Inhorn has described as the "patriarchal fertility mandate," marriage and motherhood were expected of all Egyptian women (1996, 12–13). Yet Umm Kulthūm challenged this patriarchal system in ways that were potentially threatening and confusing, much like John Lennon did by reversing and ridiculing gender roles during his househusband years in the late 1970s (Mäkelä 2004, 202–203).[7] Umm Kulthūm did not marry as a young woman, even at a time when the shirking of marriage seemed inconceivable. While an ambitious young woman might aspire to remain single, like the young doctor Suhayr in Muḥammad Khurshid's play *Maṣīruhum Ilaynā* (Their Destiny Is Ours), ultimately she is expected to marry. Suhayr's eventual concession to this expectation reflects the fact that few Egyptian women chose a path other than marriage (Badran 1995, 136–37). Umm Kulthūm's life choices did not demonstrate a need for sexual contact with men, and she did not fulfill the reproductive role prescribed for women. She further challenged expectations by adopting men's roles as breadwinner and active member in public life when women's work was a subject of controversy (Moghadam 2003, 116). Even as some women engaged in professions such as education, the female intellectuals writing in the Egyptian women's press saw a woman's place as being in the home and strived to elevate it by transforming the housewife's duties into a profession (Baron 1994, 166).

Umm Kulthūm's unconventional life choices have challenged many authors and filmmakers. A recent dramatic account, directed by a woman committed to addressing women's issues (Abu-Lughod 2005, 92), was unusual in highlighting Umm Kulthūm's choices in a neutral manner, neither lauding nor criticizing them. Throughout the thirty-seven-part Ramadan television series *Umm Kulthūm*, men are portrayed as making decisions while women connive and console. Yet Umm Kulthūm behaves differently. Having ascended to the presidency of the musicians' syndicate, she sits at a desk giving orders. She is the only woman in the series to do so.

While some observers have turned to rumors of homosexuality to make sense of Umm Kulthūm's choices—particularly her eschewal of marriage, the sanctioned framework for sexual activity and reproduction—these choices can be explained in another way. Under what Valentine Moghadam has termed a "patriarchal gender contract," Umm Kulthūm's early entry into marriage would have obligated her to submit to her husband's authority, including restrictions on her movements and behaviors (2003, 126). Such subordination would have been particularly detrimental to her early career, as her husband could have prevented her from singing in public. Although difficult to imagine given the success and social status she had attained by the 1940s, the possibility that this could have taken place was substantiated by press coverage of her midlife engagement and subsequent marriage. The announcement of her engagement to Maḥmūd al-Sharīf in 1946 included the journalist's question to Umm Kulthūm, "Do you plan to stop singing?" and her response, "This is his issue and he does not want me to stop singing." The notion was apparently prominent enough in the general public's mind that the belated announcement of her later marriage, to Ḥasan al-Ḥifnāwī in 1954, assured newspaper readers that she would continue singing (al-Maḥallāwī 1999a, 71, 89). Confirming that a husband could have prevented her from singing, the poet Aḥmad Rāmī's son Tawḥīd explained that his father would have done so had he married Umm Kulthūm (Qaṭāmish 2000). The priority Umm Kulthūm set on preserving her career over her marriage was confirmed by her niece Saʿdīyah Hānim, who explained that Umm Kulthūm refused marriage to Rāmī because she did not want to marry at all and wanted to devote herself totally to her work (Surūr 2000). Such a prioritization was both unusual and audacious when Egyptian women of all classes were expected to become mothers and working women normally left their jobs permanently after the birth of their first child (Inhorn 1996, 39).

It goes without saying that Umm Kulthūm's choices represented a significant deviation from Egyptian cultural expectations. While her careful shaping of much of her public image assisted authors in fashioning her as a national monument, her personal choices left them with the task of filling the void created by her failure to marry early and rumors of her homosexuality. In this respect, her reception challenges Tyler Cowen's assertion that deceased stars often receive greater praise than their living counterparts because they "possess no further capacity to embarrass or disappoint the critics" (2000, 86). When describing Umm Kulthūm's hybrid public persona, Nadia Habib explained that "she produced herself in that 'in-between' space . . . in order to reconcile the discrepancies between her public and private self, between her modest rural origins and her rise into the urban upper-classes." However, she did a less thorough job of reconciling the discrepancies "between her gendered location and her unique reworking of its implications" (1995, 31). During her lifetime, the singer had remarkable success in circumventing the cultural restrictions that typically regulated the behavior of Egyptian women in the twentieth century. She entered a profession that historically had cast a shadow of moral disrepute on women and carved out a repertory, audience, and performance style that enabled her to maintain high artistic standards and an honorable reputation. While marriage and childbirth were requisite for young women to maintain financial security and avoid social stigma, Umm Kulthūm lived into her fifties before entering a sustained marriage and she never bore children. For some observers of today, she represents an attractive alternative to the conservative religious rhetoric gaining increasing attention from young viewers across the Arab world. One Arab blogger expressed concern regarding the "mind-numbing" potential of Islamic televangelists' rhetoric for Arab women. She concluded, "If I have to choose between [the preachers] Sheikh Qardawi and Amr Khalid, I'll choose Umm Kulthūm" (A. 2005). While the singer's successful charting of a public career in the face of long-existing cultural restrictions may inspire some twenty-first-century women, it has left most authors and filmmakers with the challenging task of reconciling her unconventional life choices with her gendered location in the decades following her death.

Locating Umm Kulthūm

One of the challenges facing authors and filmmakers seeking to portray Umm Kulthūm is the lack of a category in which to locate a woman who shirked her responsibilities of marrying and bearing children at a young age. Since the twentieth century, observers in the Arab world have struggled to construct new categories to deal with women's behaviors that do not fit the norms of a patriarchal society. Early in the century, the president of an Egyptian women's organization noted with unease that in Europe a "third sex" was emerging, consisting of women who dismissed their maternal duties and addressed work as their top priority. Such an "unnatural, unfeminine woman" challenged the binary categories of "man" and "woman" and threatened to "upset the natural order" (Baron 1994, 147–48). Writing nearly a century later, Muntasir Mazhar still strived to keep women's "problematic" behaviors—controlling their husbands, emulating men, possessing self-confidence, exhibiting aggression, disliking housework, and lacking maternal instincts—out of the normative category of "woman" by distinguishing those exhibiting them as lesbians (Massad 2007, 264).

Although she was often distinguished from "ordinary" women, Umm Kulthūm was not portrayed in print and film as belonging to an undesired "third sex." Writer Majīd Ṭirād cast her difference as an asset, rather than a weakness, when he attributed to her the understanding that she was "not of the same disposition as other women and could live her whole life for her art" (1999, 44). Aḥmad Zakī ʿAbd al-Ḥalīm, after discussing Umm Kulthūm's youthful public appearances as a boy singer, stressed and applauded the fact that "Umm Kulthūm was different in every way." He too linked her "personal" difference, so vulnerable to criticism, to her artistic difference, so worthy of praise (1987, 121). Umm Kulthūm's friend and biographer Niʿmāt Aḥmad Fu'ād situated the singer outside the two gender categories altogether. She rooted the singer's "sacrifice" of a conventional female identity in her receipt of a boy's upbringing, including dressing in boys' clothes to hide her gender and attending men's gatherings "as one of them." Fu'ād blamed not the singer but others, those who raised her, for causing this early distortion that "anesthetized the demands of femininity in her and awoke aspiration of the person" in her. Fu'ād defined this third category of "person" as a valued space, where Umm Kulthūm was able to focus her attention on the development of her art (2000, 268–69).

Many writers suggested that Umm Kulthūm operated not only outside conventional gender categories but also beyond the human realm. Novelist Sélim Nassib had his narrator, the poet Aḥmad Rāmī, describe her as a hermaphrodite divinity (2006, 85).[8] Several other authors attributed this perception to her audience, claiming that listeners "used to imagine . . . that she was created from a substance other than that of humans" (*Umm Kulthūm: Qiṣṣat ḥayātihā*, 1977, 40; Shūshah 1976, 73). Jūrj Ibrāhīm al-Khūrī rejected the common explanation that public disapproval of her marriage to Maḥmūd al-Sharīf was based on his lack of adequate status. Instead, he argued that such outrage originated in the belief that she was a goddess, and "a goddess does not marry" (2000, 55–56). He implied that her audience had already accepted her "deviations" from her gender role during her lifetime, and he set this as a standard for her later reception. This attempt to classify the singer as extrahuman helped shift attention away from the ways in which her life choices deviated from society's expectations and focused it instead on her unusual talents and extraordinary accomplishments.

A number of authors found another category to accommodate Umm Kulthūm's avoidance of marriage: that of the ascetic. Despite celibacy being discouraged in Islam, it was more than possible to make the quality seem admirable (Golley 2003, 111). Ramaḍān, for instance, deemed the singer's avoidance of marriage a form of "fasting." Characterizing sexual intimacy with a man as a physical requirement, he portrayed her self-deprivation as high selflessness (n.d., 274–77). Many writers expanded on Fu'ād's earlier assertion, first made in the 1970s, that Umm Kulthūm lived "like a nun in the *miḥrāb* [prayer niche] of art" (N. Fu'ād 2000, 268–69).[9] Among them, al-Khūrī identified the pleasure the public took in her art as the motivation behind her asceticism (2000, 55–56). Other writers explained that Umm Kulthūm "knew that she was the beloved of the Arab public. Therefore, she paid a tax on that love, in that she sacrificed her happiness for a long time and lived as a nun in the *miḥrāb* of art to make others happy with her vocal art" (*Umm Kulthūm: Qiṣṣat ḥayātihā* 1977, 39; Shūshah 1976, 73). Expressing a similar sentiment, Sa'īd 'Uthmān likened her to "a candle [that] is consumed by fire to light what is around it" (2000, 85). As if metaphorical destruction through self-sacrifice did not generate a sufficiently sympathetic image of the singer, Nassib cast her as a victim of physical deterioration. Rāmī, his narrator, identified the throat as the locus of the emotions that are normally "given" to a man and described the actual tumor diagnosed in Umm Kulthūm's throat as the product of years of frustration, solitude, and chastity (2006, 154). In the quest to place the singer in a suitable category, commentators encouraged admiration for her self-sacrifice, quite the opposite of the logical interpretation that she had sacrificed cultural expectations of marriage in order to preserve her art and her independence.

During the past two decades, many authors and filmmakers have preferred to inflate details of the singer's romantic life, rather than cast her as an ascetic. As monogamous heterosexual love has remained a clear ideal, the notion of a woman who did not need to love or desire a man is still foreign to many (Booth 2001a, 64–65). Shortly after her death, one interviewer finally asked a journalist who had been close to Umm Kulthūm, "Was it necessary for Umm Kulthūm to love a man?" ("Dhikrayāt" 1975, 7). An answer in the negative was difficult for many to accept, so biographers would recount her marriages and amorous relationships with a host of men.[10] Often they would elaborate on rumored heterosexual relationships to drive home the point.

Authors regularly have drawn attention to the singer's ability to attract suitors. While luring readers with the promise of new information about the private life of a national icon, headlines like "Unknown Love Story between the Prince of the Fans and Umm Kulthūm" have secured her heterosexual image through men's desire, in this case that of the prominent journalist Muḥammad al-Tābi'ī (Ṣalāḥ 2000; Ḥ. Sālim 1981). In the Ramadan television series, no fewer than six men sought her affections. By focusing on just two of these men at any given point in the drama, the writers not only maintained tension, interest, and credibility, but they also created a continuous portrait of the singer as the object of male desire. As in written accounts about Umm Kulthūm, the jealousy of her male suitors features notably in the series. 'Ūd player and composer Muḥammad al-Qaṣabjī, for example, proved a useful tool of validation in both the series and written accounts.[11] One recurring anecdote has al-Qaṣabjī driven by love and jealousy to follow Umm Kulthūm in a taxi from one side of the city to the other and back as she rode with Maḥmūd al-Sharīf (Khalīl 1992, 217; Raḍwān 2000, 47).

Rather than simply casting Umm Kulthūm as the object of others' affections, many recent accounts have developed her role as a desiring subject. Ḥanafī al-Maḥallāwī described her youthful search for true love and romantic letters that she wrote to Zakariyā Aḥmad (1999a, 15, 24). Muḥammad Fāḍil's 2000 film *Kawkab al-Sharq* set her romantic attachments to several men in the foreground. In one scene, she walks arm-in-arm with Sharīf Ṣabrī Pāshā, the man she hopes to marry. Another scene casts her sympathetically as the victim of a different love interest's abandonment. Fāḍil's film not only offered an unambiguous depiction of the singer's heterosexuality, but it also portrayed her as an "appropriately" vulnerable, emotional, and affectionate woman. Presenting the active role the singer played in her romantic matters, al-Maḥallāwī cast her as initiating and pushing forward her relationship with Maḥmūd al-Sharīf (1999a, 82, 84). 'Abd al-Nūr Khalīl characterized her as a woman who knew her type of man. In his description, she was an ideal woman—an "authentic rustic woman, an eastern woman with all of her inherited traditions, who wants a strong captivating man who—and whose command—she obeys as a husband" (1992, 144).

The poet Aḥmad Rāmī figures centrally in the long line of relationships imagined for Umm Kulthūm by writers and artists. Muḥammad Rif'at al-Muhāmī seized on Rāmī's characterization of the singer as a "dream girl" to sustain the fantasy of a romantic union between the two of them (1979,

38–39). Sélim Nassib's novel, inspired by the poet's life, methodically traces the course of their relationship, using Rāmī as a narrator and casting his songs as a public diary, with lyrics written time and again in response to his emotionally trying encounters with the singer (2006).

The Ramadan television series offered a carefully developed portrayal of the two artists' emotional connection, stimulating viewers' desire to see their romance fulfilled. Following a rift with Rāmī, prompted by Umm Kulthūm's discovery that she had recorded lyrics previously rejected by her rival 'Abd al-Wahhāb, episode sixteen fuels viewers' yearning for the poet and singer to reconcile and confess their feelings for one another. While recuperating in the hospital in episode seventeen, Umm Kulthūm calls for Rāmī, and at al-Qaṣabjī's urging, Rāmī finally visits her. Red rose in hand, he begins to confess his feelings, and they reconcile. When he returns home, Rāmī's sisters prompt him to try on one of a pair of rings they have brought for him. Even as 'Aṭīyāt, a suitable young woman, has been introduced to Rāmī in the sixteenth episode, the viewer intuits that one of the rings will be for Umm Kulthūm. In episode eighteen, the poet and singer engage in a serious seaside conversation. He finally asks, "Shall we marry?" but Umm Kulthūm stalls, and the two are interrupted by al-Qaṣabjī before she boards a ship abroad, without giving an answer. The poignant scene leaves Rāmī on shore waving good-bye and then retreating alone. In time, Rāmī's sister urges him to view 'Aṭīyāt as a reasonable bride. Yet as the plans unfold, al-Qaṣabjī evinces more excitement about the upcoming marriage than Rāmī himself. When Umm Kulthūm returns from her trip, she learns of the poet's marriage. She tries to hide her feelings but then abruptly leaves a showing of her new film *Widād* after becoming aware of her hand with its ringless finger. The scene efficiently has her acknowledge and aspire to the convention of marriage. In a series that so diligently portrays the singer's strength and self-control, this revealing moment of emotion provides a convincing counterpoint to viewers' curiosity about how she could reject so many men.

With the passage of decades since her death and the increasing contributions of younger writers, recent biographical efforts have been composed amid a changed cultural context. An exploration of the singer's romantic life, which might have seemed scandalous soon after her death, has come to seem acceptable, if not expected. At the same time, accounts in the past two decades have been constructed and interpreted within a conceptual framework that includes a homosexual identity. This identity has been defined with increasing clarity since the 1990s through the activism of international gay rights organizations and a Western taxonomy based on categories of "normal" and "deviant" sexuality.[12] As a result, a homosexual categorization for Umm Kulthūm has emerged as something to be expressly avoided in order for her to retain her status as a venerated national icon.

Mother for a Nation

Film and written accounts of Umm Kulthūm addressed her eschewal of motherhood alongside her purported romantic interest in men. Without the typical early marriage, and without formal adoption procedures in Egypt, Umm Kulthūm forfeited the opportunity to demonstrate the essence of her identity as a woman through childbirth and motherhood. As Inhorn has outlined, under the patriarchal fertility mandate "all women are expected to marry and become mothers." A wide range of literature on Egypt supports Inhorn's assertion that motherhood is considered "the most important role for women and the perceived essence of a woman's identity" (Inhorn 1996, 12–13). Since the early twentieth century, Egyptian writers and intellectuals have cited the family, motherhood, and the raising of children as priorities for women. A "cult of domesticity" in the early twentieth century idealized the role of mother, as writers in the women's press identified the mother as the primary force shaping children (Badran 1995, 63; Baron 1994, 159). Numerous articles instructed women on how to be efficient and skilled mothers, and women were likely chastised when they neglected their maternal duties (Badran 1995, 140). Even when advocating employment for women, writers in the women's press promoted an essentializing argument that a "maternal sensibility" would help female teachers understand students more effectively than would their male counterparts (175–76).

The centrality of motherhood to female identity was sustained late into the twentieth century. For example, the protagonist in Yūsuf Idrīs's 1987 novella *Abū al-Rijāl* reflects that a "man is a man because he is chivalrous and generous, and courageous." He continues, "The woman is a woman not on account of her femininity and her coquetry, but by her greater role that she be the greatest mother for a more evolved humanity. *Motherhood* like manliness is not an objective or a description; the two are rather values, high degrees of emotional and rational human conduct, even corporeal conduct" (Massad 2007, 329; emphasis mine). Here, the concept of motherhood stands in the place of womanhood or femininity. Women's continuing definition through motherhood can also be observed in the popular reception of Fayrūz, about two generations younger than Umm Kulthūm. She has been cast as a devoted mother despite, or perhaps in response to, her son's claims of her frequent absence from the home. While many aspects of her reception, such as her angelic nature, can be traced to her dramatic roles onstage, her portrayal as a mother stands in contradiction to her stage roles, which often called for her to play women who delayed marriage and sacrificed the health of their children (Stone 2008, 146, 150–52). Her portrayal as a maternal figure may thus be seen to serve as a corrective to her performances onstage and at home.

According to Egyptian mores, Umm Kulthūm's lack of children left her an incomplete woman. As Golley concluded recently, "Childless women are not very much respected in Arabic countries" (2003, 142–43). In her study of infertile Egyptian women, Inhorn explained that a childless woman "feels, and is viewed as, less than a normal female—a 'pseudo-male,' who is more masculine than feminine by virtue of her uncooperative reproductive organs." Both her sexual and gender identities are "marred, for, without claims to motherhood, she can never be viewed as a complete woman, who has fulfilled her God-given adult role in life" (Inhorn 1996, 10). After Umm Kulthūm's death, authors sought to fill the void created by her lack of a child. Collectively, they mounted a concerted attempt to rectify her gender identity and, in doing so, have enhanced her status as a national icon.

Posthumous representations of Umm Kulthūm as a maternal woman not only demonstrated her feminine instincts but also ameliorated her failure to fulfill cultural expectations of biological reproduction. Many accounts set her as the possessor of "natural" maternal feelings (al-Marīnī 1975, 23; al-Disūqī 1978). One Egyptian writer who had the privilege to meet both Asmahan and Umm Kulthūm as a child characterized the former as a beautiful woman who sang when the writer was sick, but characterized the latter as "a favorite" with children "because she had time to play with us" (Marsot 2002, 108). Another commentator seemed to be describing the matriarch of a large family, rather than a childless woman, when he asserted, "Motherhood flowed in her pericardium. Her love for children possessed her thoughts and feelings" (*Umm Kulthūm: Qīthārat al-'Arab* 1978, 47).

To bolster their claims, authors culled anecdotal and visual evidence from Umm Kulthūm's public and private life. Zakariyā offered a touching anecdote from the singer's trip to Morocco. Having spotted a young boy crying in the crowd gathered to see her, she stopped her car and got out to console him. He admitted to her, "I was crying because I lost hope of seeing Umm Kulthūm," at which point she took him back to her hotel to comfort him (1983, 157–8). Another writer revealed a maternal moment from a rehearsal. In a section titled "Umm Kulthūm the Mother," she informed readers that Umm Kulthūm embraced and played with members of a children's choir during a rehearsal in order to ease their fears about performing (al-Amīr 1983). Other publications regularly featured photographs of Umm Kulthūm acting as a mother—holding, kissing, and playing with babies and children from both within and outside her extended family.[13] The grouping of a dozen such photographs under the title "Mama Thūmah" suggested that readers were seeing the singer's true nature rather than carefully arranged photo opportunities (2000, 106–11).

Many biographers strengthened Umm Kulthūm's maternal image indirectly, by portraying her as a pitiable woman who had lost the opportunity to be a mother (al-Marīnī 1975, 23). In a Beirut publication, she was described as being a woman "who won everything and lost the greatest thing—she lost motherhood. How often she longed for a child . . . but she was deprived of a child and deprived of a newborn" (*Umm Kulthūm: Qīthārat al-ʿArab* 1978, 47). Abū Bakr al-Marīnī captioned a photograph of the singer holding a newborn as follows: "Umm Kulthūm and a kiss of tenderness for a child—she missed the joy of motherhood because she did not have children in her lifetime" (1975, 256). The caption leveraged the photograph not only to demonstrate that the singer possessed natural affection for children but also to suggest that she was drawn to others' children to compensate for having none of her own. As with her decision not to marry, some portrayed her as deliberately relinquishing the opportunity to become a mother for a greater goal. Majīd Ṭirād asserted that she "sacrificed her happiness in service of her art and her public and forbade herself her right to build a family as women generally do" (1999, 44).

Anecdotes from Umm Kulthūm's private life supplemented those from public appearances in the effort to portray her as a "normal" woman with maternal instincts and to finesse her eschewal of childbirth. As noted in an earlier chapter, authors often recounted her taking children into her home and acting as an unofficial adoptive mother.[14] Accordingly, both the film *Kawkab al-Sharq* and Sélim Nassib's novel showed children around her (2006, 190). Salwá Jumjūm not only used an interview with the singer's niece Saʿdīyah to showcase her maternal treatment of the young members of her extended family, but also teased readers—through headline, setup of the interview, and final question—with the rumor that Saʿdīyah may actually have been her daughter (1981). Such a suggestion—shocking and scandalous out of context, because it would have implied a child out of wedlock—served in this case not to discredit the singer, but rather to dangle the possibility that she had fulfilled her maternal duty and become a complete woman.

An alternative method of reconciling the singer's life choices with her gendered location was to expand her maternal role to a national scale. Ḥāzim Ṣāghīyah deemed the singer to be the public's desexualized mother (1991, 60–61). Both Moustapha Chelbi's account (1977, 311) and Sami Alkassim's documentary *Far from You* cast Umm Kulthūm as one of Egypt's metaphorical parents. Alkassim's documentary paired her with Jamāl 'Abd al-Nāṣir, whose status as a perceived father to the Egyptian nation helped drive calls for him to stay in office after his announced resignation in June 1967 (Hussein 1977, 262; Kimche and Bawly 1968, 246). Umm Kulthūm's designation as a national mother was rooted in the historical conditions of her life. In the first place, she had filled the void created by 'Abd al-Nāṣir's wife's absence from the public stage. Having gained a platform, she used it to display ideals for the rest of the nation. Her emphasis on productivity and thrift after the 1967 war not only reinforced the regime, but also expanded on a national scale the ideals of household management promoted by women writers and activists in the early twentieth century (Baron 1994, 157).

Representations of Umm Kulthūm as a mother for Egypt also extended a long discursive history of the nation as figurative family. In the early twentieth century, Egyptian nationalists adopted kinship idioms to foster a sense of relatedness, belonging, and loyalty binding individuals separated by ethnic, racial, class, and religious divisions. While imperialist leaders had used fatherly gestures to inspire loyalty, nationalists answered by exploiting maternal imagery and idioms in several ways. Deemed "mothers of the nation," women were understood, in biological and cultural terms, to "reproduce" the nation. The education of girls was set as essential for the creation of mothers who could effectively raise children—especially devoted sons—and instill in them a love for their nation (Baron 2005, 5, 36). The nationalists' depiction of Egypt as a woman, the perception of the national leader as a father, and the maintenance of stratified and patriarchal relationships in daily life both reinforced and extended the scope of this kinship language. The pervasiveness of such relationships in the religious, political, and educational institutions of daily life led the Syrian-born sociologist Halim Barakat to describe Arab society as "the family generalized or enlarged" (1993, 118) and Joseph Massad to describe the citizens of Egypt as "children" (2007, 313).

Alongside the nationalists' use of kinship idioms, a maternal leader emerged in the early twentieth century. Ṣafīyah Zaghlūl, wife of the nationalist Wafd Party leader Sa'd Zaghlūl, acquired the name "Mother of the Egyptians" after her husband was arrested and deported. According to one account, she acquired the epithet when a man who was wounded protesting British rule said to her in his final moments, "I am going to die far from my mother." When Ṣafīyah asked, "My son, am I not also your mother?" he responded, "Yes, but you are also the mother of all Egyptians." An alternative account has female demonstrators saying at her door, "'Ā'ishah was the Mother of the Believers (*Umm al-Mu'minīn*), Ṣafīyah is the Mother of the

Egyptians (*Umm al-Miṣrīyīn*)." However the name was first used, it became widely adopted in the 1920s (Baron 2005, 140–41, 246). Emerging as a powerful maternal nationalist icon, Ṣafīyah helped create a sense of solidarity among a divided people.

Despite her very different social background, Umm Kulthūm's career, persona, and reception paralleled those of Ṣafīyah Zaghlūl in many respects. Both women controlled their images carefully and manipulated cultural symbols to stress their virtues, variously, as "authentic" villager, cosmopolitan international traveler, educated woman, and aristocrat. Religiosity and philanthropy were prominent parts of both women's images as well. And both spoke out on political matters: Ṣafīyah when Sa'd was arrested and deported, and Umm Kulthūm following the 1967 war. Each woman also sought to quiet national unrest by stressing that the public should focus on their professional tasks and leave governing to the country's leaders. During their respective lifetimes, both figures emerged as the most visible women in the press, as Queen Nazlī, wife of King Fu'ād, and Taḥīyah, wife of 'Abd al-Nāṣir, stayed out of the public eye. While both women raised children of their extended families as their own, neither bore children, creating a void that called out to be filled by the national community (Baron 2005, 135–39, 144–45). Given these parallels, it is not surprising that authors and dramatists have established a connection between the two women (al-Jawādī 1985, 42). In the Ramadan television series, Ṣafīyah Zaghlūl calls the singer to congratulate her after she receives a national award. The face-to-face meeting that follows not only provides concise coverage of the nation's history, but it also allows the aged "Mother of the Egyptians" to pass the torch of maternal leadership to the singer, who is at the height of her vocal powers.

Rather than using a modern model to illuminate the singer as a national mother figure, some authors have turned to the pharaonic imagery once used by nationalists in the early twentieth century.[15] Having survived the death of King Fu'ād, the removal of King Fārūq, and the death of 'Abd al-Nāṣir, Umm Kulthūm became a prime candidate to promote, alongside the country's ancient monuments, the longevity of Egypt's culture and territory. Authors played with the meanings of the singer's and the Sphinx's names to articulate the relationship between the country's ancient eternal parents (al-Malākh 1985). The Sphinx's Arabic name, Abū al-Hawl, means "Father of Fear."[16] Photos of Umm Kulthūm posing near the Sphinx were posthumously captioned "Two majesties: the father [*ab*] and the mother [*umm*]" (Abū al-Khayr 1975, n.p.). While such images cast the singer and her art as fixed and "authentic" elements of the national heritage, the values she represented became the focus of other treatments, such as that by Ni'māt

Aḥmad Fu'ād, who elaborated on an episode from ancient Egyptian mythology to explore Umm Kulthūm's role as a national mother figure. Fu'ād offered an extended comparison of Umm Kulthūm and Isis, the mother of Horus.

In both of them from Egypt there was the unlimited gift of motherhood.
In both of them from Egypt there was work as an anthem to life.
In both of them from Egypt there was triumph over hardship.
In both of them from Egypt there was enduring patience with pride.
In both of them from Egypt there was perseverance and the power of persistence.
In both of them from Egypt there was refusal of defeat and the pursuit of victory.
In both of them from Egypt there was the stream of the Nile to dawn and the light of day. (1975)

Fu'ād's interpretation was enhanced by a photograph of Umm Kulthūm singing with a stage backdrop portraying ancient Egyptian monuments during her concert to rescue the Philae Temple. Many of the singer's values, as spelled out by Fu'ād, were rooted in the public image that she crafted with particular care after the 1967 war. As Fu'ād elaborated the similarities of the missions of Umm Kulthūm and Isis, the mother of Horus, the singer's postwar response emerged more clearly as central to her maternal role:

Umm Horus [the mother of Horus] rose above great sadness when Seth cut Osiris to pieces, and she traversed the country collecting his limbs to bring life back to him.

Umm Kulthūm rose above great sadness in 1967 when the Sinai was cut off from Egypt. She traversed the country collecting money—for the cost of weapons—to return to Egypt what was lost in land and blood, to return to Egypt after the night, the break of day. (1975)

Whereas Fu'ād highlighted Umm Kulthūm's postwar patriotism from an Egyptian perspective, authors from other Arab nations elaborated on her value as a maternal symbol of regional unity. She acquired the name "Umm al-'Arab," meaning Mother of the Arabs (*Umm Kulthūm: Qīthārat al-'Arab* 1975, 161; Ben Hammed, 1997, 159). The name reinforced an etymological connection between *umm* (mother) and *ummah,* referring to a nation as a community of people. As Ṣafīyah Zaghlūl's title "Umm al-Miṣrīyīn" (Mother of the Egyptians) echoed the older name "Umm al-Mu'minīn" (Mother of the Believers), which referred to the Prophet Muḥammad's favorite wife, 'Ā'ishah, Umm Kulthūm's title "Umm al-'Arab" echoed the established phrase "al-ummah al-'arabīyah" (the Arab nation). By incorporating these nicknames, authors and observers credited the singer with building a community among Arabs through shared mutual devotion just as an Arab

Umm Kulthūm poses with the Sphinx. *Photo courtesy of Farūq Ibrāhīm*

mother holds a family together through strong emotional ties with her children (Barakat 1985, 31–32).[17]

Although "Umm al-ʿArab" could be dismissed as simply a pun on the singer's name, it encapsulated significant feelings and ideals in modern Arab history. One such ideal was unity sought through pan-Arabism. As Maḥmūd al-Saʿdnī explained, "If ʿAbd al-Nāṣir is the father of unity in this twentieth century, Umm Kulthūm is its mother" (1975b, 91). When a Sudanese journalist called her the "Mother of Arabness" during her trip to his country in late 1968, his language suggested a vision of the Arab world as a single overarching society, rather than an assortment of independent nation states that assert their differences and distinct identities, often the more so in times of crisis (Yūsuf; Barakat 1993, xi). Upon the singer's death, writers recollected her as a powerful unifying force among Arabs.[18] Hammadi Ben Hammed's account featured an artist's rendering of her dress as a patchwork made up of hundreds of people representing different Arab nationalities (1997, 156), while Chant Avedissian presented her as the focal point of a united Arab nation in his "al-Waṭan al-ʿArabī" (2008, featured on the cover).

While Ilyās Saḥḥāb was careful to note the limitations of the singer's role as a symbol of Arab unity, a host of other accounts inflated that role and the power contained within it (1980, 27–28). The author of one recent account repeated former Lebanese prime minister Sā'ib Salām's assessment that "she established national, fraternal, and emotional Arab unity before its establishment politically or constitutionally in a working fashion" (Ramaḍān n.d., 14). Others reiterated the *London Times*'s declaration that Umm Kulthūm was, "perhaps with the exception of 'Abd al-Nāṣir, the greatest embodiment of the feelings of Arab unity in the modern Middle East" and *Life* magazine's characterizations of her concerts as pan-Arab festivals that brought the entire region to a halt.[19] For Egyptian and Arab authors, the acceptance by Western observers—who were often characterized as the imperialist enemy—of Umm Kulthūm's role in strengthening Arab cultural and emotional unity certified its existence. Accounts of her unifying powers persisted more than a quarter-century after her death, when Muḥammad Sa'īd called her the "uniter of Arab hearts and feelings" (2002, 15, 27) and a photo caption credited her voice with "establishing Arab unity from the gulf to the ocean."[20]

The singer's own public performances gave authors material with which to shape her posthumous image, not only as a uniter of Arabs but also as a devoted patriot and religious woman. One writer used an anecdote from her trip to Tunisia to demonstrate the existence of Arab emotional unity. The singer attended a concert given by an Andalusian ensemble. As the musicians performed religious songs, Umm Kulthūm began humming along, and the ensemble leader pulled her into the group, encouraging her to continue. Tears fell from the singer's eyes as she sang the lyrics "Help us, O Prophet," and her voice seized everyone's attention. As the other voices fell silent, she continued her supplications. The Tunisian prime minister's wife fainted, the first lady cried audibly, and President Ḥabīb Būrqībah silently wiped his tears. Such an anecdote defined Egypt's 1967 defeat as an Arab defeat and demonstrated the emotional bond tying Arabs across national boundaries. In characterizing the scene's meaning, the writer concluded, "She sang the suffering of Egypt and the Arabs" ("Istaqbalatha" 1988).

Portrayals of Umm Kulthūm as "Mother of the Arabs" evidenced the expansion of a desire for national identity onto a regional scale. By striving to embody Arab cultural unity during her later years, the singer helped commentators and listeners project a larger palette of needs and emotions onto her art. Nadia Habib noted that listeners' projections were facilitated during her lifetime when they were "not mediated by her image and its materiality." After Umm Kulthūm's death, the greater degree to which her physical image could be manipulated further made possible her representation as a maternal icon of regional cultural unity (1995, 50–51). Some observers recognized in her "twin images of Mother Egypt and erotic partner" and characterized her singing as "both motherly and alluring" (Fishkoff 1996; Monioudis). Artists carefully manipulated these two aspects of her image to render her a symbol of regional cultural unity. Ḥijāzī's caricature emphasized her alluring qualities, while others focused on her maternal ones (Shūshah 1976, 110–11). Artists' matronly and less erotic renderings of a 1960s-era Umm Kulthūm effectively communicated her value as "Umm al-'Arab," the Arab nation's metaphorical mother (*Umm Kulthūm: Qīthārat al-ʿArab* 1975, 161; Ben Hammed, 1997, 159; *The Mother of the Arabs* 2005). Images that depicted her as "weathered" with age highlighted her strengths of experience, knowledge, determination, and persistence. While in the early twentieth century male artists had represented Egypt as a young woman to generate in their young male audience a romantic attachment to the nation and mobilize the country's youth (Baron 2005, 70–73, 78), artists of the later part of the century often erased Umm Kulthūm's body as a potential object of desire to convey her symbolic maternal role after the 1967 defeat.

While Umm Kulthūm was shown to embody regional cultural unity, her art was seen as spurring local manifestations of Arab nationalism. Because much of the region confronted the forces and effects of colonial domination for decades, her music was deemed an important tool for "preserving belief in the future" beyond such domination (I. Saḥḥāb, 1980, 28). One Tunisian writer explained, "The struggle of the Tunisian people was unceasing, fed by the feeling of Arabism and Islamism, even more than Tunisian nationalism in the narrow sense. The reviews, books, and works written by Laṭīfah al-Zayāt, Ṭaha Ḥussayn and many other writers, and the songs of Umm Kulthūm . . . contributed to revive our sentiment of Arabism" (Melligi 1975). Upon the singer's death, the Tunisian minister of foreign affairs cast the public's active engagement with her music as crucial to the battle against French colonialism after the 1930s. In explaining her significance for a local battle within a larger Arab nation, he turned to a chain of superlatives: "In front of the eyes of the Tunisians, Umm Kulthūm incarnated Arab nationalism and Arab authenticity. . . . In Umm Kulthūm they found that which they imagined the most beautiful, the most elevated, the most noble, in a word, the most Arab" (Melligi 1975). In this view, the singer's music and image constituted a focal point for defining Arab values.

Along similar lines, authors and filmmakers repeatedly cast Umm Kulthūm as the embodiment of a nostalgic fantasy of Arab will, unity, and strength in the face of imperialist powers. Ilyās Saḥḥāb remembered her as a symbol of "shared Arab nationalist sentiment" at a time when Western colonialism tried to "obliterate the traces of Arab nationalism" (1980, 27–28). Such statements confirm a long-running pattern of casting women as metaphors and symbols, rather than metonyms, of nations (Stone 2008, 144). Yet, against this trend, some accounts showed the singer herself as a potential catalyst for retaliation against the imperialist powers. Saʻd Sāmī Ramaḍān claimed that when Umm Kulthūm went to Britain in 1949 for a surgical procedure that carried a slight risk of damaging her voice, the British Foreign Ministry asked doctors not to proceed, fearing that the Arabs might revolt against Britain if she were to lose her voice (Ramaḍān n.d., 194). The Egyptian film *Kawkab al-Sharq* replicated the scene as occurring in an American hospital.

Such representations activated the closely joined feelings of Arab honor and humiliation that had long been associated with imperialist occupation. British soldiers' assaults on individual Egyptian women in the early twentieth century, construed as assaults on the nation as a woman, had amounted to a national humiliation that called for the defense of national honor (Baron 2005, 42–50). As Baron explained, "Honor came to define the parameters of the collective and was at the core of its identity: those who shared honor belonged to the nation; those who did not or were not ready to defend and avenge national honor would be excluded" (7). Both the zenith and nadir of Egyptian and Arab national honor were defined through imperialist powers. ʻAbd al-Nāṣir's most glorious moments—the evacuation of the British, the nationalization of the Suez Canal, and international condemnation of Britain, France, and Israel during the Tripartite Aggression—brought legitimacy to him and honor to Egypt and the Arab nation. Following Umm Kulthūm's death, accounts portrayed her emergence as a devoted defender and redeemer of national honor after ʻAbd al-Nāṣir attributed the moment of greatest humiliation, the 1967 defeat, to imperialist collusion.[21] By spotlighting her fundraising concerts, authors showed the ways in which the singer enlisted Arab sibling nations both to mount retribution for the dishonoring of Egypt and to articulate their collective support through financial contributions, as well as emotional outpourings. Such efforts helped listeners project onto her songs a longing for honor (Zakariyā 1983, 6).

Umm Kulthūm's perceived role as a redeemer of national honor marked the continuation of a shift in the way honor has been defined in terms of gender. Historically, honor has both originated from and enhanced masculinity in times of war and revolution (Baron 2005, 7). Within Egypt, though, it has also been tied to female sexuality and women's bodies through notions of family honor. When a discourse of national honor emerged in the early twentieth century, it was initially based on ideals of family honor. Yet women nationalists worked to shift the emphasis away from an honor grounded in female sexuality to one rooted in rank and dignity (42, 54, 56).

Umm Kulthūm's postwar efforts and reception similarly promoted a notion of national honor that was not tied to women's bodies. While she was represented by others (and herself) as the leading female agent in a psychological campaign to reclaim national honor after the 1967 defeat, the values guiding her endeavors were portrayed as transcending gender. During an extended period marked as the preparation for a resumed military conflict, she was shown to have displayed "gender neutral" values of patriotism, work, self-sacrifice, and perseverance.

In posthumous accounts, Umm Kulthūm's patriotism—particularly during her later career—was inflated through her portrayal as a national mother willing to sacrifice herself for the sake of her children as she defended national honor. As Nawar al-Hassan Golley has explained, "The term 'mother' symbolizes, foremost, ultimate sacrifice, endless giving, giving up the self for the sake of the family, for the husband and children" (2003, 142). The construal of the singer as mother of a nation pushed that "ultimate" sacrifice to yet another level altogether. What authors *did not* do in discussing her willingness to sacrifice herself for her "children" and her national family was to reveal the ways in which her decisions enhanced her own career. To an even greater extent than other "motherly" representations, the admiration for Umm Kulthūm's self-sacrifice emanating from these narratives obscured the logical interpretation that she had sacrificed heteronormative expectations of marriage and childbirth in order to preserve her art, success, and independence.

In emphasizing the singer's patriotic self-sacrifice, a number of authors turned her Paris trip into an act of antagonism. A recurring anecdote has her willing to face violence during her Paris visit, where she would mount her defense of national honor. When her Egyptian lawyer wanted her concerts canceled out of fear that she would be attacked by "Zionist extremists"—or, in some accounts, the Mossad (Israeli intelligence) and its supporters in Europe—she retorted, "If you do not finalize the arrangements, I will finalize them myself!" (Farag 2000c; 'Abd al-Rasūl 2000). Muḥammad Salmāwī's account of the singer's confrontation with a Westerner while on her Paris trip demonstrated her determination to defend her country's honor on an even more dramatic level. Salmāwī explained that during a concert intermission, the head of the Olympia theater, Bruno Coquatrix, asked Umm Kulthūm, in front of her ensemble, to stop the concert announcer's talk of Arab victory over Israel and the liberation of Jerusalem and occupied Arab lands. In reply, Umm Kulthūm claimed that she herself was the source of the announcer's rhetoric. "If you thought that I came to Paris in order to sing, you were mistaken," she said. "What brought me here is art's patriotic duty." In a dramatic flourish, Salmāwī ended the anecdote with Umm

Kulthūm ordering her musicians to gather their instruments and the announcer resuming his calls for liberation (1997). Ironically, such accounts posited the singer as a woman devoted to sacrifice over self—during an event that was initially motivated more by self than by sacrifice.[22]

As these personal conflicts, symbolic of international ones, boldly enhanced Umm Kulthūm's role in defending and redeeming national honor, so did the erasure of a key part of her postwar campaign. While her war effort concerts "returned a part of the lost dignity" (A. Ṣālih 1970, 29), the same could not be said for her work in support of the Palestinians. After the singer's death, most authors made no mention of her support for Palestinian liberation, focusing instead on her patriotism for Egyptian or, more broadly, pan-Arab causes. While writers reminded readers of her dedication to the reclamation of *Egyptian* land, in particular her plans to present a new song about the victory over Israel following the October War ("Life and Songs" 1975, 4), they largely omitted her support of *fidā'iyīn* efforts to reclaim Palestinian land.[23] Her manager and nephew Muḥammad al-Disūqī never acknowledged that money had been generated for the Palestinian Fatah organization at concerts. Instead, he maintained, "The money we received—every bit of it—went to the government's war effort" (Farag 2000c). Fu'ād al-Manṣūrī took the reader back to one of the singer's Libyan concerts but eliminated any mention of Fatah or Yāsir 'Arafāt in his account of the announcer's comments, instead focusing on the death of the Egyptian military leader 'Abd al-Mun'im Riyāḍ (1998).

In being represented posthumously as a symbol of national honor, Umm Kulthūm helped sustain a key nationalist narrative, along with having her status as patriot and woman strengthened. As discussed, she was posited as a successor to Ṣafīyah Zaghlūl as "Mother of the Egyptians," helping feed the perception that she was part of a continuing line of resistance in the face of imperial domination. Her representation as the "Mother of the Arabs" and the "Mother of Egypt" kept vital the concept of nation as figurative family, promoting a unified front in opposition to foreign occupation (Baron 2005, 143). Meanwhile, maternal portrayals of the singer through pharaonic imagery and idioms evoked a sense of territorial continuity despite centuries of foreign rule.

At the same time, Umm Kulthūm's representation as a timeless regional matriarch helped mask the failures of the 1960s. Following the destruction of 'Abd al-Nāṣir's image as Arab leader and the deflation of Arab political unity in the later 1960s, the singer's performances served to demonstrate emotional and cultural unity. They invoked longing and hope for the recovery of what had been lost through the war. Noting the unity that her 1968 Baalbek concert created among Arabs across the region, a Lebanese newspaper explained, "She is the past, the splendor of the past, and restoration" (Y. 1968, "Hiya al-rūḥ"). This nostalgic invocation of an unrealized Arab political unity lingered after her death, surfacing in an Arab author's recollection that she provided a *miḥrāb*, or prayer niche, guiding Arabs to "turn their hearts toward Egypt, the *qiblah* (direction of prayer) of Arab unity" (Kashak 1975). A similar notion appeared in a young man's music video of one of the singer's patriotic songs intended to urge armed resistance to the U.S. military presence in Iraq ("Omkolthoum-iraq"). In the video, the tone is set with images of a maternal Umm Kulthūm caught in an enraptured moment of performance, hands raised as if in prayer. Her voice then accompanies borderless topographical maps that convey the producer's pining vision for an undivided, decolonized Middle East.

By sustaining an anti-imperialist narrative and nostalgic longing for a unity that was never fully realized, Umm Kulthūm's actions and reception turned attention in the years following her death away from the internal reasons for the failures of 1960s. In effect, she came to be seen and represented by Arab writers and artists as the achiever of Arab unity, an area in which 'Abd al-Nāṣir had failed after the 1961 breakup of the political union with Syria. Nicknames like "Uniter of the Arabs" and "Mother of the Arabs" encapsulated her success.[24] Yet, in perpetuating this unifier image—like the perpetuation of 'Abd al-Nāṣir's explanation of imperialist collusion as the cause of the 1967 war, a claim that remained in textbooks for decades—writers have demonstrated a failure to come to terms with the internal causes for the defeat and the failure of Arabs to unite politically (Podeh 2004). Domestic challenges of the period included an economic downturn that prevailed before the war, 'Abd al-Nāṣir's inability to control General 'Abd al-Ḥakīm 'Āmir, and the priority of legitimizing the regime over guaranteeing individual freedoms. A rare voice acknowledged Umm Kulthūm's contribution to this overall failure. Wrote Ḥāzim Ṣāghīyah, "In brief, the Sufism of Kulthumian singing expresses an Arab desire that approaches madness in the interrogation of a previous memory." The writer thereby charged Umm Kulthūm with promoting a retreat from the world and its confusions (1991, 99, 104).

Of the varied and contradictory representations that authors and filmmakers have offered in order to reconcile Umm Kulthūm's life choices with her identity as an Egyptian woman, their portrayals of a national mother are among the most complex. Noting the frequency with which women stars have been tapped to aid postcolonial nationalist movements, Christopher Stone pointed to the paradox of betrayal that they suffer. These women are needed for nation-building, but they are then scorned by society due to their problematic, often shameful status as performers and artists (Stone 2008,

139–41). This has not been the case for Umm Kulthūm, whose posthumous portrayal as a national mother figure has enhanced, rather than tarnished, her overall image. Perhaps Egypt did not need such a figure per se, but the concept of a national mother provided a way to comprehend and categorize a woman who had failed to meet the cultural norms of early marriage and childbirth. While Fayrūz's association with the celestial and the spiritual—the moon, angels, prayer, and the Virgin Mary—made her acceptable as a national symbol by desexualizing her (150–52, 154), Umm Kulthūm's representation as a national mother figure helped make her acceptable as a woman by endowing her with a defining feature of womanhood.[25]

Maternal representations of Umm Kulthūm after her death have connected in intricate ways to her self-portrayal during her lifetime. In some ways, they have extended her own efforts. Many have woven together strands of her careful self-presentation, implicitly integrating her demonstration of maternal compassion, patriotic self-sacrifice, and cross-class appeal. When Zakariyā effused that "Umm Kulthūm lived her life as a symbol of the unity of feelings among the sons of our Arab *ummah* through her art" (1983, 7), he not only cast her as a national mother but also acknowledged her agency in shaping her image as a symbol and promoter of Arab unity. Yet maternal representations also negated some of Umm Kulthūm's important accomplishments during her lifetime. The "mother" label constrained her by making her appear to conform to what have been deemed the most important and "essential" of women's roles, selectively highlighting her abilities to nurture, guide, and unite people.

The singer's maternal representations have also had contradictory implications beyond her life and reception as an individual. Despite her personal success in navigating cultural expectations during her lifetime, women's reproductive roles have been affirmed through posthumous accounts. Her portrayal as the symbol of a nation and its honor reinforces heterosexualism (Peterson 2000, 64–70). Her casting as a national mother figure reinforces the contemporary characterization of women as wombs and the expansion of womb into woman (Booth 2001a, 66–67). On the other hand, in being presented as national mother, Umm Kulthūm stands as an important exception to the patriarchal relationships that pervade Arab society and the paternal conception and behavior of political leaders, employers, and teachers alike (Barakat 1985, 45–46).

Despite the contradictions, listeners continue to turn to the "maternal" and other representational strategies adopted by authors and filmmakers during the three-plus decades since the singer's death. Some find her unconventional life choices an attractive and admirable model amid increasingly voluble conservative rhetoric in the Arab world. For others, the anomalies of her life provoke discomfort. Many settle for explanations that either contradict long-standing cultural norms or negate her remarkable accomplishment of leading an unusually independent life as a woman. In the absence of a definitive place to locate this icon, the many competing interpretations can only be sustained, further enriching her significance as a presence in the region.

CHAPTER 6

An Evolving Heritage

Umm Kulthūm's glowing treatment in many biographical and dramatic accounts has obscured how old-fashioned her music and image seemed to some by the end of her career. In 1970, one contributor to the Lebanese newspaper *al-Nahār* attacked her, warning that "she must not sing in Baalbek because she lowers the level of the festival" (al-Khūrī 2000, 97). Her conservative style was made only more apparent by the emergence of new popular idioms beginning in the 1970s and continuing through the next three decades. Several of these popular styles, including *sha'bī* and dance-pop, drew on elements of Western popular music. Up to the early 1980s, Western popular music in Cairo, as well as Beirut and Damascus, could still be regarded as peripheral. Yet it was one of several styles that mixed with the central current of Arabic music represented by the repertory of Umm Kulthūm. The fusion of these idioms had previously been seen in the compositions of Muḥammad 'Abd al-Wahhāb, who often drew on several different styles of music within one song (Racy 1981). Such intermixing grew in prominence in the mid- and later 1980s. The Arab pop sound that resulted often featured traditional Arabic rhythms articulated through hand claps, finger cymbals, and a drum machine, combined with Western pop instruments and harmonic language. The most broadly and continuously successful of the artists to emerge in the 1980s was 'Amr Diyāb. His success into the 1990s and beyond illustrated the expansion of Western elements: he took advantage of the music video, or "video clip," and Western clothing fashions.[1] As Arab satellite television stations proliferated in the late 1990s, so did the prevalence of the video clip, prompting older singers to update their look and younger ones to model themselves after Western stars. This included young women performers dressing like their scantily clad counterparts in the West.

As the age of the *muṭrib* (a singer in the *ṭarab* tradition) and the long, orchestrated song gave way to that of the video clip star and the three-minute pop hit, one might have expected Umm Kulthūm's music and legacy to become an ever more distant cultural artifact in the decades following her death. Such an occurrence would have followed the musical precedent in Egypt whereby musical styles have been abandoned after about thirty years. Music created in the 1910s, for one example, was rarely performed live by the 1940s (el-Shawan 1980, 186). Yet to the contrary, young listeners in Egypt are remarkably knowledgeable about the singer's musical and cultural contributions. As one official in the music industry characterized these young listeners' response, "Maybe in their thirties they'll turn to her, like they've just discovered Beethoven."[2] For some listeners, the process begins earlier. One young Egyptian began listening to her performances in his twenties as he began to "meditate on big questions"—such as the difference between religion and ideology—and discovered answers in her songs.[3] Young listeners articulate a distinction between music that calls for such intellectual appreciation and music with which they feel a visceral connection. A young Egyptian half-jokingly asked his fiancée, "Who do we like more, Umm Kulthūm or Shakira?" The fiancée quickly chose the latter but then proudly described her recently inherited cassette collection of Umm Kulthūm's concert performances.[4]

Regardless of its exact timing, a young person's "awakening" to Umm Kulthūm is the result of contemporary memorialization practices. As a graduate student explained through a revealing self-correction, "We grow up with her. And we like her. Or, at least, we are used to hearing her."[5] This experience of becoming accustomed to and eventually appreciating her music grows from many practices of memorialization: official and popular, physical and sonic, seemingly durable and obviously fleeting. The range of actual memorials, including physical monuments, traditional performances of her songs, and stylistic reinterpretations, has succeeded not only in engaging younger generations within Egypt but also in expanding the singer's international audience in the Middle East, Europe, and North America. While the creators of some memorials have sustained the persona that she worked so hard to establish during her final years, others have challenged her self-structured legacy, offering revisions of her image and repertory adapted to a range of contemporary cultural and political needs.

Monuments of Multisensory Experience

An array of physical memorials has sustained Umm Kulthūm's legacy both within and beyond Egypt. As she used her fundraising concerts of the late 1960s and early 1970s to forge relationships with international leaders, she spurred official commemoration to begin during her lifetime. The singer's expression of surprise at finding no mosque near her hotel in Tunis prompted local officials to begin establishing one in her name in affirmation of her public piety ("La mosque" 1975; Melligi 1975).[6] The renaming of a Sudanese girls' school after the singer, during her lifetime, marked her international stature, charity, and maternal persona. Although some memorials proved impermanent, many remained, and additional monuments followed in the years after her death. The music conservatory in the Tunisian city of Hammam Lif still sits on Rue Om Kalthoum, and a street of the same name in the country's capital places the singer in a pantheon of Arab icons alongside Ibn Khaldūn and Ḥabīb Būrqībah.

Umm Kulthūm, through her efforts to strengthen her relationship with fans abroad, laid the foundation for later attempts to create a memorial culture in her honor. When she gave concerts outside Egypt, the first of multiple generations of parents chose to preserve her legacy by naming their children after her (Tawfīq 1968b; Yaḥyá 1968a). Many of these infant namesakes helped generate a ritualized public performance of motherliness, piety, and compassion associated with the singer. In a Khartoum hospital, she held and kissed each infant named Umm Kulthūm, recited the opening chapter of the Qur'ān over her, and asked God to give her happiness and health ("Umm Kulthūm tuqabbil" 1969). Having transformed the name from an odd, unfashionable reference to one of the Prophet's daughters into a proudly worn, modern signifier of accomplishment and talent, the singer now has living monuments across the Arab world to carry her legacy well into the twenty-first century (M. 'Awaḍ 1969b, 10). While the larger Arab world honored the singer through these physical memorials, controversy surrounded Egypt's failure to do so. A plethora of memorials was proposed at the time of her death, including an Umm Kulthūm conservatory for singing that would house a museum and a public library of her recordings, and an Umm Kulthūm theater ("Thalāth iqtirāḥāt" 1975; "Masraḥ kabīr" 1975). A quarter-century later, observers still deplored the absence of any such memorials. The singer's birth village had been slated to carry her name, but in 2000 a journalist observed, "There is little to remember Umm Kulthūm by today in Ṭammāy al-Zahāyrah." Although villagers eagerly directed this journalist to the location of the singer's house, she found only an empty lot, where the structure had long since disintegrated ("Tudfan" 1975; Farag 2000a). Many lamented the government's failure to convert her Cairo villa into a museum, an opportunity that was lost entirely once the Nile-side property was sold and razed for commercial development ('Abd al-'Āl n.d., 21; M. 'Awaḍ 1987, 3–4).[7]

More than a quarter-century after the singer's death, the injustice of her Zamalek villa's destruction was finally addressed through the establishment of a memorial on the site and the inauguration of a museum on the island of Roda, in the middle of Cairo. In a 2003 ceremony, a statue of Umm Kulthūm was unveiled where her home once stood. This symbolic site, however, became a humbling and dissonant setting for the singer's likeness—she now stands precariously in the middle of an intersection only to witness taillights racing irreverently past her toward an urban highway. The energy generated during her performances is imperceptible, as she stands stilted, expressionless, and silenced. While during her lifetime Umm Kulthūm was able to mold her speech and conduct into a whole that seemed able to appeal to the entire nation, here her characteristic gestures and demeanor have been stilled. Owing to incongruities between noble subject and hassled location, between the intensity of the singer's performances and the lifelessness of her statue's likeness, this memorial may remind drivers of the singer's existence, but it does nothing to resurrect the essence of her persona and the power she wielded over her listeners.

In contrast, that persona and commanding presence have been dramatically brought to life through the Umm Kulthūm museum. After years of public attacks directed toward the Egyptian Ministry of Culture for its delays in creating a museum to commemorate the singer, plans at last were laid in 1989 as part of a series honoring Egypt's great musicians, including Muḥammad 'Abd al-Wahhāb and 'Abd al-Ḥalīm Ḥāfiẓ. Yet the plan still failed to take shape as years passed by, and the singer's signature possessions were auctioned off for charity in a fitting extension of her own humanitarianism ("Arab World" 2000). In late 2001, funded by a group of Arab businessmen and outfitted under the direction of the Ministry of Culture, the museum finally opened.

For some, the ultimate form of the museum may still disappoint. Unlike many Western museums, the space is relatively small. There are no long pathways inside to slow a visitor's pace, prompt reflection, and invite the synthesis of facts and artifacts into a meaningful personal narrative. The space lacks large wall displays that delineate important phases in Umm Kulthūm's career using eye-catching text and images. Display cases do little to establish a historical context for her musical achievements. As for the context of the Egyptian music industry overall, the exhibit confines itself to a few record players, musical instruments, and radios intermingled with the singer's own personal artifacts. Little attention is given to other performers with whom she shared the airwaves, and her contributions are not placed in a larger historical narrative including the singers who came before and after her.

Despite these limitations, the museum has served its purpose in educating young Egyptians, European tourists, and visitors from the Arab world since its opening. A side room offers a variety of collections in two formats.

In 2003, a statue of Umm Kulthūm was dedicated in front of the site where her villa once stood. The site is now occupied by a hotel and commercial building named after her. *Photo by author*

Appealing to tech-savvy young visitors, touch-screen computers allow users to customize their experiences by browsing dozens of video recordings, audio recordings, and photographs. Video recordings of the singer's concert performances display her intense interactions with audiences and exhibit her vocal virtuosity. Time lines offer a narrative overview of her life. In the same room, a library of print materials demonstrates both Umm Kulthūm's value and the value of preserving her cultural contributions. The museum's director, who is frequently on hand, proudly tells visitors that the library's shelves house "all that was ever published about her" in domestic and international newspapers. A glance at the collection of roughly one hundred bound volumes of articles supports his claim, and most visitors do not spend enough time looking through them to discover the substantial duplications that inflate the collection. Numerous books, biographical treatments, and histories of Arabic music reinforce the observed impression of thoroughness and give evidence of the state's substantial effort to create an adequate memorial in the singer's name.

The museum's most powerful educational tool is found in the small theater into which employees quickly usher arriving visitors. In the absence of wall displays delineating Umm Kulthūm's achievements, the film constitutes the primary narrative component of the museum. Eschewing a straight chronological telling, the poignant film begins not with Umm Kulthūm's birth and childhood but rather with a dramatic portrayal of combat juxtaposed with her fundraising trips following the country's defeat in the June 1967 war. In the arresting introduction, the midcentury image of Egypt as the political and military center of the Arab world is upheld, with Egypt taking the brunt of the blows in the war. The singer's carefully crafted role as a deeply patriotic citizen of international stature is also set in the foreground. Footage from her fundraising trips across the Arab world calls attention to her efforts to ease the psychological and financial blows incurred in the defeat, which included the loss of revenue from tourism and Suez Canal shipping, as well as the stunning destruction of Egypt's air force. Scenes from the singer's trips to Paris and Moscow suggest that her appeal extended far beyond the Arab world, while her receipt of a Pakistani award testifies to her significance within the broader Islamic community. The film's rejection of the rags-to-riches story found in most biographies and films is significant. While the commonly told narrative foregrounds the singer's village roots and embodiment of "authentically" Egyptian values, the museum film instead highlights her patriotism and international success. By emphasizing her charitable actions after the war, the film has fed young Egyptians' eagerness to introduce the singer to foreigners as a selfless patriot rather than simply a great singer.

For older visitors, the museum does much to satisfy the desire for nostalgic entertainment, rather than additional knowledge. Components like the film and the relatively modest displays of objects mainly confirm prior knowledge while validating many adults' understanding of Umm Kulthūm's place in the history of Egypt and the Arab world. As studies have demonstrated, people often reject museums' attempts to deconstruct the myths surrounding their subjects. In something more of a *re*construction, at the Rock and Roll Hall of Fame and Museum, visitors seeking information and displays on their favorite artists encountered mannequins bearing only faint resemblances to the icons they represented. Challenging visitors' desires for the validation of nostalgia and myth, these displays left many feeling cheated (Santelli 1999, 241–42).

The Umm Kulthūm museum is designed to avoid making adult visitors feel defrauded or challenged through deconstruction of its subject. For example, the constituent parts of the museum—its collections, grounds, and building—collaborate to feminize its subject. In contrast to the military music ensemble uniform, smoking jacket, and swords chosen to represent Muḥammad ʿAbd al-Wahhāb in his museum, gossamer scarves, diamond jewelry, and stylish handbags evoke Umm Kulthūm's presence. At the center of the museum, an eye-catching case houses a colorful array of concert dresses that sustain the singer's conservatively feminine presentations of self.[8] The floral pattern of one dress serves as a motif throughout the museum grounds: flower beds and bougainvillea both prepare visitors and punctuate their experience of this overtly feminine memorial as they approach and leave the building. Peaceful views of the Nile strengthen this evocation of femininity while recalling the importance of the river in the singer's life and its place in her repertory.

After crossing the threshold of the museum, one feels on a visceral level the feminine presence. A lengthy *promenade architecturale* shapes the visitor's experience in several phases prior to reaching the museum door.[9] Passing through the first gate and walking by a long line of small shops on the Manastirli Palace grounds, one soon forgets the cars, noise, and dirt of the commercial and residential areas of Roda. The calm Nile-side setting prompts a slower pace on the walk toward the distant ticket office. The lengthy path is lined with vibrant flora, and reflected sunlight allows visitors to dwell with their senses on the colors, shapes, and textures of this vivid outdoor setting. This slow approach only intensifies the contrast upon crossing the museum's threshold: the bright open feminine space changes into a dark, confining one. Black ceilings and dark gray walls create a cave-like interior. Lengthy, dark display cases subdivide the museum's small chambers into narrow passageways that give the visitor a closed-in feeling. Curved walls complete the womblike embrace.[10]

Although the museum has been criticized for failing to capture Umm Kulthūm's "classicism, grandeur, or grassroots decency," it does preserve an important facet of the persona she constructed—her motherliness (Rakha and el-Aref 2001). The film emphasizes this trait by portraying Umm Kulthūm surrounded by children in Sudan and guiding her country through its postwar crisis by summoning therapeutic displays of Arab cultural unity through the enthralled crowds that she drew abroad. As photographic collages and awards stress her postwar activities across the region, the museum's collections, film, interior design, and grounds work together to memorialize Umm Kulthūm as the Mother of Egypt, if not the Mother of Arabs. By accommodating the singer to the cultural norm of productive heterosexuality, the museum stands alongside authors' and dramatists' efforts to counter rumors of her homosexuality and her failure to produce children of her own.

As a memorial with multisensory elements, the museum has an "unofficial" or popular counterpart in the many Umm Kulthūm cafés that exist in

In the Umm Kulthūm museum, the case that holds a collection of her concert dresses constitutes just one of many curved design elements. Sunlight streaming in through the glass doors contrasts with the extreme darkness of the museum. *Photo by Yahia Shawkat, courtesy of the Aga Khan Trust for Culture*

Egypt and abroad. Established and maintained by ordinary business owners, the typical Umm Kulthūm café is constructed as a kind of shrine, displaying pictures of the singer on its walls and pumping her performances through its speakers. While cafés in Egypt historically have been the province of older men who pass the hours drinking tea, smoking, and playing games, the capital's Umm Kulthūm Café and Kawkab al-Sharq Corner have recently attracted an expanded clientele. The original Umm Kulthūm Café at Tawfiqīyah Square, which opened in the mid-1960s, now regularly draws college-age couples, families, and men of all ages. Widely known by young locals, Cairo's Umm Kulthūm cafés do not simply pay homage to the singer but also perpetuate her legacy among this youthful audience. Cafés in Berlin, Paris, and Toronto do so for an increasingly international crowd, reviving the interest that was sparked across Europe and the broader English-speaking world in the late 1960s when fans called for additional concerts abroad.

While European and American customers often see the world's Umm Kulthūm cafés as hip venues in which to show off their taste for "exotic" culture, others use them as a therapeutic environment in which to cope with the pain of being cut off from family, friends, and home. This is particularly the case in Baghdad, where the loss of loved ones to death and emigration, a disintegrating economy, and the constant threat of escalating violence turned "home" into unpleasant and unrecognizable territory. With its decades-old sounds and images, the city's Umm Kulthūm café has provided a familiar retreat that allowed its patrons to seek refuge in their memories. As the café's owner succinctly observed, "They come here to escape. Umm Kulthūm is another world" (Oweis 2003). To take maximum advantage of the site's ability to allow for recreation of a moment from the past, men often sit in the same spot where they gathered with friends in the 1960s and 1970s when Umm Kulthūm was alive. The sadness in her singing infuses their hopelessness and pessimism with pathos: men stare blankly into space, hold their heads down, and cry at the sound of her voice (Goldenberg 2003; Oweis 2003; Miller 2002). In a short work of fiction, refugees fleeing the world's famine, oppression, and poverty similarly seek the singer's melancholy soundtrack in a north London café, with the aim of reflecting on those they left behind, reassessing the old problems they have exchanged for new ones, and wondering if they will ever return home (Rose 2005). In fiction as in reality, the café's symbolism guides patrons through a ritual of consumption and reflection in which the intake of soothing drinks, familiar images, and sad melodies allows them to engage in a psychological and emotional recalibration of their identity amid otherwise unfamiliar surroundings. Like the museum, Umm Kulthūm cafés nourish the legacy that the singer strived to establish during her final years, but as a locus of ritualized reflection, they also offer patrons a powerful way to deal with the disorientation that results from physical and virtual displacement.

State Curatorship

While physical monuments have carried Umm Kulthūm's legacy into the twenty-first century, her presence on a sonic level has required constant renewal. Although she was never forgotten by her fans, her prominence in Egypt waned after her death as Anwar and Jīhān al-Sādāt sought a new artistic front to reflect the change in political leadership. While Tunisia was commemorating the singer's passing by hosting an international singing competition in her honor, Egyptian radio reduced the broadcasting of her performances (al-Asrār 1976; Melligi 1975). Yet despite any temporary fading of her songs from the radio rotation, the steps taken by the singer to hasten her passage into the *turāth* ensured that she would be remembered musically. The Firqat al-Mūsīqā al-'Arabīyah (Arabic Music Ensemble) began performing her early repertory in 1969 and continued to do so for more than a decade after her death. In the Mubārak era, which began in 1981, a remarkable resurgence has occurred in the singer's presence across Egyptian media, as a variety of musical practices have preserved her legacy for younger generations. One can now view her concerts of the 1960s on satellite television, hear remixes of her romantic songs in Nile-side restaurants, and watch aspiring young singers tackle her challenging repertory on the country's answer to *American Idol*.

During the Mubārak years, the Egyptian state has emerged as an influential curator of the country's musical heritage. While many artists have contributed to the Egyptian canon, a few have acquired a special place in its ranks. Along with two other popular musicians of the mid-twentieth century, Muḥammad 'Abd al-Wahhāb and 'Abd al-Ḥalīm Ḥāfiz, Umm Kulthūm has been resurrected by the Ministry of Culture and state media outlets as a powerful icon inextricably linked with the era of 'Abd al-Nāṣir.[11] The plan to construct museums in Cairo celebrating these three figures ('Abd al-Wahhāb's museum is housed in the National Arab Music Institute near Ramses Square, and the planned museum for 'Abd al-Ḥalīm Ḥāfiz has yet to be built) focused on an ideal means of stimulating and validating nostalgia for that era (Santelli 1999, 242). In many ways, Umm Kulthūm's treatment is representative of national media leaders' multifaceted approach to preserving the cultural legacy of these icons through radio, recordings, and physical monuments. In broadcasting and distributing the three musicians' audio recordings and films, the state-run media engages in sound financial policy, especially when considering the dizzying competition, including satellite television, internet media, and traditional outlets supported by free media capitals in the Arab world. Considering all these alternatives on the media smorgasbord, efforts have been undertaken to ensure that young Egyptians know Umm Kulthūm's name, voice, and music.

The Egyptian media have preserved a remarkably thorough collection of Umm Kulthūm's performances and made that collection accessible to the public through both commercially available recordings and radio broadcasts. State-run Sono Cairo retail stores across the capital and in other large cities have made available for purchase her live and studio performances on both cassette and compact disc. Recordings include her film songs, religious songs, romantic repertory, and patriotic anthems. As part of a broad revival of 1960s-era media policies that flooded the market with cheap cultural products and political books, Sono Cairo has enabled Egyptians to buy a piece of this cultural inheritance based on their means—whether they can only afford a few cassettes of favorite songs or an extensive CD collection.[12] Radio broadcasts from Egypt have drawn on the thorough collections of audio recordings preserved in the state radio archives. Also in Egypt, an eponymous radio station has steadily broadcast four hours of Umm Kulthūm performances daily. Another devoted to classic songs has consistently featured an Umm Kulthūm segment every afternoon and evening. In the Mubārak era, then, for anyone who has an old radio or a few hours to spend in a neighborhood café, a wide range of Umm Kulthūm's songs is readily accessible. By programming everything from her earliest recordings of the mid-1920s to her final ones of the early 1970s, radio has preserved and made available to younger listeners the full scope of her diverse repertory. Over the past three-plus decades—even given the reduced airtime during al-Sādāt's tenure—the singer's place on the Egyptian airwaves has centered primarily on her lyrically and musically concise film songs of the 1940s, as well as a patriotic song from the 1930s ("'Alā Balad al-Maḥbūb") and a religious song from the 1950s ("'Araftu al-Hawá"). Two groups of longer songs have also been broadcast frequently: her romantic songs of the 1960s, which feature strong contrasts, dance rhythms, Western influences, and lengthy instrumental sections, and many of Riyāḍ al-Sunbāṭī's tightly knit neoclassical compositions, which rely on motivic coherence and lean instrumental introductions.[13]

Through such thorough collections, state media have strived to preserve for consumers treasured moments from the past. When Sono Cairo created master copies from the singer's older records, a German company showed that the sound quality could be improved through rerecording the instrumental portions of her performances. Sono Cairo rejected the proposal, insisting instead on preserving the "rich quality" of those old recordings. As a result, the company retained the hissing of the needle, which itself was considered a "part of the heritage" and a means of evoking a bygone era (Farag 2000b). The Egyptian state radio archive has also preserved the original commentary of broadcasters on recordings of Umm Kulthūm's live concerts. Still aired on radio today, these detailed, often lengthy commentaries have directed listeners' attention to specific occasions and values from the past through narrations of the attendance of noteworthy audience members, such as Jamāl 'Abd al-Nāṣir; by conveying the emotions stirred by major state holidays, such as Revolution Day; and even by describing Umm Kulthūm's concert attire. Moreover, Egyptian radio has helped preserve the emotional atmosphere of Umm Kulthūm's legendary evening concerts by programming—every evening, to this day—her live performances of a long song, usually from the 1940s or 1960s. The efforts of those who produce and mediate sonic memorialization of the singer have, therefore, extended beyond mere preservation of artifacts and into an attempt to recreate the experience of a moment from an increasingly distant past.

Radio practices such as those employed by state broadcasting have spurred listeners to move beyond acts of consumption to collection. Detailed radio schedules, such as those published in the weekly magazine *al-Idhā'ah wa al-tilīfizyūn* (Radio and Television), coupled with regular broadcasts of the singer's full-length live performances, prompted listeners to record radio programs. Homemade recordings often possessed a bonus value in comparison with those sold through Sono Cairo outlets, as they included original broadcasters' commentaries, ample audience response, and more lightly edited performances that often extend to two hours. This easy access to material cut from Sono Cairo recordings prompted listeners to create their own personal archives from radio broadcasts. As listeners accumulated recordings of perceived extra value and became archivists in their own right, they acted as custodians of personal collections, passing them on to their children, who might, in turn, preserve them for future generations.[14] These accumulating physical manifestations of a sonic cultural artifact attested to the value that was placed on Umm Kulthūm's music, demonstrated collectors' musical taste, and reinforced the state media's efforts to portray the singer as one of the country's most significant cultural icons.

Egyptian radio broadcasting has also played a crucial role in educating younger listeners about Umm Kulthūm's musical and cultural contributions. In the past two decades, the anniversary of her death has prompted commemorative, explicitly educational programming on stations normally devoted to contemporary popular music, news, and sports. In 2003, the radio station al-Sharq al-Awṣat (Middle East) broadcast a lengthy interview with Umm Kulthūm photographer Fārūq Ibrāhīm, a series of segments exploring the significance of individual songs, a technical discussion of Riyāḍ al-Sunbāṭī's compositions, and an excerpt from a drama about the singer's life. Ṣawt al-'Arab (Voice of the Arabs) emphasized her later career by broadcasting a set of recordings from 1968, including the presentation ceremony for a Tunisian state award and her interview of the Egyptian minister of religious endowments from her guest appearance as a radio host for the program *The Microphone with. . . .* The programming of the youth-oriented station al-Shabāb typified efforts to engage and educate listeners born after the singer's death. Programmers cleverly sandwiched a solid introduction to the icon between sports updates and candy bar commercials. Excerpts from many of the singer's live performances and studio recordings gave young listeners a broad familiarity with her output and her intense connection with audiences, while hosts and guests recounted her biography, outlined her partnerships with several leading composers, surveyed her patriotic songs, and summarized each of the films in which she starred. The director of the Umm Kulthūm museum enticed listeners to continue learning by offering detailed accounts of the museum's exhibits and its use of current technology.

Contemporary Performances and the Dynamics of Exchange

The state's efforts to preserve and promote Umm Kulthūm's legacy have been enhanced and complemented by the creative decisions of individual artists, including many outside Egypt. Umm Kulthūm's repertory functions as musical currency—shared knowledge that is widely recognized and exchanged across the Arab world (Baty 1995, 39–40). Young listeners across the region have been engaged by cover performances (as well as original recordings) that have contributed to a body of "audiographic" representations of the legendary singer (Baty 1995). The Lebanese singer George Wassouf, the Tunisian Dhikrá, and the Algerian Fella Ababsa stand among those performers who have appealed to young audiences with sophisticated, visually absorbing concert productions during the past two decades. Their cover versions have strengthened Umm Kulthūm's place in the *turāth*, while her songs have provided a means of broadening the cover artists' audience outside their home countries. Their cassettes and CDs are readily available in Egypt, and they give live performances to great acclaim in the broader Arab world. These professional singers have also established an attractive model for their aspiring successors, who may wish to make their ascent through performing cover songs. Keeping up a competitive international format that was established in the Arab world shortly after Umm Kulthūm's death (Melligi 1975; al-Maḥdī 1993, 174), the region's *American Idol*–style shows have enticed ordinary teen and twenty-something singers to shift from consumption to active performance of her songs in public displays of respect and remembrance.

These cover performances have bound young singers to Umm Kulthūm in an exchange that is beneficial both to them and to the singer's legacy: the icon has offered the allure of instant legitimacy to those willing to risk being measured against her own performances, and, in return, younger singers have ensured her recognition by subsequent generations. A rehearsal scene from *Idol* knockoff *Star Academy 1* showed the stakes of this exchange process for young singers. When the young Moroccan Sofia Marikh announced that she would sing "Inta 'Umrī," an immediate "Whoa!" from contestants and staff reflected surprise, respect, and anticipation, but soon the response turned to snickering and coaching during her weak performance. Meanwhile, the stakes for Umm Kulthūm were exposed when the young Lebanese-Armenian pop singer Maria announced her intention to record video clips for several of the Egyptian icon's songs. In seeking artistic legitimacy after receiving popular and critical rebuke for producing provocative music videos, Maria turned to Umm Kulthūm's legacy as a reservoir of sonic and moral redemption. Yet her plan was quickly branded a "grave intentional offense to the star's history," and Umm Kulthūm's heirs—along with her surviving colleagues—initiated legal action to halt the contamination-by-association that would have resulted from a cover by the disreputable pop star ("Maria Angers" 2007; "Maria Vows" 2007). Recognizing that even Umm Kulthūm's carefully constructed conservative image was not immune to posthumous damage, ordinary listeners rushed to her defense. Citing the injuriousness of a performance by a singer perceived to have shady morals, a viewer of Lebanese pop star Nancy Ajram's televised rendition of "Alf Laylah wa Laylah" rebuked "these youngsters who want to exercise their abilities at the expense of the Lady of Tarab." Others who felt disturbed by the potential of Ajram's performance to taint the icon's memory exhorted her to "stay away" from Umm Kulthūm ("Nancy Ajram"). Such public discomfort exposed the fine line separating the fashionable artistic exchanges needed to sustain Umm Kulthūm's active place in the *turāth* from the tawdry ones that pose the risk of injuring her idealized reputation as mother of a nation and exemplar of morality.[15]

A number of artists have capitalized on this mutual exchange by offering musical memorials that stray significantly from Umm Kulthūm's style without offending the sensibility of her legacy. For instance, Egyptian drummer Yaḥyá Khalīl and Palestinian musician Michel Sagrawy offered instrumental jazz reinterpretations of her songs. Sagrawy and his band members claimed to "vividly recall the life and career of an exceptional musician" with their "In Memory of Om Kalthoum" (Sagrawy 2006).

While jazz renditions such as Sagrawy's garnered flattering publicity, efforts by others have generated controversy by updating her music and placing it in new entertainment contexts that conflict sharply with the persona she worked so hard to construct during her final years. Beginning in 2001, young artists in the Middle East issued an attention-getting group of Umm Kulthūm remixes. Leading this trend was the Lebanese DJ Saʿīd Murād. In April 2001, he released his first album, "Two Thousand and One Nights," which included remixes of Umm Kulthūm's "Alf Laylah wa Laylah" and "Laylat Ḥubb." Egyptian DJ ʿAmr Ismāʿīl offered remixes of "Fāt al-Miʿād," "Inta ʿUmrī," and "Amal Ḥayātī." While most DJs focused their efforts on songs from the 1960s, Ismāʿīl also tackled the much older song "Mā Dām Tuḥibb," which Umm Kulthūm first recorded in 1940.

As these artists expanded audiographic representations of Umm Kulthūm's work, observers expressed concern over the context in which the music was performed. Lebanese critic Ibrāhīm al-Arīs asked, "Is it right for a modern person to take phrases from the music introduction to one of the songs of Umm Kulthūm and turn it into a dance rhythm which moves the young people of today in nightclubs?" (Hammond 2007, 175). While the particular development to which al-Arīs responded was recent, he was echoing centuries-old concerns over the corrupting potential of music depending on when, where, and among whom it is performed.[16] In al-Arīs's view, music might have corruptive potential in a contemporary nightclub that promoted illicit behavior under increasing Western influence. The Sharm al-Shaykh club scene in which DJ 'Amr Ismā'īl worked illustrated both a questionable context and a glaring conflict between Umm Kulthūm's image and the contemporary consumption of her music. After the area was targeted for development in the 1990s as a diving and desert safari destination, house and techno music permeated the local hotel-entertainment complexes. An iconic, stationary red double-decker bus pointed club-hopping Europeans to the Bus Stop venue in the Naama Bay area of town, where Ismā'īl wove his Umm Kulthūm remixes into a house and techno playlist designed to get thousands of tourists dancing in the waterfalls and pool of the Sanafir hotel complex. Incorporating live drummers, Brazilian dancing, and a light and laser show, Ismā'īl recreated a scene that one might have experienced in Ibiza or Mallorca. The effect was that Umm Kulthūm remixes were driving intoxicated, scantily clad young women to dance, while the complex's owner, 'Adlī al-Mustaqāwī, was profiting handsomely in the process. The story did not end at the Bus Stop: Ismā'īl soon took his extravaganza to the Sanafir's Echo Temple, an open-air desert theater enveloped by mountains. While conceived by some visitors as "the ideal place to send our SOS messages of 'Love, respect, and tolerance' through the Sinai Star Gate to the entire Universe" ("Sanafir Hotel"; Lanier 2001), the setting was viewed by others as grossly inappropriate for music from the *turāth*.

Critics derided the DJ remixes on stylistic grounds as well. Ibrahım al-Arīs linked perceived musical and moral decay when he asked, "How can it be right for someone to violate the old melodies and make them contemporary so that their classic form is turned into techno?" (Hammond 2007, 15, citing *al-Ḥayāt* January 2002). In al-Arīs's view, this act constituted a "deformation of the heritage" (15, 175). His assessment echoed others' concerns about how Arabic music might evolve. The blurb on the back cover of Muḥammad Qābīl's *Mustaqbal al-ughnīyah al-miṣrīyah* (The Future of Egyptian Singing) depicted Egyptian song as suffering attacks from the "excesses in television images," the loss of artistic value given the increasing emphasis on dance, and the ascendance of Gulf, Levantine, and North African singing (1999).

Criticism of remixes of Umm Kulthūm's music, however, ignored their value as adaptations of art from the past with new value in the present (Kirshenblatt-Gimblett 1995, 369–72). Remixes have carried her music and awareness of her own musical contributions to a wider international audience. Outside Egypt, the dance remix redirected non-Arab and second-generation Arab listeners toward Arabic music. Murād's "Alf Laylah wa Laylah" took clubs across France, the United Kingdom, and Spain by storm, satisfying a European taste for the "exotic," piquing interest in Umm Kulthūm's original recordings, and fostering an expanded audience for them. DJs and producers also gave Umm Kulthūm renewed relevance for younger generations in the Middle East. As teenagers in the 1990s, Bassim Fikrī Kamal, 'Abd al-Salām al-Shubukshī, Maḥmūd al-Maṣrī, and Muḥammad Najīb were at most occasional consumers of the icon's music. Yet the example of professionals like Sa'īd Murād, coupled with increasingly accessible audio software, transformed them into creative artists who honored Umm Kulthūm through active engagement with her music. With this inspiration and new names, Cairo-based DJ Bisso and DJ Abdo, DJ Big Boss of Sharqia, and DJ Hussam of Syria—all born in the 1980s—soon offered their own dance-oriented versions of the icon's classics from decades before they were born. By prompting ordinary young listeners to engage with Umm Kulthūm's music, high-profile DJs extended her own efforts to redefine her significance for successive generations of Egyptians through her production of romantic monologues, populist *ughnīyāt*, neoclassical *qaṣā'id*, and patriotic anthems, along with her reconstructed postwar image.[17] Remixes also enhanced and transformed the value of Umm Kulthūm's music outside the nightclub context derided by critics. By inserting Umm Kulthūm remixes in carefully constructed buildups of Arabic dance music at upper-class Nile-side hotel weddings, DJs regularly helped twenty-something couples and their parents share a collective physical and emotional response to updated versions of prized songs from the *turāth* (Atia 2002). In doing so, they took part in cultivating an appreciation of the heritage in a multigenerational setting and intensified its presence as a pride-worthy element of Egyptian culture.

Criticisms of Umm Kulthūm remixes also obscured the many ways in which they actually continued practices from earlier in the twentieth century. The reliance on dance rhythms that al-Arīs deplored had gained increasing prominence as early as the 1960s in music now considered part of the *turāth*, including many of Umm Kulthūm's songs (Danielson 1997, 181–82). While the remix might have been seen as a "deformation" of that heritage and radically different from the central domain represented by her music (Racy 1981, 11), in reality it furthered a process of stylistic mixture that

Beginning of "Inta Omri d.j. mix." Music by Muḥammad ʿAbd al-Wahhāb, lyrics by Aḥmad Shafīq Kāmil. Premiered in 1964 and remixed by Elie Attieh. 2004. *Inta Omri,* Take 5 Music T5M 4103 390 162. Compact disc.

had been used in the mid-twentieth century. Composers like Muḥammad 'Abd al-Wahhāb had often incorporated Western elements—sometimes as unexpected as a hoedown—along with more traditional Egyptian ones.

Both professional and amateur artists have used their creativity to adapt distinctively "Eastern" features of Umm Kulthūm's songs to the largely Western formal and rhythmic idioms of the dance remix, often producing remarkably effective stylistic integrations. Among the amateurs, Montreal-based DJ Alpacinooo generated a *masmūdī ṣaghīr iqā'ah* (a rhythmic pattern commonly used in Egyptian music) from drums and hand claps to produce the dance remix's rhythmic propulsion in his reinterpretation of "Sīrat al-Ḥubb." In his "Alf Layla wa Layla East Dancing Balady Remix," DJ miXm@n isolated the sharp rhythmic profiles of the song's central themes to generate effective transitions. Professionals like Lebanese house specialist Elie Attieh successfully adapted the more challenging components of Umm Kulthūm's performances, such as the improvisatory instrumental solo. In his "Inta Omri d.j. mix," Attieh preserved the ametrical feeling of the song's opening improvisatory *qānūn* solo by withholding an articulated drumbeat, setting the *qānūn*'s implied beat at an extremely slow tempo, gradually introducing a rhythmically active synth, and metrically displacing the *qānūn*'s descending gestures to disguise a faster quadruple meter.

Criticism of such artful stylistic integrations obscures both the historical expansion of the *turāth* and the continuity of the ways in which this music has been constructed. Nevertheless, by placing Umm Kulthūm's voice, music, and legacy in new entertainment contexts, DJs and producers have generated tensions between these newfound settings and the public persona that the singer worked so hard to establish during her lifetime. Through professions of piety, tasteful modes of dress and conduct, and carefully crafted statements of self, she presented herself to her public as a woman of morals, modesty, and conservative values, an image contradicted by the changing ways in which her music has been consumed. In an ironic trade-off, DJs have renewed her relevance for listeners who were born after her death, but they have done so by betraying the values she embodied in her careful public self-presentation.

A Living Reincarnation

As many perceived the Egyptian tradition of singing to be under attack from remixes, music videos, and other trends in popular music, artistic and political leaders strived to cultivate commendable young singers who could preserve the music already deemed to be a valuable part of the *turāth*. Muḥammad Qābīl's *The Future of Egyptian Singing* (1999) charted the accomplishments and potential of dozens of young Egyptian singers nurtured through the Association of Young Talents. Qābīl recounted the achievements of the Arab Radio and Television Network, which featured thirty episodes of young singers performing selections from the *turāth*. The young talents focused on the musical heritage of 'Abd al-Ḥalīm Ḥāfiz, Muḥammad 'Abd al-Wahhāb, and Umm Kulthūm. The physical layout of Qābīl's book made clear the young singers' responsibility: wedged between the iconic figure of Umm Kulthūm on the cover and the challenges presented by dance-oriented video clips described on the back, the new generation was charged with carrying on her legacy and the broader tradition of Egyptian song against the ascendance of a popular idiom that appealed to the country's youth.

While these singers sustain the *turāth*, they are also presented as having the potential to garner more than musical significance. One young singer was fashioned as a virtual living reincarnation capable of revivifying both Umm Kulthūm's patriotism and her broader cultural meaning. After entering the Arab Music Institute in Egypt, fourteen-year-old Amāl Māhir was selected as one of the voices of Umm Kulthūm in the wildly successful Ramadan television series (*Umm Kulthūm*) discussed in earlier chapters. She soon found herself performing in front of President Mubārak himself in summer 1999 while recording Umm Kulthūm's songs for the sound track to the series (Khalil 1999). Governmental support for the young talent quickly followed this encounter. Mubārak gave her a substantial cash award and directed Egyptian radio to assist in her professional development (I. Ḥījāzī 2001; Hassan 2003). Māhir then began a steady stream of performances at celebrations attended by the president, first lady, and government ministers. Although artistic leaders had given Māhir the opportunity to perform in the series, the subsequent development of her career owed much to Mubārak's support and attention.

Mubārak's interest in Māhir could be interpreted as appreciation for a skilled voice and tasteful image in an era of tawdry, often untalented "video clip" singers. Egyptian academic Ashraf Galal expressed a typical view of female pop stars appearing on such clips, identifying moral decay in the ascendance of the music video and bemoaning not simply "the absence of Arab identity and positive values" but, more disturbingly, "a complete cancellation of higher meaning and values" (Hammond 2007, 173, citing *al-Ḥayāt*, April 20, 2004). However, the context of Mubārak's first encounter with the young singer suggests that Māhir represented something more specific to the leader than vocal talent alone. Mubārak first heard her not as a singer but as a performer striving to replicate Umm Kulthūm's sound. The television series and its enthusiastic reception attested to Māhir's success in emulating her model. Viewers criticized many aspects of the series, including the lead actress's excessive weight, as well as the show's failure to elucidate Umm Kulthūm's personal life and characterize her humor and audacity (Rakha 2000). Yet critics refrained from critiquing the sound track, despite the great challenge of providing new performances of Umm Kulthūm's songs in scenes ranging from her childhood to the 1930s. The bulk of this task fell on Māhir, and her remarkable recreation of Umm Kulthūm's vocal mannerisms was essential to the credibility of many scenes. Her deft handling of ever more elaborate solos gave credence to the young Umm Kulthūm's rise in status in the 1910s through encounters with rural elites. In scenes from the 1920s, Māhir's careful enunciation of consonants underscored the belief that Umm Kulthūm's singing skill was rooted in her early training in Qur'ānic recitation. After her emergence in the series in late 1999, Māhir kept Umm Kulthūm's songs as a staple of her own live performances, and her exacting reproduction of the icon's vocal nuances earned her the moniker "Umm-Kulthoum-sound-alike" (Atia 2000a).

The Mubāraks' support for Māhir's development recalled the al-Sādāts' cultivation of Yasmīn al-Khayyām as a replacement for Umm Kulthūm in the early 1970s, when they sought a new leading artist to underscore the change of political leadership.[18] President for nearly two decades, Mubārak had no need to underscore a change of leadership on the eve of the millennium. What he did face was a crisis of legitimacy (al-Awadi 2004, 197). Lacking charisma and international achievements, he had legitimized his political leadership in the 1980s by stressing the rule of law and maintaining a social contract in which the government provided goods and services in exchange for the public's political docility. This social contract eroded in the 1990s when a series of economic crises prevented the vast majority of Egyptians from seeing improvements in living standards. Economic reforms failed and instead exposed rampant corruption. And Mubārak's increasing use of coercion against Islamist groups undermined his claims to legal legitimacy (al-Awadi 2004). Faced with a public that questioned his leadership capabilities and perceived him as unintelligent, he struggled to find effective means to continue legitimizing his leadership (Shehata 1992, 85–87).

During the 1980s and 1990s, the Mubārak regime sought to legitimize itself by stressing selected historical continuities with the 1952 revolution, even as it enacted a de-Nasserization in the realm of policy. In state speeches, links to a nationalist past were normally articulated through devices like Mubārak's self-casting as the "harbinger of the third phase of revolution" responsible for completing the transformation to democracy (Hatina 2004, 115). Yet connections were also sought through the promotion of cultural symbols from the revolutionary era, including Umm Kulthūm. Mubārak himself engaged in such promotion explicitly by writing the preface to one of Umm Kulthūm's biographies (Mubārak 1995). Given this context, Amāl Māhir offered an engaging new tool with which to rebuild legitimacy. Māhir's consistent revoicing of Umm Kulthūm in her performances provided an aural, physical, and emotional link to the revolution that was more engaging than staid state speeches and the printed word. The nostalgia that Māhir was capable of generating served to recall powerful cultural myths of national honor and Arab unity and retain them as part of the national consciousness.

The immaculate timing of Māhir's emergence also enabled her to participate in Egypt's highly touted millennial celebration of 2000, during which her identity was fused with another on an international stage. Planned by the Ministry of Culture to rehabilitate the country's image as a safe tourist destination after the Luxor terrorist attacks of 1997, the celebration featured an elaborate multimedia production at the pyramids of Giza. Although the $9.5 million commemoration of the two-thousandth anniversary of Christ's birth was considered irrelevant and wasteful by many Egyptians, it proved effective as a public relations gambit by drawing foreign tourists and gaining the country international television airtime. Extending from the evening of December 31, 1999, through the morning hours of January 1, 2000, the concert program featured the work of French musician Jean-Michel Jarre and performances by local and national artists. Jarre's contribution, inspired by ancient Egyptian mythology, portrayed the twelve dreams of the sun during its nighttime passage through the dark underworld on the eve of the millennium. In Jarre's evening multimedia segment, dreams about human attributes such as wisdom, courage, and purity were portrayed through the objects in which the sun had concealed them, such as a tree, blood, and snow. With the sun's dream about memory—portrayed through the object of the voice—Jarre offered a tribute to his childhood obsession, Umm Kulthūm. He used laser beams to project her portrait onto the Cheops pyramid. When her recorded voice faded away, the live voice of Amāl Māhir emerged as the legendary singer reincarnated. In a fitting parallel, Umm Kulthūm, known as the "Star of the East," was thus reborn in sound during the sun's own rebirth as it readied to rise again in the east.[19]

Māhir's subsequent appearances were designed to strengthen the perception that she was Umm Kulthūm reincarnated. In addition to giving numerous performances sponsored and attended by government agencies and officials, including the Mubāraks, Māhir sang at the opening of the Umm Kulthūm studio in the state radio and television building, at the opening of the Umm Kulthūm museum, and on the anniversary of the singer's death in

2003. As if confirming the mythological connection between voice and memory, Māhir's penchant for replicating the finest vocal and gestural nuances of Umm Kulthūm's performances—down to her use of hoarseness and vocal cracking—brought forth listeners' memories of Umm Kulthūm's era ("Firqat").[20] Māhir's convincing performances led at least one observer to credit her with the ability to "deliver the feelings of Umm Kulthūm to us as if she were Umm Kulthūm herself" (ʿA. Ṣādiq 2003). So compelling was Māhir's embodiment of the icon that a novelist constructed an entire scene based on her musical powers. In Perikles Monioudis's novel *Land*, Māhir performs at a concert in Alexandria to which audience members have come expecting to hear Umm Kulthūm. Despite the actual performer's youth, the audience sees the elder icon in her. Through her performance, which the narrator describes as a "reincarnation," Māhir enables the audience to be reunited with the Umm Kulthūm they so longingly remember.

Māhir's role as Umm Kulthūm reincarnated continued as her performances expanded to include new patriotic songs alongside the icon's repertory. While some of this new material promoted Egyptian patriotism, much of it came during the waves of official and popular Egyptian support for the Palestinian intifada in 2000 and 2002. Māhir's new songs included "Yā ʿArḍinā Filisṭīn" ("Our Land, Palestine") and "Ukhtī Wafāʾ" ("My Sister Wafāʾ"). The latter was one of many songs hurriedly recorded in April 2002 as ʿUmar Baṭīshah, head of Egyptian radio, spurred the production of patriotic songs, coverage of the intifada, and fundraising programs for Palestinians (Bar'el 2002). Penning the lyrics of "Ukhtī Wafāʾ" himself, Baṭīshah expressed sentiments similar to those in Umm Kulthūm's own "Aṣbaḥa ʿIndī al-Ān Bunduqīyah" ("Now I Have a Rifle"), which she recorded in 1969 to promote the Palestinian resistance movement. The lyrics, written by the Syrian poet Nizār al-Qabbānī, hold up the *fidāʾī* (freedom fighter) as a role model and hero. In the song, Umm Kulthūm gives voice to a youth's yearning to join the *fidāʾīyīn* through the climactic lines "Take me to Palestine with you, men, I want to live or die like men." As sung by Umm Kulthūm, al-Qabbānī's lyrics, which never assign a gender to the aspiring freedom fighter, prefigure Baṭīshah's praise of the female Palestinian suicide bomber Wafāʾ Idrīs, who carried out her mission on a Jerusalem street in January 2002. Māhir herself built on this lyrical connection by choosing Kulthumian gestures and vocal mannerisms to deliver the lyrics "My sister Wafāʾ / Heartbeat of greatness / Blossom who was once on earth and now resides in heaven. . . . You chose *shahāda* [martyrdom] / In death you have brought life to our will" ("Ukhtī Wafāʾ").[21] The young singer intensified the connection with the icon's repertory by performing the song at the opening of the Umm Kulthūm studio in the Egyptian Radio and Television Building in early 2003.

At the same time, Māhir, in her public statements, embraced the patriotism that was such a prominent aspect of Umm Kulthūm's persona. While Umm Kulthūm displayed her patriotism through her fundraising concerts for Egypt after the 1967 war, she also issued many statements promoting the Palestinian resistance. Māhir echoed Umm Kulthūm's comments in support of the Palestinians as she justified her own performances, lamenting that "the suffering of the unarmed Palestinian people exceeds what a man can bear" (Hassan 2003).

In serving as the reincarnated Umm Kulthūm, Māhir helped prop up cultural ideals that were seen to be threatened and also prompted nostalgia for past decades. In the 1990s, the Oslo peace process between the Israelis and Palestinians seemed as if it would alter many political constants in the region. The process prompted vibrant debate about the future of the Arab world and the meaning of Arab identity following a possible peaceful resolution of the Palestinian-Israeli conflict. Amid this uncertainty, those feeling unease about change could turn to the memory of Umm Kulthūm for constancy and comfort (Hammond 2007, 167). Concurrently, during this period of nostalgia for 'Abd al-Nāṣir and the independent modernity that he had come to symbolize (al-Ali 2001, 165),[22] Amāl Māhir's revival of Umm Kulthūm's sound, movements, and rhetoric called forth an idealized vision of the 1950s and 1960s, including the never entirely fulfilled ideals of egalitarianism and Arab unity that the elder singer represented. Such a channeling by Māhir helped divert Egyptian popular attention from the faults of the current regime, including rampant poverty, unemployment, a lack of truly democratic elections, and decades of emergency law allowing indefinite imprisonment without trial.[23] In the words of one moved concertgoer, Māhir's performances offered Egyptians a way to "regain the golden era" ('A. Ṣādiq 2003). Response to her performances pointed to the real work of Sono Cairo, which had produced recordings of the elder singer with the stated desire "to preserve Umm Kulthūm as she was, not recreate her" (Farag 2000b). Rather than updating her performances by cleaning up the sound, the company retained the hissing that evoked a past era and helped listeners briefly escape from present-day problems. Māhir's state-supported rise and the media's preservation of Umm Kulthūm's performances did not simply capture music from the past, as Sono Cairo's statement suggests. Instead, they reproduced it in ways that addressed contemporary needs.

Competing Visions

While the Egyptian state cultivated Amāl Māhir as one facet of its promotion of Umm Kulthūm, artists and listeners around the world claimed the icon's music as part of their heritage and became custodians of that heritage in their own right. They capitalized on the "enhanced use value" of Umm Kulthūm's music and image, imbuing them with a diverse range of political and social meanings and adapting them, sometimes in contradictory ways, to respond to their own contemporary political needs (Buxton 1990, 429). For decades, Egyptian radio broadcasts reached beyond the country's borders to the rest of the Arab world. Egyptian recordings have been distributed internationally and satellite channels have regularly broadcast films of the singer's concerts, as well as the Ramadan television series. From its initial broadcast in late 1999, the biographical drama boosted record sales among consumers born after Umm Kulthūm's death and motivated young members of the Arab diaspora to learn more about Umm Kulthūm's songs and the Arabic language (Sabra 2000; Atia 2000b).

Taking advantage of this access to her music, both artists and ordinary listeners have challenged the dominant domestic vision of Umm Kulthūm's contemporary political significance and reinterpreted her music as an evolving cultural heritage. Rosalind Nashashibi, an artist of Palestinian–Northern Irish background, used her perspective to challenge the East-West binary in a short film called *The States of Things*. By joining the audio of one of Umm Kulthūm's old romantic songs with footage of a used-clothing sale, Nashashibi disturbed and confused viewers, leading them to ask, "Where is this?" and "Who are these people?" (Halasa 2003). In Nashashibi's rendering, Umm Kulthūm's voice proved a powerful tool to challenge the notions of cultural difference that shape everyday lives. Within Egypt, Umm Kulthūm as muse helped Hudá Luṭfī produce a sizable collection of artwork featuring the icon. Exploring issues of gender and politics, her pieces, like Nashashibi's, have been designed to make viewers ask questions. The multimedia *Democracy Is Coming!* featured Umm Kulthūm, in her prime, looking askance as jets zoom by overhead. The striking, deceptively simple image can be read as a critique of the U.S. invasion of Iraq in 2003, or in one of several other ways. The singer's look of disappointment, set against a gloomy gray background, might either prompt reflection on the Mubārak regime, its restrictions on political freedoms, and the democracy that Egypt has yet to enjoy, or on the unfulfilled promises of the 'Abd al-Nāṣir era.

Even among a diasporic population that may seem disconnected from the Arab musical heritage, the singer's music can be a powerful political tool. A young Palestinian listener in America blogged, "the last thing i ever imagined myself doing was listening to oum kalthoum in non-remix form." But he had defied his own prediction and used his experience of her voice and his interpretation of her lyrics to engage in a lengthy reflection on the

Palestinian issue and its troubling disconnection from Arab nationalism (al-Falasteenyia).

Some artists have reversed Umm Kulthūm's long-standing position as a government tool and turned her music against leaders. To do this, they looked not to a song with politically charged lyrics but to a romantic one that guaranteed instant recognition even outside the Arab world—and even when divorced from its lyrics. Her romantic songs, such as "al-Aṭlāl" ("The Ruins"), often allowed for multiple interpretations, like John Lennon's political songs, which often invoked the parties involved—the "us" versus "them"—in vague terms without ever specifying what political action needed to be taken. This was why "Imagine" could be sung at a Conservative Party conference in Britain in 1987 to greet Margaret Thatcher and, at the same time, chanted as a peaceful call for mobilization against a conservative agenda in Communist Eastern Europe (Negus 1996, 194–96). Similarly, contrasting political motivations have driven artists to reinterpret "Inta 'Umrī" ("You Are My Life"). Arguably the most popular of her songs, and the product of a long-awaited collaboration with her former rival Muḥammad 'Abd al-Wahhāb, "Inta 'Umrī" features typically romantic lyrics, such as "Whatever I saw before my eyes saw you was a wasted life."

The Israeli Arab rock band Khalas selected an instrumental metal cover version of "Inta 'Umrī" as the opening track on its 2004 album *Mā 'Adish Fīhā* (We've Had It). As the band members were quick to remind interviewers, Umm Kulthūm was the "opium of the masses" who brought Egypt to a standstill during her concerts (Bin Nun 2004). Khalas performed "Inta 'Umrī" to invoke and, at the same time, reject such inaction in its past and current forms. Following the slowdown at the end of the song's introduction, the icon's "sedative" vocals were replaced by the band's original protest music rebuking Arab leaders who "sit and do nothing." Thus, the band not only co-opted the "Voice of 'Abd al-Nāṣir" but also used her music to denounce the region's contemporary leaders. While the band members recognized Umm Kulthūm as a legitimate part of a broader Arab heritage, their cover version provided a much-needed antidote to the idolatry and hagiography that have characterized most print and media accounts of the Egyptian icon.[24] They preserved both Umm Kulthūm's music *and* the leftist 1960s critique that branded her performances a musical narcotic responsible for anesthetizing Egyptian and other Arab listeners to the impending reality of the 1967 defeat. The band constructed its performances not simply to enact cultural heritage but to challenge its dominant vision.

Also claiming the broad Arab cultural heritage as his own, the young Palestinian-American hip-hop artist Iron Sheik tapped Umm Kulthūm's repertory to register his protest against American leadership. In his 2004 song "Low Expectations," he attacked George W. Bush's foreign policy and the legitimacy of his presidency. Musically, he chose a string melody from "Inta 'Umrī" to accompany a proclamation by Bush from the second presidential debate of 2000. As "Low Expectations" opens, Bush claims, "I think one way for us to end up being viewed as the ugly American is for us to go around the world saying, 'We do it this way. So should you.'" A rapid shift from sampled applause to laughter highlights the ultimate hypocrisy of the then presidential candidate's statement, and a second instrumental melody from "Inta 'Umrī" ushers in the first of Iron Sheik's extended verses of critique. Alternating strings and *nāy* propel a litany of alleged offenses committed by the president, who is described by the rapper as an unintelligent, illegitimately elected leader who used his power to wreak havoc in Iraq:

Is our children learning, they're learning from the best
using Bushian grammar on that English test
He might be dyslexic but what the heck, he's an evil idiot
with no respect for humanity.

The ascending octave leaps in the verses' instrumental theme condense suddenly to obsessively oscillating half-steps as the opening string melody returns in the chorus. Iron Sheik's voice—overdubbed and panned hard left and right—builds tension to an unexpected interruption before the jab of the song's final two words:

We got a joke as a President, but I can't laugh
that fool of a man's behind a bloodbath.
We got a joke as a President leading this nation.
Low expectations!

Perhaps the most sustained competing vision of Umm Kulthūm's contemporary political significance was created by the Israeli and Moroccan singers Zehava Ben and Sapho. These Sephardic musicians claimed Umm Kulthūm as part of their heritage and promoted a selective version of her persona and cultural contributions to further their shared agenda for Middle East peace. Born to Moroccan immigrants in a crime-and-drug-infested neighborhood of Beersheba, Israel, Zehava Ben established herself as a successful singer of popular Mediterranean music. Riding the rising wave of Mizrahi (Eastern) music, in 1995 she released the album *Zehava Ben Sings Arabic*, which included selections from Umm Kulthūm's repertory. Ben's album contributed to a growing trend in Israel in the mid-1990s that enabled one to hear Umm Kulthūm's songs in a West Jerusalem disco, an avant-garde dance production, and a festival performance by Sapho herself (Helm 1994).

Ben and other Israeli artists turned to Umm Kulthūm's repertory as part of a broad effort to cultivate greater appreciation of Sephardic culture represented by Jews of Middle Eastern descent. Although Middle Eastern Jews made up more than 60 percent of the Israeli population, their Sephardic culture had been ridiculed and marginalized while media maintained the dominance of Ashkenazi culture (roughly speaking, the culture of Jews from Germany and other areas in non-Iberian Europe). In general, Arab culture was stigmatized. Motti Regev characterized the common attitude toward Arab music itself as "one of exclusion and denial" up to 1994, noting that media practices helped transform Arab music into a "marginal presence" by producing its absence (1995, 441–45). In turn, the attitude toward Arab culture and music was extended to marginalize Mizrahi music created within Israel because of its perceived similarity to Arab popular music (Regev and Seroussi 2004, 205). Although a sizable body of Mizrahi music emerged in the 1970s and early 1980s, it was largely ignored by the media. Despite this cultural climate, several generations of Sephardic musicians have worked to elevate the status of Mizrahi music.[25] Within this process, Zehava Ben and musicians of similar background have claimed Umm Kulthūm as part of a larger Mizrahi heritage constructed in opposition to Ashkenazi culture. Part of what spurred Ben and others in their endeavor was the regional scope of the Egyptian singer's cultural contribution, physical presence, and reception—all heightened through her Arab world concerts in the late 1960s and early 1970s. As one musician noted, "Zehava is Mizrahi (Eastern), and Umm Kulthūm's music is Mizrahi, not Egyptian or Moroccan or Syrian" (Fishkoff 1996).[26] Even though Umm Kulthūm's music was neither an integral part of the local Moroccan heritage of Ben's ancestors nor written in her native Hebrew, Ben nevertheless claimed it to achieve her own goals, including the elevation of Sephardic culture within Israel.[27]

As noted, peace was another goal driving artists like Ben to perform Umm Kulthūm's repertory in Israel. Claiming that their shared cultural link with the surrounding Middle East was a path for peace, many Sephardic Jews began to promote cultural methods of integrating Israel and the Arab world in the 1990s (Helm 1994). At the Jaffa Peace Festival in 1995, Ben performed "Inta 'Umrī," explaining, "I am for peace, and maybe my songs can serve as a bridge between people" (Agassi 1997; Strich 1996). Sapho—a Moroccan-born Jew who opposed the Israeli presence in the Palestinian territories—used her singing of Umm Kulthūm's songs as "a statement in favor of peace and liberation." Amid Israel's mid-1990s negotiation of peace agreements with Jordan and the Palestine Liberation Organization, she took "al-Aṭlāl" ("The Ruins"), a song that Umm Kulthūm had repeatedly performed to stir desire for renewed warfare in the aftermath of the June War of 1967, and upended it to promote her peace agenda. As she explained, "Singing "al-Aṭlāl' in Jerusalem was a political act that allowed me to cry out my desire for peace. I'm a Jewish woman singing an Arab woman's music, and I believe in peace" (Fishkoff 1996). As the peace process progressed and the audience for Mizrahi music broadened in the 1990s, artists like Ben and Sapho could no longer be chastised for singing "music of my enemy" (Helm 1994).

In seeking to overcome the accusation that she was singing "the enemy's music" and to claim the mantle of Umm Kulthūm, Ben was compelled to engage in a process of erasure. The credibility of the CD cover of *Zehava Ben Sings Arabic,* which featured her face embedded in Umm Kulthūm's head, required that viewers adopt an extremely narrow view of the Egyptian's output. Ben not only portrayed her own efforts as apolitical, but she extended that portrayal to her late Egyptian counterpart, claiming that "most of Umm Kulthūm's songs are about love." Ben thereby removed the icon from her cultural context, transforming her into a sonic artifact, while recalling that "she gave a beautiful gift to Egypt—her voice" (Fishkoff 1996). To make the Egyptian singer a more palatable model in a country where she was seen by many as an anti-Israeli symbol, Ben erased from her own account not only Umm Kulthūm's many patriotic songs, such as "Aṣbaḥa 'Indī al-Ān Bunduqīyah," but also the political interpretations of her romantic and religious songs, such as "al-Aṭlāl," her anti-Israeli public statements, and her participation in propagandist campaigns. Through this process of erasure, Ben was able to incorporate Umm Kulthūm's repertory into a well-received peace program and position herself as "an advocate of reconciliation" ("Zehava" 2003).

As Ben's continued peace platform and performances of Umm Kulthūm's repertory offered the Egyptian singer new political relevance, they also distinguished Ben's own musical products in a crowded market.[28] One online retailer foregrounded the added value of Ben's music when it enticed consumers to purchase her recording as a way of participating in her efforts for peace. As described effusively on the website, "We are especially glad to introduce her to an international audience, as she is working openly for peace between Israelis and Palestinians, not just speaking but also doing. She performs in front of Palestinian audiences, singing in Arabic songs they love, such as in this cassette" ("Oriental Music"). Israeli filmmaker Erez Laufer underscored the singer's distinctiveness by subtitling his documentary on Ben *The Solitary Star.* On the hundredth anniversary of Umm Kulthūm's birth, al-Jazeera's inclusion of Ben in programming reflected the special status she had attained in the eyes of Arabs as an Israeli symbolizing the repossession of cultural territory in former Palestinian lands ("Zehava" 2003).

The contradictions inherent in Zehava Ben's and Amāl Māhir's interpretations of Umm Kulthūm boldly illustrate the diverse ways in which the late singer's songs and persona have been appropriated in an evolving cultural heritage. Māhir merged her adoption of Umm Kulthūm's patriotic persona and musical nuance with her promotion of attempts to reclaim territory through military means and popular violence. In contrast, Ben used the icon's repertory and a highly selective reading of her persona to prompt an unofficial remapping of territory. As Amy Horowitz has argued, Ben's covering of Umm Kulthūm's music allowed her audience "to invest in otherwise contradictory elements, to momentarily realign nonaligned political positions," such as Muslim and Jew, Israeli and Egyptian. In creating these brief realignments, Ben's performances enabled listeners to temporarily cross "seemingly impenetrable borders" (2005, 223–24). While Māhir's performances drew listeners' attention to the past and stale calls for renewed combat, Ben invited listeners to realize scenes in a peaceful future. Māhir's efforts and the official support she has received preserve Umm Kulthūm's music and image in ways that help legitimize President Mubārak's government and direct public attention away from faults in domestic leadership. In contrast to this conservative use, non-Egyptian artists like Ben have claimed Umm Kulthūm's music as part of their cultural heritage and offered stylistically diverse cover versions of songs that express their own responses to contemporary political concerns. Though offering starkly different images of Umm Kulthūm, Māhir and Ben alike have strengthened her contemporary relevance for young listeners in their respective communities and helped sustain her cultural and political legacy into the twenty-first century. These divergent cases suggest that Umm Kulthūm's music and persona will continue to be adapted to meet changing needs in the years to come. Sapho's 2006 performance of Umm Kulthūm's repertory in Beirut aptly illustrated this process; the singer offered her rendition as a statement of support and a gesture of understanding in one of the first international concerts to be held in the city after the July War in 2006 between Israel and Hezbollah (Nasr 2006).

Artists like Ben and Māhir have helped preserve Umm Kulthūm's memory decades after her death. Along with physical monuments, memorials in sound have sustained and altered her posthumous image and legacy. These memorials articulate her relevance in multiple, often contradictory ways. While the singer has lost the degree of control over her image that she exerted in her lifetime and for many years after her death, she has retained cultural and political significance within an increasingly international context.

Many of these redefinitions of Umm Kulthūm's cultural relevance continue to test apparent boundaries between art music and popular music, between the music of now and the music of the heritage. When Shakira danced to a portion of "Inta 'Umrī" in 2007 during the Paris stop on her *Oral Fixation* tour, she challenged the dichotomy posed by the young Egyptian fiancé: "Who do we like more, Umm Kulthūm or Shakira?" In his question, the two icons stood for the supposedly distinct categories of "classical" music (music calling for intellectual appreciation) and "popular" music (music calling for a visceral response). Yet performances like Shakira's give support to Racy's view that Arab music and popular music exist as intersecting domains rather than discrete, binary categories. Whether one views Arab music as still being the dominant, central domain, or sees it as having been surpassed and supplanted by the Arabpop that appeals to an increasingly young population, Umm Kulthūm's music continues to bridge these two domains as it circulates in various contemporary interpretations in the Arab world and beyond.

While some observers have seen *ṭarab*-based music as ending with 'Abd al-Ḥalīm Ḥāfiz and remaining distinct from more recent popular music (Stokes 2002, 597), others have stressed points of continuity. Articulating connections between *ṭarab*-based music and Arabpop, pop stars such as 'Adawīyah and Ḥakīm positioned themselves as the successors of 'Abd al-Ḥalīm (Hammond 2007, 28). Adopting this view, one artist identified the young remixers as a "new generation of composers" and stressed that they have not altered Umm Kulthūm's voice (175). A long-range view might foresee new, "popular" versions of Umm Kulthūm's music—versions that continue long-existing practices of music creation—being ultimately absorbed into the *turāth*.

Regardless of the perspective one adopts, the reception of Umm Kulthūm's work continues to defy the simple pop-classical categorization that Racy warned scholars to avoid. Her legacy is constructed through both government-supported preservation efforts normally associated with "classical" music and individual and commercial efforts typically construed as "popular." The collective work of many, this expanding range of physical and sonic memorials eludes such binary categories to preserve her legacy and supply her music and image with multiple meanings for disparate audiences on an increasingly international scale.

Epilogue

When recounting Umm Kulthūm's life, authors have often exaggerated the break in her public appearances after the June War and even claimed that she retired from singing. In doing so, they sought to enhance the value of her postwar efforts and emphasize the depth of her fidelity to the nation. While these writers' claims contradict contemporaneous accounts of the singer's actual efforts in the weeks following the war, they do prompt a question worthy of consideration: What if she *had* retired?

Had the singer's career ended along with the defeat, she would be remembered rather differently than she is today. She would be recalled as an exceptional artist, but not as an iconic patriot. Accounts of her artistic accomplishments would surely acknowledge the many patriotic songs that she recorded in the decades preceding the war, but her personal patriotism would warrant much less notice. While her colleague and onetime rival Muḥammad ʿAbd al-Wahhāb asserted that "the public applauded and cheered Umm Kulthūm as if she were a national leader and not a singer" (al-Najmī 1993, 210), she would be remembered as simply the latter had she retired after the 1967 defeat.

Umm Kulthūm would also be recalled as something of a two-dimensional figure had her career ended earlier. Her prewar charitable efforts would have been insufficient to outweigh her personal gains from the contractual arrangements that she negotiated so shrewdly. Seen as self-interested, she would have enjoyed a minimal humanitarian reputation. Instead of being lauded as a national mother figure who guided the country out of its defeat, the singer likely would be remembered uncomfortably as an exceptional but selfish artist who contributed to the defeat itself.

Overall, today's icon would be seen as a far less perfect figure. She would be the target of more intense criticisms that she had intoxicated people with her performances and turned their attention away from domestic and international realities. While critiques deeming her concerts to be a "drug that leads Arabs to linger in truancy" and "one of the reasons for the defeat of 1967" are rarely repeated today (I. Saḥḥāb 1980, 19, 22), they would perhaps have become central to the way she was received both in her later years and after her death.

Had Umm Kulthūm stopped singing after the 1967 war, the temporal and geographic span of her art, image, and significance would be deemed narrower than they are today. Rather than being seen as someone who transcended eras and leaders, along with the values for which they stood, she would likely be tied more tightly to the era of ʿAbd al-Nāṣir. Symbolizing his failures rather than perseverance and triumph in the face of defeat, she would have been substantially less revered and suffered a more noticeable decline in popularity in the decades after her death. Having earned less of an international reputation in her lifetime, her posthumous international presence would likely have been comparably small.

Yet instead of retiring, Umm Kulthūm continued singing, and the final years of her career entailed two conterminous but contradictory processes. During her lifetime, she became an archived part of the cultural heritage and a museum subject. She also remained an active artist responding to the changing political and cultural needs of the late 1960s and early 1970s. When her style risked being regarded as outmoded in Egypt, she turned to an array of younger composers, reinvigorated her career by tapping into her international fan base, and redefined her cultural and political significance within Egypt and the Arab world.

The years of her later career also witnessed the singer's remarkable agency in shaping her image during her lifetime and much of the way she would be remembered after her death. As Walīd ʿAwaḍ stated so concisely, "Everything that she did was the result of intelligent choice" (1975, 116). Her public appearances and statements support his claim. The singer was keenly aware of her audience and the context in which her statements would be interpreted. She tailored them accordingly. In Egypt, for example, she played up the propaganda value of her postwar efforts and remained silent about the prewar planning of her Paris concerts. Once in Paris, however, she downplayed the concerts' propagandist potential and instead focused on their conception before the war. An exchange from one of her Paris press conferences illustrates her careful shift of emphasis.

Daily Mail reporter: Do you believe that your presence occurring now after the war between Israel and the Arabs gives it a political goal?
Umm Kulthūm: We agreed on the visit before the war.
Daily Mail reporter: In this situation your visit has a greater meaning.
Umm Kulthūm: I hope so. (Tawfīq and Ibrāhīm 1967)

When speaking directly to Egyptian journalists, she had declared, "I will say to each European I meet that every centime, penny, or cent he gives to Israel is turned into a bullet that kills an Arab" ("Umm Kulthūm fī Faransā" 1967). Yet there is simply no record that she ever followed through on her promise. In direct contrast to exaggerated posthumous accounts of her antagonistic encounters with Europeans in Paris, the guarded and carefully chosen words from her Paris press conference demonstrate her determination to appeal to the public there.

While the singer's postwar efforts have been distinguished as the "most important" part of her career by an Egyptian government website ("Umm Kolthoum"), much of her activity during this period represented remarkable continuity from her career before the war. She simply demonstrated an incredible ability to execute a number of her prewar plans in a radically different political context. Both her Paris concerts and concerts in the Arab world had been conceived in the months and years preceding the war. She continued to pursue these and other efforts initiated earlier in her career out of self-interest. Observers, however, perceived and represented these efforts as a dramatic and admirable transformation illustrating the ultimate in self-sacrifice. Journalists helped readers see the singer as operating beyond herself, and existing as more than herself. As one journalist reflected, "Umm Kulthūm was, in each step she took, the voice of Egypt responding, the Arab issue aroused, and the story of Egypt on every tongue" (S. Fuʿād 1968, 9).

Yet much of the singer's posthumous legend rests on her own great care in articulating the significance and intention that she wanted to be attributed to these efforts. She described her work as being for Egypt, rather than for herself. In her words, "I wanted to say to the whole world, 'This is Egypt. Everlasting with its history, ancient unspoiled character, and culture. Sound in its leadership, people, and struggle; steadfast in the face of the difficult challenge and the harsh trial.'" She took pains to shape interpretations of her Paris concerts in particular. She professed, "No one can describe the extent of my pride when I went to Paris, stood in the middle of Europe, and raised my voice in the name of Egypt. I cannot forget the sights of thousands of Arabs who gathered in that hall and came from the corners of Europe in order to confirm the meaning that I wanted to give it. 'We are still standing on our feet. Our heads are still raised. Our voice is still resounding'" (Qandīl 1969a, 58–60).

Such pronouncements did not alter the fact that her efforts dramatically enhanced her own fame. Entire issues of weekly magazines were devoted to her after the war. After using the postwar period to intensify her regional status, she was claimed by Arabs as an Arab phenomenon. An Iraqi writer readily extended the reach of the singer's peasant roots and her cultural contributions when he reflected, "This village girl from our pure Arab countryside was able to captivate the heart and feelings of the Arab millions . . . she was able to occupy a page in the history of our eternal Arab vocal *turāth*" ('Abd Fatḥī 1985, 5).

Other continuities run from Umm Kulthūm's later career to her posthumous reception. Many of her efforts in the postwar years served to bolster the Egyptian regime and control public outrage. Decades after her death, the Egyptian media used her music and image to address the public anger that simmered at the outset of the Iraq war in early 2003. In Egypt, where the war was felt as a blow against the entire Arab world—against "us"—the editor of the magazine *al-Kawākib* used the singer to validate and check feelings on the street with the April 1 issue. He played to readers' emotions by printing the opening lines of "Asbaḥa 'Indī al-Ān Bunduqīyah," followed by his own commentary (italicized below), under Umm Kulthūm's photograph:

Now I have a rifle, take me to Palestine with you.
    to hills that are sad like the face of the Magdalene,
to the green domes and the prophet's stones.
    for twenty years I have been searching
for a land and an identity
No—for sixty years,
    and not only did Palestine not attack first,
but neither did Iraq. (Maḥmūd Sa'd 2003)

In addition to Umm Kulthūm's lyrics, the editor used the singer's image and legacy to rechannel public outrage. At the time of the issue's publication, public anger was being stirred up by *sha'bī* singer Sha'bān 'Abd al-Raḥīm's *al-Ḍarb x al-'Irāq* ("Attack on Iraq"). The title track's expression of widely felt anti-Americanism resulted in the rapid sale of one million bootleg cassettes (Michael 2003). Yet the laundryman-turned-singer's skyrocketing fame generated controversy. His widely successful 2001 hit "I Hate Israel" had been followed by rumors of an ode to Osama bin Laden. His politically charged lyrics were so provocative that he became the subject of parliamentary debate and the potential target of a broadcasting ban in 2001 (Gordon 2003, 85). Now, two years hence, Sha'bān, affectionately known as Sha'būlā, called the United States on its double standards by asking, "Will you disarm? Why not? It would be great. Inspect Iraq? Go ahead and inspect Israel."

As a massive police presence was used to contain carefully monitored antiwar protests in Cairo so that rage directed toward the United States did not turn against the Egyptian regime itself, the magazine cover used Umm

Kulthūm to check Sha'būlā's ability to stoke public anger. Elegantly dressed in an ivory suit, discreet earrings, and her signature jeweled sunglasses, Umm Kulthūm dwarfed the gaudily clad, greasy-haired Sha'būlā, making him look silly. Her presence appeared to draw from him a reverent expression totally at odds with his musical voice. A caption situated the musical newcomer squarely in the context of a well-respected lineage: "Patriotic Song from the Lady to Sha'būlā." While Sayyid Darwīsh—the youthful male icon of early twentieth-century patriotic song—would have lent credibility to Sha'būlā in the cover's visual composition, the choice of Umm Kulthūm doubly weakened his credibility. On the one hand, the visual juxtaposition of an artist known for her outstanding ability to express the meaning of her songs with one known for not even understanding the words of his brought into focus Sha'būlā's illegitimacy as a respected artist. On the other hand, his portrayal as a descendant of the voice of 'Abd al-Nāṣir undermined his inflammatory potential as a bold and subversive artist.

As an alternative to Sha'būlā, a pop star who distressed the Egyptian regime, radio and print media turned listeners' attention to the deceased icon, who could be used as needed to control the mood on the street. Extensive radio airplay and print media coverage of her song "Baghdad"—a song she recorded in 1958—prompted Egyptians to seek her lyrics for the inspiration found in their uplifting, if delusional, assurances of victory in the face of the Iraq war. By directing listeners to the voice of a deceased singer no longer capable of reacting to political events and more readily framed by others, the media used her music and her patriotic legacy to validate and contain public anger.

A source of both political utility and continued interest even for younger listeners born after her death, Umm Kulthūm's image and music remain vital parts of both Egyptian and Arab culture. With her iconic image so powerful and her art deemed a repository of "Arab soul and Arab authenticity" (Melligi 1975), the singer is likely to remain a rich source for contemporary appropriations. Having made herself newly relevant for her national and regional audiences in a time of political, economic, and psychological crisis, she sustained her career and shaped much of the way she would be remembered after her death. As she did, she ensured her lasting presence as part of an evolving national, regional, and ultimately diasporic heritage.

Notes

Introduction

1. Jane Hill, personal communication, February 12, 2003.

2. This assessment, made by al-Laythī (1952, 34), was quoted by Danielson (1997, 162–63).

3. Like Baty, I use the verb "remember" in order to transcend generic divisions often separating the written from the oral, the textual from the graphic, the aural from the visual, the formal from the informal, and the fictional from the factual (1995, 40).

4. The Arabic term "naksah" refers to a period of illness after a recovery from an earlier one. The government translator charged with finding an English euphemism for the defeat rejected the logical option "relapse." He was concerned that foreigners would not understand that the initial sickness was the prerevolutionary period, and that the recovery had taken place from 1952 to 1967. He settled on the word "setback," which has since become the standard translation (Moftah 2002). English publications refer to the conflict itself as the Six-Day War, while Arabic publications refer to the June War.

5. Discussing a recent example of such a response to crisis, Don McLeese observed that Hurricane Katrina "jolted artists out of their comfort zones and complacency, spurring many to new peaks of creativity and productivity" (2008, 213).

6. As outlined clearly by Danielson (1997), these groups of songs include the romantic works of Aḥmad Rāmī and Muḥammad al-Qaṣabjī in the late 1920s and 1930s, the populist songs of Bayram al-Tūnisī and Zakariyā Aḥmad and the neoclassical *qaṣīdah*s of Riyāḍ al-Sunbāṭī in the 1940s, and the patriotic songs of the 1950s.

7. Biographies published during the past two decades have treated both contemporary political figures and historical cultural figures (Wallach and Wallach 1997; Hunsberger 2000). Factors cited as working against the production and criticism of auto/biography in the region have included the absence of historicism, the emphasis on the well-being of the community over that of the individual and individualism, and the viewing of non-Western autobiographies as imitations of Western ones (Zonis 1991, 62–63; Golley 2003, 56). However, as Fay has argued, the Arab under-

standing of history and historiography as biography challenges Eurocentric claims that the autonomous individual or subject, as the product of Western humanism and the Enlightenment, was unavailable to the region (2001a, 2).

8. This achieved celebrity stands in contrast to both ascribed celebrity accorded by a famous family name and the attributed celebrity stemming from concentrated media attention (Rojek 2001, 17–18).

9. While Dyer developed his taxonomy of media texts in the area of film studies, it has been applied to music by Mäkelä (2004, 20–21) and Frontani (2007, 3–5).

10. It is rather unusual for an artist to obtain such wide-ranging control over her media texts. A comparable example is Charlie Chaplin, who gained not only a high degree of control over the production and distribution of his films but also of promotional texts. The rise and fall of his career, including the rise and fall of his control over his star image, is thoroughly explored by Maland (1989).

11. For example, aristocratic English women in the seventeenth century were expected to lead lives centered on motherhood and family, and their autobiographies reflect this private focus (Pomerleau 1980, 27–28).

12. When Baker performed in France during World War II, she abandoned her banana G-string for evening gowns and was seen as a godmother to soldiers (Regester 2000, 46–47). Elvis's postwar phase has been neglected by biographers in preference to his early and Vegas years (Doll 1998, 32–33, 40, 180). Although Lennon used his new househusband image to question masculinist myths of rock music culture and to set up the private sphere as an ultimate site of "truth," his death left this project unfinished and his reception as a heroic martyr left it forgotten (Mäkelä 2004, 206, 210).

1. "A New Umm Kulthūm"

1. The events outlined here have been documented in detail by Oren (2002, 1–169).

2. This overconfidence is discussed by Oren (2002, 84, 92, 97). False optimism turned into actual deception after the war's outbreak. Egyptian and other Arab newspapers boasted that Egyptian forces had downed dozens and even hundreds of Israeli planes (*al-ʿAlam* [Rabat], June 5, 1967, special edition, 1; al-Ṭāwīl 1967; "Farḥat" 1967; Oren 2002, 177–78).

3. Riyāḍ al-Ṣunbāṭī quickly composed a musical setting for lyrics that Ṣalāḥ Jāḥīn had adapted from his 1961 diwan, and the song was put together in just one week ("Umm Kulthūm tataghannā bi al-jihād" 1967).

4. Edited versions of these performances can be heard on "Salū Qalbī," Ṣawt al-Qāhirah 94SDCD01B06 compact disc, and "Ḥadīth al-Rūḥ," Ṣawt al-Qāhirah 94SDCD01B67 compact disc. She had premiered "Ḥadīth al-Rūḥ" in May 1967.

5. These public reactions were documented in detail by Oren (2002, 286, 288) and Hussein (1977, 260, 262).

6. Public responses outside Egypt were described by Morris (1967), Fawaz (1998), and Munro (2000, 67).

7. Authors expressing skepticism about the spontaneity of the demonstrations

included Lambert (1967), Lacouture (1973, 311), and Stephens (1971, 507). Kimche and Bawley maintained that while much of the public's reaction was genuine, its organization was spurred by the Arab Socialist Union. The authors also noted that the huge placards carried by workers shortly after the speech would have taken hours to prepare (1968, 245–46). More recently, Beattie identified the role of the Arab Socialist Union in facilitating protesters' transport to Cairo and of radio in presenting 'Abd al-Nāṣir's resignation as the goal of an American-Zionist conspiracy (1994, 211).

8. 'Abd al-Nāṣir subsequently acknowledged this allegation of imperialist collusion to be untrue. Nevertheless, the myth persisted for decades (Podeh 2004).

9. This speech was largely written by Muḥammad Ḥassanayn Ḥaykal (Aboul-Enein 2005).

10. 'Abd al-Wahhāb, for example, still in Beirut in mid-July, sent his wife to Cairo to donate £E 5,000 in his name and offered a year's housing for a family displaced from the canal (al-Malākh 1967a). Outside Egypt, other Arab artists offered musical responses to the war. Fayrūz and 'Āṣī and Manṣūr al-Raḥbānī entered a period of heightened musical productivity, with Fayrūz being awarded the key to the city of Jerusalem (Stone 2008, 95).

11. Statements about broadcasting practices are based on radio schedules published in the magazine *al-Idhā'ah wa al-tilīfizyūn*.

12. Umm Kulthūm's work with the NAEW extended a long-standing tradition of Egyptian women's philanthropic work during wartime. Women's organizations conducted social welfare and philanthropy during the Balkan Wars of 1911–12 (Baron 2005, 37).

13. Umm Kulthūm's efforts were documented by al-Malākh (1967b, 1967e) and other Egyptian journalists ("Umm Kulthūm tukhātib" 1967; "Umm Kulthūm tusāfir" 1967; *al-Idhā'ah wa al-Tilīfizyūn* August 5, 1967, 11).

14. She reduced the length of her concerts to two songs in December 1968.

15. One such play was Mikhail Ruman's *al-Zujāj* (The Glass), in which a young man, representing the activist movement, wants to rid his neighborhood (Egypt) of corruption, nepotism, and the status quo overall ('Abd al-Nāṣir's regime).

16. A month after the war, both prices and taxes were raised, diminishing the average citizen's purchasing power by 5 to 9 percent. Rice, lentils, and oil doubled in price (Kanovsky 1970, 290).

17. Limited Egyptian airstrikes on Israeli positions in Sinai and the sinking of the Israeli destroyer *Eilat* (October 21) demonstrated that the battle *was* continuing (Aboul-Enein 2002).

18. Farūq Ibrāhīm, personal communication, March 16, 2003.

19. When asked later by an Egyptian interviewer about the genesis of her Paris concerts, she obfuscated, indicating only that she had been invited to give the performances and not that the invitation predated the war (Nāṣif 1968c).

20. Her Paris performances and interviews were broadcast on radio and television throughout December, and she also continued to participate in the NAEW's charitable work (Tawfīq and Shafīq 1967b; R. Ṣāliḥ 1967; "Ughnīyah min Bārīs" 1967; "al-Tajammu' al-waṭanī" 1967).

21. The protests were documented by Aboul-Enein (2002) and Ansari (1986, 144), among others (Erlich 1989, 192; Beattie 1994, 214–15; "Aftermath of the War"; "Flood Waters" 1968, 278).

2. For Country or Self?

1. This idea was generated in 1967, when the journalist Fūmīl Labīb proposed that Egyptian artists give fundraising concerts in the Arab world (1967a). Umm Kulthūm had mentioned her willingness to sing in the Arab world to raise funds for the war effort in late summer of the same year (Abū Zayyid and Ḥussayn 1967, 5).

2. The Pakistani award was given to honor her work to liberate the occupied lands as well as her concerts for the war effort. She also sang Pakistani poet Muḥammad Iqbāl's "Ḥadīth al-Rūḥ ("Li mādhā" 1968).

3. This "feedback cycle" has been discussed in detail by Racy (1991; 2003).

4. Tender, moody, singing, and clownish types of listeners were identified and described by Umm Kulthūm earlier in her career (Racy 2003, 59, 63; N. Fu'ād 2000, 302–304).

5. For example, her performances of "al-Aṭlāl" in December 1966 and January 1967 elicited more restrained responses from her audience, which in turn prompted her to offer fewer repetitions and variations of sections of the song.

6. This interpretation contrasts with Danielson's (1997, 186). Umm Kulthūm's trips coincided with the anniversary of the Moroccan king's ascension, 'Īd al-Naṣr and 'Īd al-Istiqlāl in Tunisia, and Sudan's independence day. She did not comply with some Sudanese listeners' desire that she sing the *qaṣīdah* "al-Sūdan" during her visit to the country ("Kayf yasta'ad al-Sūdān" 1968), and she also avoided performing songs with lyrics by Kuwaiti and Lebanese poets—"Yā Dārnā Yā Dār" and "Hādhihi Laylatī"—in those respective countries.

7. The 15,000 Israeli troops who entered the town, the base of the Palestinian Fatah organization, were largely repelled by a Jordanian army of comparable size, along with approximately three hundred *fidā'iyīn*. The heavy mythologizing of the battle as a *fidā'iyīn* victory is traced by Andrew Terrill (2001).

8. This reluctance is illustrated by the rejection of 'Abd al-Nāṣir's proposal of a two-party system by members of the Arab Socialist Union's Supreme Executive Committee in August 1967 and the comparatively limited reforms introduced through the March 30 Program following the riots of February 1968 (Farid 1994, 81–89; Hussein 1977, 300).

9. By crossing the canal in August and surprising the Israelis with a heavy artillery barrage in October, Egyptian forces ushered in the first part of what came to be known as the war of attrition. The war was intended in part to restore anti-Zionist prestige to the regime and the army and to channel the patriotic feelings of members of the public (Khalidi 1973, 61–62; Hussein 1977, 318).

10. Najāt al-Ṣaghīrah, for example, participated in Kuwait's effort to generate funds for the war effort, raising KD [Kuwaiti dinars] 12,000 through a concert in Kuwait ('Aṣamat 1968d).

11. She had given occasional concerts abroad between the 1930s and 1960s, including appearances in Iraq and Syria. After the war, ʿAbd al-Ḥalīm Ḥāfiz (Ḥāfiṯh) also made appearances in the region, including performances in Tunisia in July 1968 and Morocco in July 1969.

3. Sustaining a Career, Shaping a Legacy

1. Although ʿIṣmat counted eighteen months since her concert on June 1, 1967, she had actually given a concert in Cairo's Qaṣr al-Nīl hall in May 1968 as well as her annual charity concert to benefit tuberculosis patients in April in Alexandria. She donated a portion of the proceeds from both concerts to the war effort (*al-Jumhūrīyah* May 12, 1968, 12; al-ʿAbbāsī 1968a).

2. These efforts supplemented previous autobiographical statements, which included a series of articles in the magazine *Ākhir sāʿah* in 1937–38 and the narration of her life story to Niʿmāt Aḥmad Fu'ād, whose work first appeared in 1952. Umm Kulthūm told her life story to the writer Saʿd al-Dīn Wahbah and allowed the filming of concert footage in 1969. While the scenario was completed and filming begun, the project was later aborted due to difficulties in finding an actress to play the lead role (Tabārak 1990, 37–38; "Ḥayāt" 1970; Māhir 1971a).

3. Umm Kulthūm's work with ʿAwad illustrates how autobiographical texts are often hybrid products, voiced by several people and edited in varying visible and invisible ways by writers, translators, and editors alike (Golley 2003, 81–82).

4. Muslim women have not had recourse to formal adoption procedures because the Qur'ān and prophetic tradition mark the practice as *ḥarām*. While informal adoption is a widespread way of aiding lost, abandoned, and illegitimate children, these children do not take the adopting adults' names and cannot collect an inheritance from them (Sonbol 1995, 59–64).

5. Umm Kulthūm entered into a number of short, contractual marriages in her youth in order to travel abroad and to address her father's concerns regarding propriety. She ended the marriages after her travels and her father's death (al-Muhāmī 1979, 38–39; *Umm Kulthūm: Qīthārat al-ʿArab* 1975, 34).

6. Umm Kulthūm's cousin had asked her to help obtain medical care for her infant son, ʿĀdil, in 1965, whereupon Umm Kulthūm took the child into her home and oversaw his upbringing and education for several years. Umm Kulthūm also took in her brother's granddaughter and minded her schooling from the age of nine (M. ʿAwaḍ 1969a, 1969b, 128).

7. Such "dogged" pursuit was exemplified by her vigorous defense of her own rights in a court case over royalties brought against her by composer Zakariyā Aḥmad and her deliberate extension of her performance in a Revolution Day concert in order to prevent ʿAbd al-Ḥalīm Ḥāfiz from performing (Danielson 1997, 162–63; Rosenbaum 2004, 328).

8. Several explanations have been offered for her abandonment of this project after nearly a decade. While Umm Kulthūm acknowledged that others were better poised to recite the entire Qurʿān and Riyāḍ al-Sunbāṭī suggested that the two of

them were frustrated in their attempts to find a new style of recitation, others have maintained that religious authorities failed to authorize the project (Qandīl 1968d; al-Khūrī 2000, 180–81; Shūshah 1976, 80; Danielson 1997, 192; ʿAfāf Yaḥyá, personal communication, March 2, 2003).

9. This legal conflict is discussed in more detail by Danielson (1997, 162–63).

10. Inglis extended the concept of idiosyncrasy credit, developed by organizational social psychologist Edwin Hollander (1958) in his study of leadership in small groups, to the entertainment industry to explain how The Beatles transformed themselves from idols to innovators.

11. In the 1930s and 1940s, music composed up to two decades earlier was considered part of the *turāth*. By the 1960s and 1970s, the *turāth* had been expanded to include repertories from the 1930s and 1940s, and it now includes music from the 1960s and 1970s (el-Shawan 1980, 47).

12. The relationship between the Egyptian leadership and the PLO is discussed by Cobban (1984, 45–47, 204–205), Shemesh (1996, 103–104), and Hussein (1977, 319–20).

13. Scheduled broadcasts were published in *al-Idhāʿah wa al-tilīfizyūn*, April 12, 1969.

14. French and German television recorded her performances in Baalbek in 1970 (unlabeled article in *Dār al-Hilāl* clippings file 65).

15. Sāmīyah Ṣādiq, personal communication, September 11, 2003.

16. Many additional explanations have been offered for the rift between Umm Kulthūm and the first couple, ranging from the singer's addressing the new president without the official titles of protocol, to using his name in a pun that was interpreted as a lack of respect, to her refusing to sing in his honor ("Kānat fī khilāf" 1975; Ramaḍān n.d., 76).

4. From Artist to Legend

1. Her funeral and commemorative programming were documented by Jighām (1975a) and others ("ʻal-Anwār'" 1975; "Dhikrayāt" 1975; "Musalsalat" 1975; *al-Anwār* February 9, 1975).

2. For example, al-Khaṭīb drew heavily on the work of al-Naqqāsh, and content from *Umm Kulthūm: Qiṣṣat ḥayātihā wa mukhtārāt min aghānīhā* (1997) was drawn from Shūshah's writing.

3. References to Umm Kulthūm are made in plays by Linin al-Ramlī (1982, 71) and Jalāl Muḥammad (1991, 30), both of which are cited by Gabriel M. Rosenbaum (2004, 329).

4. The battle involving the two women's charitable projects was portrayed by Muḥammad Salmāwī (2000), Ḥanafī al-Maḥallāwī (1994, 36, 234–36, 240; 1999b, 137), and Saʿd Sāmī Ramaḍān (n.d., 76).

5. Sāmīyah Ṣādiq, personal communication, September 11, 2003.

6. Tallies of her patriotic efforts were offered by Maḥmūd ʿAwaḍ (1987, 7), Majīd Ṭirād (1999, 43–44), Muḥammad Saʿīd (2002, 23), and others ("Umm Kulthūm wa qiṣṣat" 1975).

7. Such characterizations were offered by Kamāl Raḍwān (2000, 63–64), Ṭāhir al-Bahī (2000), Muḥammad al-Disūqī (1992), and Ḥussayn ʿUthmān (1977).

8. Accounts of her retirement and seclusion have persisted from the days following the singer's death into the twenty-first century ("Umm Kulthūm wa qiṣṣat" 1975; Tabārak 1975; *Umm Kulthūm: Qīthārat al-ʿArab* 1975, 36; al-Maḥallāwī 1994, 166; al-Manṣūrī 1998; Hammond 1999; Farag 2000c; ʿAntar 2001; al-Makāwī 2003). Ḥussayn ʿUthmān, for example, claimed that she had admitted to spending two weeks in seclusion after the war (1977). She was sick and bedridden for one week during the war, but just four days after its end, a letter from her expressing support for ʿAbd al-Nāṣir appeared in a weekly magazine. By the next week, the text of her new song was published and she had donated £20,000 (sterling) of her own money from Kuwait broadcasting to the war effort.

9. Her patriotic songs of the 1950s were largely omitted in previous episodes, and their conflation with her domestic fundraising concerts allowed them to be incorporated efficiently in the series.

10. The ruins had associations with Roman, Hellenistic, Phoenician, and Lebanese civilizations (Stone 2008, 16).

11. Other characterizations of her as the fourth pyramid were made by Simone Bitton (1996), Muḥammad al-Shādhilī (2000), and Muḥammad al-Makāwī (2003).

12. These processes have been documented by Laila Shukry el-Hamamsy (1975, 296), Beth Baron (2005, 68), and Lila Abu-Lughod (2005, 152).

13. She also mediated to make Tammāy al-Zahāyra one of the first rural villages to have pure water, offered financial support to its needy families, funded the rebuilding of two dozen homes destroyed by fire, and personally intervened to obtain medical care for a teenage villager ("Umm Kulthūm ism al-qariyah" 1975; *Umm Kulthūm: Qīthārat al-ʿArab* 1975, 85–88; "Niṣf milyūn" 1975; "Umm Kulthūm wa ḥamalāt al-khayr" 1971; Ramaḍān n.d., 31).

14. These images have been reproduced in publications from the 1970s to 2000 (Abū al-Khayr 1975, n.p.; Shūshah, 1976, 268; "Min albūm" 1978; Danielson 1997; Farag 2000a).

15. Muḥammad Wajdī Qandīl, personal communication, March 8, 2003.

16. The economic impact and perception of al-Sādāt's policies are discussed by Galal A. Amin (1989, 110–11), Raymond A. Hinnebusch, Jr. (1985, 238–39, 246–49), and John Waterbury (1983, 207–13).

17. An exception is "Wa Dārit al-Ayyām," which she performed in her first concert following ʿAbd al-Nāṣir's death and subsequently became a way of evoking his memory.

18. ʿAmr Ibrāhīm, personal communication, February 22, 2003.

19. The couple supported the young singer Yasmīn al-Khayyām as part of a strategic campaign to remove Umm Kulthūm, seen as an unwanted icon of the earlier regime, from the stage (al-Maḥallāwī 1994, 38, 176–80, 186–207; 1999b, 137).

20. More broadly, Ziyād al-Raḥbānī's works composed for his mother to sing were intended to expose "the dissimulation that was the Raḥbānī nation" (Stone 2008, 2). While his father and uncle's works promoted a "fantasy of a monolingual

and monocultural Lebanon," the younger Ziyād's music addressed the country's linguistic diversity, while challenging the notion of the 1960s as a national golden age, formed through a nostalgic response during the civil war that began in the 1970s (2, 93). In one instance of critique, Ziyād's play *Happiness Hotel* likened the effects of the heritage, which included his parents' works, to that of marijuana (102).

21. According to many accounts, she stopped singing for an entire year after ʿAbd al-Nāṣir's death. In fact, she postponed the beginning of her next season by only one month, singing in January 1971 rather than December 1970, as originally scheduled.

5. Mother of Egypt or Erotic Partner?

1. The caption, taken from the lyrics of the Aḥmad Rāmī and Riyāḍ al-Sunbāṭī song "Yallī Kāna Yashjīk Anīnī," also appeared on banners carried at her funeral, where it was presented as Umm Kulthūm's message to her mourners (F. Saḥḥāb and I. Saḥḥāb 2003, vol. 3 196).

2. ʿAbd al-Wahhāb's accomplishments as a composer have been remembered more than his success as a singer, as evidenced by his common designation as *al-mūsīqār* (composer). Despite Umm Kulthūm's early efforts at composition and active role in shaping her mature repertory, she was rarely referred to as a *mūsīqārah*. A photograph of her from the 1932 Congress of Arabic Music in Cairo captured an event in honor of "*al-mūsīqārah*" Umm Kulthūm (F. Saḥḥāb 1997, 190).

3. Plays about the singer's life, performed in Europe between 2002 and 2004, also portrayed her as a lesbian (Ayad 2003). The plays, written by the Egyptian ʿĀdil Ḥakīm and directed by the Tunisian Lutfī Ashūr, were based on Sélim Nassib's novel *Oum*, which was first published in French in 1994. While the novel suggests that the singer had an intimate relationship with her husband and Maḥmūd al-Sharīf, it also places her in two intimate scenes with women. Described in an ambiguous manner, these scenes can easily be interpreted as implying her participation in homosexual encounters (Nassib 2006, 54–55, 60, 171–72). The weekly Israeli television drama *Florentene* also reinforced rumors of Umm Kulthūm's homosexuality by using her voice as the sound track when the masculinist sex symbol Maor is persuaded by his friends to "play gay" to avoid performing his annual military reserve service (Stein 2000, 38).

4. Fārūq Ibrāhīm, personal communication, March 16, 2003. The singer's marriage to Ḥasan al-Ḥifnāwī, a dermatologist more than a decade her junior, was characterized in print as a loveless "relationship of collegiality, friendship, and shared life under one roof more than a relationship of marriage" (I. M. Ibrāhīm 1975). By the time she married, a taxonomy of normal and deviant sexuality had begun to take hold from the West, as illustrated by Najīb Maḥfūẓh's 1957 novel *al-Sukkarīyah* (Sugar Street).

5. Raḍwān's "*shudhūdh*" (deviance) is a shortened form of "*shudhūdh al-jinsī*" (sexual deviance). A literal translation of the European expression, the phrase was used by Arab translators of psychology books and Arab behavioral psychologists in the mid-twentieth century. The phrase remains the most common and widely un-

derstood way of referring to the Western concept of homosexuality, even though it can refer to a much wider array of practices (Massad 2007, 172).

6. Hanā' Kilany, personal communication, March 4, 1999.

7. Between 1975 and 1980, Lennon cultivated a househusband image as he remained in seclusion, while making and releasing no records, conducting no interviews, and only participating in two press conferences and an advertisement. To reinforce this image, he maintained that he hung his guitar up on the wall throughout these years (Mäkelä 2004, 197).

8. Nassib's novel, which, as noted before, was originally written in French (1994), was translated into several languages including Arabic (Turkiya 1999), Hebrew (Nassib 1999), English (Nassib 2006), and Italian (Nassib 1996).

9. Authors expanding on Fu'ād's assertion included Shūshah (1976, 73), Zakariyā (1983, 9), and al-Maḥallāwī (1994, 130–31).

10. Biographers offering such accounts include Khalīl (1992, 212–15), al-Maḥallāwī (1994, 28, 127; 1999a, 15, 24), al-Muhāmī (1979, 38–39), and the anonymous author of *Umm Kulthūm: Qīthārat al-'Arab* (1975, 34). Rumored husbands included Maḥmūd Mukhtār, Aḥmad Rāmī, a prominent lawmaker, and Muṣṭafá Amīn (al-Maḥallāwī 1999a, 54, 112–13). The power of marriage to affirm gender and sexual identity can be seen in books about the country's three leading singers. The lives and careers of singers who spent all or most of their adult life unmarried are treated under the provocative titles *Women in the Life of 'Abd al-Ḥalīm Ḥāfiṭh* and *Men in the Life of Umm Kulthūm* ('Āmir 1995; Khalīl 1992). Such titles not only arouse the interest of readers but also attempt to compensate for the subjects' failure to marry early in life. No such book exists about Muḥammad 'Abd al-Wahhāb, who was married several times.

11. Accounts featuring her suitors' jealousy include those by Khalīl (1992, 61–62, 217), al-Maḥallāwī (1999a, 28), Raḍwān (2000, 47), Fāḍil (2000), and In'ām Muḥammad 'Alī (2001).

12. For more on this process, see Joseph Massad (2007). The impact of Western concepts and terminology is illustrated not only in the literal midcentury translation of "sexual deviance" into Arabic but also in the creation of new Arabic words *mithlīyah* and *ghayrīyah*, based on roots of "sameness" and "difference," to approximate the Western concepts of homosexuality and heterosexuality. Massad's distinction between same-sex practices and the homosexual identity, as adopted recently from the West, is substantiated by the presence of ample Arabic vocabulary for specific sexual acts but far fewer terms designating identities. Nevertheless, the widely made identity distinction and its roots in the Mediterranean model of sexuality have been criticized for restricting and simplifying our understanding of sexuality in the Middle East (al-Kassim 2008, 301–302).

13. Examples include publications by al-Khaṭīb (1975), Muṣṭafá (1975, 49), Abū al-Khayr (1975), Shūshah (1976), al-Jawādī (1985, 71), and Ben Hammed (1997, 46), as well as "Min albūm" (1978, 18) and *Umm Kulthūm: Qīthārat al-'Arab* (1978, 85).

14. These authors include 'Abd al-'Āl (n.d., 18), 'Abd al-Muṭallib (2000), Nassib (2006, 190), and the anonymous author of "Māmā Thūmah" (2000, 106, 110).

Children she took into her home included two young members of her extended family whose parents died, her nephew Samīr, and ʿĀdil Ibrāhīm ʿAlī, the son of a relative.

15. The use of pharaonic imagery dates back to the 1880s and was used by members of the early nationalist movement to reinforce claims to territorial continuity (Baron 2005, 59–67). One example is Muḥammad Nājī's 1919 oil painting *The Awakening of Egypt; or the Procession of Isis*, in which Isis represents the nation.

16. While the Greek version of the Sphinx was a winged female monster with a woman's head and lion's body, the Egyptian form was a recumbent lion with the head of a man, ram, or hawk.

17. Such maternal representations continue to be offered by listeners and observers. For example, a YouTube contributor applied the tag "the mother of arabs" to a video of one of her live performances ("Omm Kalthoum-Inta Omri"), and a 2008 radio segment on her life was interpreted by an American listener as having been deliberately broadcast on Mother's Day (Nancy Elizabeth Currey, "Umm Kulthoum on NPR" email to SAMR-list, May 13, 2008).

18. These accounts included "Nightingale" (1975), Melligi (1975), and "Dhikrayāt" (1975, 7).

19. Western assessments were repeated in the works of Sayyid Maḥmūd (2003), al-Kurdī (1975), and ʿAbd al-ʿĀl (n.d., 27), as well as "Wafūd ʿarabīyah" (1975), "Security Problems" (1975), and "Aqwāl ūrūbīyah" (1975).

20. The photo appeared in *Nisf al-dunyā*, February 6, 2000, 61.

21. The singer was also characterized as a defender and redeemer of national honor during her later career (Nahās 1970, 7; A. Ṣāliḥ 1970, 29).

22. Posthumous portrayals of antagonistic encounters before and during her Paris trip such as those in the film *Kawkab al-Sharq* contradict her own statements.

23. Although the October War (Yom Kippur War) has also been described as a stalemate and an Israeli victory, the strong showing by Egypt's military in the first days of the three-week conflict and Egypt's regaining and reopening of the Suez Canal during the subsequent peace process were vital events that made the war such an important point in Egyptian history. While nearly all accounts of Umm Kulthūm's life laud her efforts for the Egyptian war effort following the 1967 defeat, only two of her biographers have cited her financial contributions to the *fidāʾiyīn* (al-Naqqāsh 2000, 103; al-Maḥallāwī 1999b, 78–79). Many accounts have erased her financial and verbal support for the Palestinian resistance (*Umm Kulthūm: Qīthārat al-ʿArab* 1975, 12–14; *Umm Kulthūm: Qīthārat al-ʿArab* 1978, 45–46; al-Saʿdnī, 1975a, 12–14; "Mourning in Kuwait" 1975, 1; ʿAntar 2001). Some authors do mention the song "Asbaḥa ʿIndī al-Ān Bundūqīyah." The erasure and simplification of the singer's patriotic acts has helped to fashion her as an internationally palatable figure, especially as she has gained a wider global reputation and an expanding Western audience in the decades since her death.

24. These nicknames appeared in numerous publications (*Umm Kulthūm: Qīthārat al-ʿArab* 1975, 5, 50; *Umm Kulthūm: Qīthārat al-ʿArab* 1978, 3; *Umm Kulthūm: Qiṣṣat ḥayātihā* 1977, 39).

25. These associations were established in part through Fayrūz's song lyrics and her roles onstage (Stone 2008, 150–52, 154).

6. An Evolving Heritage

1. ʻAmr Diyāb's career is outlined in greater detail by Michael Frishkopf (2003, 145–48).

2. Tarek al-Kashef, quoted by Hammond (1999).

3. Bashīr ʻAbd al-Fattāḥ, personal communication, February 18, 2003.

4. Ihāb and Hind Fatḥī, personal communication, March 16, 2003. Like many listeners in Egypt, the fiancée's father had recorded nightly radio broadcasts of Umm Kulthūm's concert performances on audiocassettes to create a substantial personal collection.

5. Ḥanān Badr, personal communication, March 2, 2003.

6. Though the mosque was built, the singer was unable to return to inaugurate it in her name during her final years.

7. The singer's stepson mounted a televised attack on the Ministry of Culture after waiting a decade for progress on the museum. Dr. Muḥammad Ḥasan al-Ḥifnāwī, personal communication, July 1, 2003. A commercial tower, the Hotel and Burj Umm Kulthūm, now occupies the site.

8. Danielson has addressed the origins and modesty of the singer's concert attire (1991, 326–27).

9. A term attributed to Le Corbusier, *promenade architecturale* refers to a space designed with particular attention to movement and sequence in order to choreograph an evolving experience for the person moving through it.

10. The museum's components were constructed in a sequence that differs from the way in which they are typically experienced. Two curved walls were preexisting features of the building, which was originally constructed as a geological museum and then refurbished and redesigned by Akram al-Majdūb and Maurizio di Paolo as the Umm Kulthūm Museum. These designers took advantage of the curved walls' potential to create a womblike environment by completely blocking off their windows with panels running the length of the interior walls, adopting a dark color scheme, minimizing lighting, and repeating the curved motif in the dress case and on the projection wall. The role of the body in understanding architecture has been examined by Gartner (1990, 83–89) and Ando (1988).

11. The state-owned Egypt Radio and Television Union has dominated broadcasting in the country through national, regional, and satellite television channels and numerous national radio networks. The lifting of the state's monopolies on television and radio broadcasting in 2001 and 2003, respectively, prompted the establishment of independent satellite channels and privately owned radio stations.

12. The recordings of many other artists, including Sayyid Darwīsh, Muḥammad ʻAbd al-Wahhāb, and ʻAbd al-Ḥalīm Ḥāfiz, are also available at affordable prices. The resurrection of cultural and media policies from the ʻAbd al-Nāṣir era has been interpreted as an attempt to "sell" neoliberal economic policies imposed on Egypt by its Western sources of funding (Jacquemond 1997).

13. Conclusions have been drawn based on programming schedules published in the weekly magazine *al-Idhā'ah wa al-tilīfizyūn* in the fall of 1982, 1987, 1992, 1997, and 2002. Results of this sampling were largely confirmed by daily listening during 2003. Danielson has addressed the enduring qualities of al-Sunbāṭī's songs composed for Umm Kulthūm in the 1960s (1997, 114–15, 174–83).

14. Hind Fatḥī, personal communication, March 16, 2003.

15. The singer's pristine self-presentation and posthumous representation as an exemplar of proper behavior were brought into sharp focus by a rare photograph of Umm Kulthūm smoking—a behavior that she publicly rejected as being destructive to one's vocal health—while watching a soccer match with her husband in 1955 (Tabārak 1990, 94).

16. The eleventh-century philosopher and theologian al-Ghazālī used criteria of *zamān* (time), *makān* (place), and *ikhwān* (associates) to evaluate the appropriateness of music, musical activities, performers, and listeners (al Faruqi 1985, 17–19).

17. Danielson has addressed the singer's efforts at redefinition (1997, 121–25, 164–68, 181–83).

18. Al-Maḥallāwī outlined the first couple's efforts on this matter (1994, 38, 176–80, 186–207; 1999b, 137).

19. The preparations for and reception of the millennial celebration were documented by el-Aref (1999) and a variety of other observers ("Egypt's" 2000; "Egyptian Court" 1999; "In front"; "Les 12 Reves").

20. 'Afāf Yaḥyá, personal communication, March 2, 2003.

21. This English translation is provided in subtitles on the online video.

22. Nadje S. Al-Ali is careful to note, however, that more ambivalent and critical attitudes exist among certain segments of the population, such as women activists who did not live in Egypt before the 1967 defeat (2001, 166).

23. Jason Brownlee has addressed the nondemocratic nature of the country's elections and efforts to stifle opposition during this period (2002).

24. Edward Said has also punctured the singer's idealized facade by offering negative reactions to her performances, shaped by his childhood exposure to Western classical music (Said 1999; de Groot 2005; Said 1993, 98).

25. Horowitz has discussed the elevation of Mizrahi music (2005, 210, 216–18). While addressing the rise of this style, Regev and Seroussi have also analyzed the "narrative of musical discrimination" that surrounded the style beginning in the late 1990s (2004, 220–24).

26. Interpolation in original.

27. The efforts of Ben and other Mizrahi musicians were aided by a distribution contract that made Umm Kulthūm's Sono Cairo albums available for sale in Israel in 1996 (Palti 2000).

28. From 1996 to 2006, Ben sang at the inauguration of Tolerance Square outside UNESCO's Paris headquarters, recorded another album of Umm Kulthūm's songs, participated in the song and video clip "We Brought Peace upon Us," and released a music video of "Inta 'Umrī."

References

Periodicals Consulted

L'Action (Tunis)
al-Ahrām (Cairo)
al-Ahram Weekly (Cairo)
al-Akhbār (Cairo)
Ākhir sā'ah (Cairo)
al-'Alam (Rabat)
al-'Alam (Tripoli, Libya)
al-'Amal (Lebanon)
al-'Amal (Tunis)
al-Anbā' (Jerusalem)
al-Anwār (Beirut)
al-Ayyām (Khartoum)
al-Bilād (Jedda)
Cairo Times
al-Dustūr (Amman)
Egypt Today (Cairo)
Il Giornale di Tripoli
Haaretz (Tel Aviv)
al-Ḥayāt (Beirut)
al-Hudá (New York)
al-Idhā'ah al-Lībīyah/al-Idha 'ah wa-al-tilīfizyūn (Tripoli)
al-Idhā'ah wa al-talfazah (Tunis)
al-Idhā'ah wa al-tilīfizyūn (Cairo)
al-Ittiḥād (United Arab Emirates)
al-Jumhūrīyah (Cairo)
al-Kawākib (Cairo)
Kuwait Times
Libyan Times (Benghazi)
al-Madīnah (Jedda)

Maroc Demain (Casablanca)
al-Muṣawwar (Cairo)
al-Nahār (Beirut)
Niṣf al-dunyā (Cairo)
Le Petit Marocain/Le Progres Marocain (Casablanca)
La presse de Tunisie (Tunis)
al-Quds (Jerusalem)
al-Ra'ī al-'Ām (Khartoum)
Ṣawt al-'Urūbah (Lebanon)
'Umān (Kuwait)
al-Ummah (Benghazi)
La Vigie Marocaine (Casablanca)
al-Waṭan (Muscat)

Print Sources and Websites

A., Amal. 2005. "Holy Accountant: Amr Khalid." *Improvisations: Arab Woman Progressive Voice.* May 1. http://arabwomanprogressivevoice.blogspot.com/2006_05_01_archive.html (accessed December 1, 2006).

al-'Abbāsī, Salāmah. 1967. "Kayf 'āshat al-Buhayrah laylat al-'amr ma'a Kawkab al-Sharq?" [How did Buhayra live the night of its life with the Star of the East?]. *al-Jumhūrīyah*, August 19, 6.

——. 1968a. "Ghannat Umm Kulthūm li ḥayāt al-maṣdūrīn" [Umm Kulthūm sang for the life of consumptives]. *al-Jumhūrīyah*, April 5, 10.

——. 1968b. "Ma'a Umm Kulthūm fī al-liqā' al-sābi'" [With Umm Kulthūm in the seventh encounter]. *al-Jumhūrīyah*, June 14, 3.

——. 1968c. "Umm Kulthūm fī al-liqā' al-rābi' min ajl al-majhūd al-ḥarbī" [Umm Kulthūm in the fourth encounter for the sake of the war effort]. *al-Jumhūrīyah*, February 3, 1.

——. 1968d. "Umm Kulthūm ibnat al-sha'b al-aṣīlah kānat al-mathal al-a'lá lil-ghinā' al-'arabī" [Umm Kulthūm the authentic daughter of the people was the highest model of Arab singing]. *al-Jumhūrīyah*, February 24, 10.

——. 1968e. "Umm Kulthūm taqḍī 10 ayyām bi al-Sūdān bi munāsibat 'īd al-Istiqlāl" [Umm Kulthūm spends ten days in Sudan on the occasion of Independence Day]. *al-Jumhūrīyah*, November 23, 6.

——. 1969. "'Ādat Umm Kulthūm ba'd adā' al-'umrah" [Umm Kulthūm returned after performing the minor pilgrimage]. *al-Jumhūrīyah,* November 3, 8.

'Abd al-'Āl, Muḥammad Maḥmūd. N.d. *Umm Kulthūm fī dhikráhā* [Umm Kulthūm in her remembrance]. al-Manṣūrah: Maktab Nūr li Ṭibā'at al-Awfsat.

'Abd al-Fattāḥ, Suhayr. 1992. *Umm Kulthum: Ḥayāt ṣawt* [Umm Kulthūm: The life of a voice]. Jedda: Manshūrāt al-Khazindār.

'Abd al-Ḥalīm, Aḥmad Zakī. 1987. *Nisā' fawq al-qimmah* [Women at the peak]. Cairo: Dār al-Fayṣal.

'Abd al-Ḥamīd, Aḥmad. 1975. "Ta'ammulāt 'an turāth Umm Kulthūm" [Reflections on the heritage of Umm Kulthūm]. *al-Jumhūrīyah*, February 19, 3.

ʿAbd al-Ḥayy, ʿAbd al-Tawwāb. 1967a. "Umm Kulthūm fī awwal ḥaflah min silsilat ḥaflāt al-milyūn ginīh!" [Umm Kulthūm in the first concert in the series of concerts of £E 1 million]. *al-Kawākib*, August 22, 4–5.

——. [1967b]. "Umm Kulthūm taqūd al-ʿamal al-waṭanī ilá al-marʾah al-miṣrīyah" [Umm Kulthūm leads the national work of the Egyptian women]. *al-Kawākib* (undated article in *Dār al-Hilāl* clippings file 65).

ʿAbd Allāh, ʿAbd Allāh Aḥmad. 1995. *Umm Kulthūm: al-Ḥubb al-kabīr* [Umm Kulthūm: The great love]. Cairo: Markaz al-Rayah.

ʿAbd al-Laṭīf, Salāḥ. 1967. "3,000 risālah ilá ʿAbd al-Nāṣir fī kull yawm" [3,000 letters to ʿAbd al-Nāṣir every day]. *Ākhir sāʿah*, July 26, 8–9.

ʿAbd al-Majīd, Samīr. 1967. "Ḥadīth maʿa Umm Kulthūm" [Conversation with Umm Kulthūm]. *al-Muṣawwar*, September 22, 5.

ʿAbd al-Muṭallib, Aḥmad. 2000. "Qariyat Umm Kulthūm: Arḍ lā tanbut al-zuhūr" [Umm Kulthūm's village: A land that doesn't produce flowers]. *Niṣf al-dunyā*, February 6, 47.

ʿAbd al-Rasūl, Ḥasan. 1969a. "Ḥadīth fī al-sayyālah wa ḥakāyah min al-ṭāʾirah al-muhtazzah!" [A conversation amid tears and a report from the shaking airplane]. *al-Akhbār*, March 28, 2.

——. 1969b. "ʿIndamā bakat Umm Kulthūm!" [When Umm Kulthūm cried]. *al-Akhbār*, March 16, 12.

——. 1969c. "Umm Kulthūm tataḥaddath sāʿah maʿa al-sufarāʾ ʿan al-ghināʾ al-ʿarabī" [Umm Kulthūm talks for an hour with the ambassadors about Arab song]. *al-Akhbār,* March 17, 2.

——. 2000. "Muwāqif khālidah li Umm Kulthūm fī ḥamlāt al-majhūd al-ḥarbī" [Umm Kulthūm's eternal stances in her concerts for the war effort]. *al-Jumhūrīyah*, February 7 (Umm Kulthūm Museum Library vol. 12, 107).

ʿAbd al-Ṣamad, Ṣalāḥ. 1969. "*al-Dustūr* fī khidmat al-qārʾi" [*al-Dustūr* at the reader's service]. *al-Dustūr*, March 16, 3.

ʿAbd al-Wahhāb, Muḥammad. 1981. "Umm Kulthūm al-insānah" [Umm Kulthūm the person]. *al-Kawākib*, February 3, 4.

ʿAbd Fatḥī, ʿAdnān. 1985. *Umm Kulthūm al-muʿjizah: Ḥayātuhā—majmūʿat aghānīhā* [Umm Kulthūm the miracle: Her life and her songs]. Baghdad: al Maktabah al Waṭanīyah/Maktabat Tammuz.

Aboul-Enein, Youssef. 2002. "Examining the Reconstruction of Egyptian Morale during the Aftermath of the 1967 Six-Day War: An Arab Perspective," *Air & Space Power Chronicles*, April 1. http://www.airpower.maxwell.af.mil/airchronicles.cc.enein.html (accessed May 17, 2006).

——. 2005. "The Heikal Papers: A Discourse on Politics and the 1967 Arab-Israeli War with Egyptian President Gamal Abdel Nasser." *Strategic Insights* 4 (4), http://www.ccc.nps.navy.mil/si/2005/Apr/aboul-eneinApr05.asp (accessed November 16, 2008).

Abū al-Faḍl, Fatḥī. 1967. "ʿḤaqq Bilādakʾ: Nashīd jadīd yanṭaliq bihi ṣawt Umm Kulthūm" ["Ḥaqq Bilādak": A new anthem delivered by the voice of Umm Kulthūm]. *al-Ahrām*, July 27, 8.

Abū al-Khayr, Salīm. 1975. *Umm Kulthūm*. Cairo: Salīm Abū al-Khayr.
Abū al-Majad, al-Sayyid. 1969. "Ghadan tughannī Umm Kulthūm li inqādh ma'bad al-ḥubb ans al-wujūd" [Tomorrow Umm Kulthūm sings to rescue the temple of love Ans al-Wujūd]. *al-Akhbār*, June 18, 3.
Abū Dhikrá, Wajīh. 1968. "Ra'aytu ḥaṭām al-jaysh al-isrā'īlī fī al-ḍiffah al-sharqīyah bi al-Urdun!" [I saw the wreckage of the Israeli army on the eastern bank in Jordan]. *Ākhir sā'ah*, March 27, 4–6.
Abu-Lughod, Lila. 2005. *Dramas of Nationhood: The Politics of Television in Egypt*. Chicago: University of Chicago Press.
Abū Naṭhārah. 1967. "Akhbār al-nās" [The people's news]. *al-Akhbār*, December 18, 8.
——. 1968. "al-Laylah Umm Kulthūm fī al-Manṣūrah fī ūlá haflātihā" [Tonight Umm Kulthūm in al-Manṣūrah for the first of her concerts]. *al-Akhbār*, February 1, 10.
Abū Sālim, Ṣalāḥ. 1967a. "Bayn al-waḥī wa al-hijrah wa al-isrā' wa ghazawāt al-nabī wa futūḥātihi" [Between the revelation, the migration, the night journey, the Prophet's conquests, and his victories]. *al-Jumhūrīyah*, December 19, 5.
——. 1967b. "Naṣṣ barnāmij al-Sīrah al-Nabawīyah fī ṣawt Umm Kulthūm" [Text of the program al-Sīrah al-Nabawīyah in Umm Kulthūm's voice]. *al-Jumhūrīyah*, December 17, 5.
——. 1967c. "al-Sīrah al-Nabawīyah fī barnāmij ghanā'ī bi ṣawt Umm Kulthūm" [al-Sīrah al-Nabawīyah in a vocal program in Umm Kulthūm's voice]. *al-Jumhūrīyah*, December 16, 5.
——. 1969. "Umm Kulthūm tughannī al-Sīrah al-Nabawīyah" [Umm Kulthūm sings al-Sīrah al-Nabawīyah]. *al-Jumhūrīyah*, June 14, 8.
Abū Zayyid, Farūq, and Fāṭimah Ḥussayn. 1967. "al-Fannān al-'arabī" [The Arab artist]. *al-Idhā'ah wa al-tilīfizyūn*, August 5, 3–6.
"Aḍwā' 'alá al-siyāsah al-dawlīyah" [Lights on international politics]. 1968. *al-Idhā'ah wa al-tilīfizyūn*, January 6, 14.
"The Aftermath of the War," http://www.country-studies.com/egypt/the-aftermath-of-the-war.html (accessed March 23, 2005).
Agassi, Tirzah. 1997. "Peace of Her Heart." *Jerusalem Post*, April 4.
"Ahamm aḥdāth fi naṭharihim" [Most important events in their view]. 1968. *al-Jumhūrīyah*, December 23, 5.
Aḥmad, Fahīm. 1967. "Umm Kulthūm satathayyar dawīyan fī Bārīs" [Umm Kulthūm will cause a storm in Paris]. *al-Idhā'ah wa al-tilīfizyūn*, September 9, 3–6.
"Akbar ḥadath tārīkhī lil-fann al-miṣrī fī Bārīs" [Biggest historical event for Egyptian art in Paris]. 1967. *al-Akhbār*, November 20, 3.
"Akhbār al-nās" [The people's news]. 1968. *al-Akhbār*, November 27, 8.
"al-Akhbār: Umm Kulthūm tufakkir fī jawlat al-muhāfiṭhāt li tanṭhīm juhūd al-mar'ah" [The news: Umm Kulthūm considers a tour of the governorates to organize the women's effort]. 1967. *al-Idhā'ah wa al-tilīfizyūn*, July 22, 20.
"Ākhir sā'ah: Miftāḥ madīnat al-Iskandarīyah li Umm Kulthūm" [Last hour: Key to city of Alexandria to Umm Kulthūm]. 1967. *al-Jumhūrīyah*, September 1, 6.

al-ʿAlam (Rabat). 1967. June 5, special edition, 1.

Al-Ali, Nadje S. 2001. "Between Political Epochs and Personal Lives: Formative Experiences of Egyptian Women Activists." In *Auto/Biography and the Construction of Identity and Community in the Middle East*, ed. Mary Ann Fay, 155–76. New York: Palgrave.

Amīn, ʿAlī. 1975. "Mudhakkirāt Umm Kulthūm kamā katabathā Umm Kulthūm maʿa ʿAlī Amīn" [Umm Kulthūm's memoirs as she wrote them with ʿAlī Amīn]. *Ākhir sāʿah*, February 12, 27–38.

Amin, Galal A. 1989. "Migration, Inflation, and Social Mobility." In *Egypt under Mubarak*, ed. Charles Tripp and Roger Owen, 103–20. London: Routledge.

al-Amīr, ʿIzzat. 1975. "al-Qur'ān fī ḥayāt Umm Kulthūm" [The Qur'ān in the life of Umm Kulthūm]. *al-Kawākib*, February 11, 30–31.

——. 1983. "Māmā Umm Kulthūm." *al-Kawākib*, February 1, 21.

ʿĀmir, Munīr. 1995. *Nisā' fī ḥayāt ʿAbd al-Ḥalīm* [Women in the life of ʿAbd al-Ḥalīm]. Cairo: Maktabat al-Madbūlī al-Ṣaghīr.

Ando, Tadao. 1988. "Shintai and Space." In *Architecture and Body*, ed. Scott Marble, et al., [n.p]. New York: Rizzoli.

Ansari, Hamied. 1986. *Egypt: The Stalled Society*. Albany: SUNY Press.

Anson, Robert Sam. 1981. *Gone Crazy and Back Again: The Rise and Fall of the* Rolling Stone *Generation*. Garden City: Doubleday.

ʿAntar, Aḥmad. 2001. *Umm Kulthūm*. Cairo: Wizārat al-Thaqāfah.

"'al-Anwār' tashhad al-widāʿ al-kabīr li Umm Kulthūm" ["al-Anwār" witnesses the big farewell to Umm Kulthūm]. 1975. *al-Anwār*, February 6, 6–7.

Aoude, Ibrahim G. 1994. "From National Bourgeois Development to Infitah: Egypt 1952–1992." *Arab Studies Quarterly* 16 (1): 1–23.

"Aqwāl ūrūbīyah fī sayyidat al-ghinā': Fāqat Idīth Biyāf ta'thīrān" [European statements about the Lady of Song: She exceeded Edith Piaf in influence]. 1975. *al-Anwār*, February 5, 7.

"Arab World Opens Its Arms to Telefood." 2000. http://www.fao.org/Food/tf2000/ART-e.htm (accessed June 8, 2007).

el-Aref, Nevine. 1999. "Prepping the Plateau." *al-Ahram Weekly*, December 23, http://weekly.ahram.org.eg/1999/461/tr1.htm (accessed June 8, 2007).

ʿĀrif, Jamīl. 1969. "40 alf mīdāliyyah dhahab li Umm Kulthūm" [40,000 gold medals of Umm Kulthūm]. 1969. *Ākhir sāʿah*, October 29, 16.

"al-Asrār allatī istaqbat Mahrajan Umm Kulthūm fī Tūnis" [The secrets kept by the Umm Kulthūm Festival in Tunis]. 1976. *al-Jumhūrīyah*, December 30 (*Dār al-Hilāl* clippings file 65).

Atia, Tarek. 2000a. "Bursts of Passion." *al-Ahram Weekly*, October 26, http://weekly.ahram.org.eg/2000/505/tim1.htm (accessed June 4, 2003).

——. 2000b. "Sabrine: Stars in Her Eyes." *al-Ahram Weekly*, February 3, http://www.ahram.org.eg/weekly/2000/467/profile.htm (accessed May 27, 2000).

——. 2002. "Hani Wahba: The DJ Will Be Determining Your Mood Tonight." *al-Ahram Weekly*, August 22, http://weekly.ahram.org.eg/2002/600/profile.htm (accessed June 8, 2007).

Atiya, Nayra. 1988. *Khul-Khaal: Five Egyptian Women Tell Their Stories*. Syracuse, NY: Syracuse University Press.

'Aṭīyah, Ṣalāḥ. 1967. "Umm Kulthūm taqūl: 'Atamannā an ughannī min Tal Abīb'" [Umm Kulthūm says: "I hope to sing from Tel Aviv"]. *al-Jumhūrīyah*, May 24 (*Dār al-Hilāl* clippings file number 65).

———. 1968. "Kayf tamma al-liqā' al-sādis bayn Umm Kulthūm wa 'Abd al-Wahhāb" [How the sixth encounter between Umm Kulthūm and 'Abd al-Wahhāb ended]. *al-Jumhūrīyah*, July 22, 6.

"'al-Aṭlāl' fawq qimmat al-haram" ["al-Aṭlāl" above the pyramid's peak]. 1969. *al-Idhā'ah wa al-tilīfizyūn*, June 28, 26.

Attar, Samar. 2002. "To Create and in Creating To Be Created: Reflections on the Mixing of Fiction and Memoir in *Lina: A Portrait of a Damascene Girl* and *The House on Arnus Square*." In *Auto/Biography and the Construction of Identity and Community in the Middle East*, ed. Mary Ann Fay, 215–26. New York: Palgrave.

'Awaḍ, Maḥmūd. 1969a. "Umm Kulthūm allatī lā ya'rifuhā aḥad" [The Umm Kulthūm no one knows]. *al-Akhbār*, February 8, 12.

———. 1969b. *Umm Kulthūm allatī lā ya'rifuhā aḥad* [The Umm Kulthūm no one knows]. 1st ed. Cairo: Mu'assasat Akhbār al-Yawm.

———. 1987. *Umm Kulthūm allatī lā ya'rifuhā aḥad* [The Umm Kulthūm no one knows]. 4th ed. Cairo: Mu'assasat Akhbār al-Yawm.

'Awaḍ, Walīd. 1975. "al-Fallāhah allatī ḥakmat al-'ālim al-'arabī" [The peasant who conquered the Arab world]. In *Umm Kulthūm: Qithārat al-'Arab*, 1975, 114–34.

al-Awadi, Hesham. 2004. *In Pursuit of Legitimacy: The Muslim Brothers and Mubarak, 1982–2000*. London: Tauris Academic Studies.

'Awnī, Duriyah. 1967a. "Kayfa ista'addat Bārīs li-istiqbāl Umm Kulthūm?" [How did Paris prepare to receive Umm Kulthūm?]. *al-Muṣawwar*, September 22, 2.

———. 1967b. "Yahūd sharqīyūn jā'ū li samā' Umm Kulthūm" [Eastern Jews came to listen to Umm Kulthūm]. *al-Muṣawwar*, November 24, 9.

———. 1998. "Umm Kulthūm tughannī 'al-Aṭlāl' lil-yahūd" [Umm Kulthūm sings "al-Atlal" for Jews]. *Niṣf al-dunyā*, February 1 (Umm Kulthūm Museum Library vol. 10, 197–200).

Ayad, Christophe. 2003. "Oum Kalsoum, icône écornée." *Libération*. January 11, 29.

al-'Azīz, Muḥammad Ḥamādī. 1975. "Sayyidat al-Ṭarab al-'Arabī" [Lady of Arab Trance]. March 20. Rabat. Reprinted in al-Marīnī 1975, 230–34.

Badran, Margot. 1995. *Feminists, Islam, and Nation: Gender and the Making of Modern Egypt*. Princeton, NJ: Princeton University Press.

Bahjat, Ahmad. 1968. "Umm Kulthūm tataḥaddath ba'd riḥlatihā ilá al-Maghrib" [Umm Kulthūm speaks after her trip to Morocco]. *al-Ahrām*, April 5, 10.

al-Bahī, Ṭāhir. 2000. "Ziyārah ilá Ṭammāy al-Zahāyrah" [A visit to Ṭammāy al-Zahāyrah]. *al-Kawākib*, February 29, 10–14.

"Bakat Umm Kulthūm fī al-thulth sā'ah al-akhīrah" [Umm Kulthūm cried for the last twenty minutes]. 1971. *al-Akhbār*, January 9, 13.

Bakhīt, Kamāl Ḥasan. 1975. "Ihtazza 'arsh al-ghinā' al-'arabī" [The throne of Arabic singing was shaken]. *al-Ayyām*, February 4, 12.

al-Bandārī, Jalīl. 1967. "Umm Kulthūm qarrarat an tadhhab ilā al-jabhah" [Umm Kulthūm decided to go to the front line]. *al-Akhbār*, May 20 (*al-Ahrām* clippings file 110).

———. 1968a. "Anā wa al-nujūm" [The stars and I]. *al-Akhbār*, April 23, 8.

———. 1968b. "Ma'a al-safīr fī intiṭhār al-safīrah Umm Kulthūm" [With the ambassador—waiting for the ambassador Umm Kulthūm]. *al-Akhbār*, April 20, 13.

Banjulūn, 'Abd al-Majīd. 1975. "Wā Umm Kulthūmāh—a'ilá al-abad?" [Oh Umm Kulthūm, forever?]. *al-'Alam* (Rabat), February 10. Reprinted in al-Marīnī 1975, 238–40.

Barakat, Halim. 1985. "The Arab Family and the Challenge of Social Transformation." In *Women and the Family in the Middle East: New Voices of Change*, ed. Elizabeth Warnock Fernea, 27–48. Austin: University of Texas Press.

———. 1993. *The Arab World: Society, Culture, and State*. Berkeley: University of California Press.

Baranovitch, Nimrod. 2003. *China's New Voices: Popular Music, Ethnicity, Gender, and Politics, 1978–1997*. Berkeley: University of California Press.

Barbas, Samantha. 2001. *Movie Crazy: Fans, Stars, and the Cult of Celebrity*. New York: Palgrave.

Bar'el, Zvi. 2002. "Boycott of the Big Mac." *Haaretz*, April 24, http://news.haaretz.co.il/hasen/pages/ShArt.jhtml?itemNo=155201&contrassID=2&subContrassID=5&sbSubContrassID=0&listSrc=Y&itemNo=155201 (accessed January 11, 2007).

Barney, Katelyn. 2007. "Sending a Message: How Indigenous Australian Women Use Contemporary Music Recording Technologies to Provide a Space for Agency, Viewpoints, and Agendas." *World of Music* 49 (1): 105–124.

Baron, Beth. 1994. *The Women's Awakening in Egypt: Culture, Society, and the Press*. New Haven: Yale University Press.

———. 2005. *Egypt as a Woman: Nationalism, Gender, and Politics*. Berkeley: University of California Press.

Baty, S. Paige. 1995. *American Monroe: The Making of a Body Politic*. Berkeley: University of California Press.

Beattie, Kirk J. 1994. *Egypt during the Nasser Years: Ideology, Politics, and Civil Society*. Boulder: Westview Press.

Ben Hammed, Hammadi. 1997. *Oum Kalthoum*. Paris: Alif Les éditions de la Méditerannée.

al-Bīlī, Nuwāl. 1967. "Mādhā qālat Umm Kulthūm fī al-Tajammu' al-Waṭanī lil-Mar'ah al-Miṣrīyah" [What did Umm Kulthūm say at the National Assembly of Egyptian Women?]. *Ākhir sā'ah*, July 19, 27.

Bin 'Abūd, al-Mahdī. 1968. "Umm Kulthūm tharwah haḍārīyah" [Umm Kulthūm is a cultural treasure]. *al-'Alam* (Rabat), March 16. Reprinted in al-Marīnī 1975, 154–57.

Bin Nun, Sagi. 2004. "Kiss the Fat Woman Good-bye." *Haaretz*, October 26, http://www.haaretz.com/hasen/pages/ShArt.jhtml?itemNo=493443&contrassID=1&subContrassID=7&sbSubContrassID=0&listSrc=Y (accessed July 21, 2007).

al-Bīṭār, Ṣalāḥ. 1967. "Wizārat al-Siyāḥah tunaṭhṭhim ḥaflāt Umm Kulthūm" [Ministry of Tourism organizes Umm Kulthūm's concerts]. *al-Kawākib*, February 14, 42.

Blundy, David, and Andrew Lycett. 1987. *Qaddafi and the Libyan Revolution*. London: Weidenfeld & Nicolson.

Booth, Marilyn. 2001a. "Infamous Women and Famous Wombs: Biography, Gender, and Islamist Concepts of Community in Contemporary Egypt." In *Auto/Biography and the Construction of Identity and Community in the Middle East*, ed. Mary Ann Fay, 51–70. New York: Palgrave.

———. 2001b. *May Her Likes Be Multiplied: Biography and Gender Politics in Egypt*. Berkeley: University of California Press.

Brophy, Brigit. 1988. *Mozart, the Dramatist*. Rev. ed. New York: Da Capo.

Brownlee, Jason. 2002. "The Decline of Pluralism in Mubarak's Egypt." *Journal of Democracy* 13 (4): 6–14.

Bruss, Elizabeth. 1976. *Autobiographical Acts*. Baltimore: Johns Hopkins University Press.

"Burqīyah min amīrat al-Maghrib li Umm Kulthūm" [Telegram from Moroccan princess to Umm Kulthūm]. 1970. *al-Jumhūrīyah*, December 2, 10.

Buxton, David. 1990. "Rock Music, the Star System, and the Rise of Consumerism." In *On Record: Rock, Pop, and the Written Word*, ed. Simon Frith and Andrew Goodwin, 427–40. New York: Pantheon.

Chakravorty, Mrinalini. 2007. To Undo What the North Has Done: Fragments of a Nation and Arab Collectivism in the Fiction of Ahdaf Soueif. In *Arab Women's Lives Retold: Exploring Identity through Writing*, ed. Nawar al-Hassan Golley, 129–54. Syracuse, NY: Syracuse University Press.

Chelbi, Moustapha. 1977. Um Kalthoum, la voix d'or de la conscience arabe. In *Les Africains*, ed. Charles-André Julien, et al., vol. 3, 285–316. Paris: Éditions J.A.

Chipman, Abram. 2000. "Janacek and Sibelius: The Antithetical Fates of Creativity in Late Adulthood." *Psychoanalytic Review* 87 (3): 429–54.

———. 2004. "Loneliness and Liberation in the Life and Stage Works of Bela Bartok." *Psychoanalytic Review* 91 (5): 663–81.

Clancy-Smith, Julia. 1991. "The House of Zeinab: Female Authority and Saintly Succession in Colonial Algeria." In *Women in Middle Eastern History: Shifting Boundaries in Sex and Gender*, ed. Nikki R. Keddie and Beth Baron, 254–74.

Cobban, Helena. 1984. *The Palestinian Liberation Organisation: People, Power, and Politics*. Cambridge: Cambridge University Press.

Cott, Jonathan, ed. 2006. *Bob Dylan: The Essential Interviews*. New York: Wenner.

Cowen, Tyler. 2000. *What Price Fame?* Cambridge: Harvard University Press.

Crane, Susan. 2002. *The Performance of Self: Ritual, Clothing, and Identity in the Hundred Years War*. Philadelphia: University of Pennsylvania Press.

Crist, Elizabeth B. 2005. *Music for the Common Man: Aaron Copland during the Depression and War*. Oxford: Oxford University Press.

Daniel, Wayne K. 2005. "Hayloft Patriotism: The *National Barn Dance* during World War II." In *Country Music Goes to War*, ed. Charles K. Wolfe and James E. Akenson, 81–101.

Danielson, Virginia. 1991. "Shaping Tradition in Arabic Song: The Career and Repertory of Umm Kulthūm." PhD diss., University of Illinois.

——. 1997. *The Voice of Egypt: Umm Kulthūm, Arabic Song, and Egyptian Society in the Twentieth Century*. Chicago: University of Chicago Press.

Darwīsh, Ṣalāḥ. 1967. "Li awwal marrah yudhī' al-tilīfizyūn al-ḥafl al-shahrī li Umm Kulthūm" [For the first time television broadcasts Umm Kulthūm's monthly concert]. *al-Jumhūrīyah*, June 1, 1, 15.

——. 1968. "Ism Umm Kulthūm 'alá mawālīd al-Sūdān" [Umm Kulthūm's name to Sudanese newborns]. *al-Jumhūrīyah*, December 29, 1.

——. 1969a. "al-Amal al-fidā'ī huwa al-ṭarīq al-amthal li i'ādāt Filisṭīn 'arabīyah" [The work of the fidā'iyīn is the model path for the restoration of Arab Palestine]. *al-Jumhūrīyah*, March 20, 11.

——. 1969b. "Fī badāyat mawsim Umm Kulthūm" [At the beginning of Umm Kulthūm's season]. *al-Jumhūrīyah*, November 28, 8.

——. 1969c. "Iḥtimām saḥafī 'ālamī bi badāyat mawsim Umm Kulthūm" [World press interest in the beginning of Umm Kulthūm's season]. *al-Jumhūrīyah*, December 6, 8.

——. 1969d. "Mafāja'āt fī ḥafl Umm Kulthūm al-thānī bi al-Sūdān" [Surprises in Umm Kulthūm's second concert in Sudan]. *al-Jumhūrīyah*, January 4, 8.

——. 1969e. "Sirr al-qur'ān fī ḥayāt Umm Kulthūm" [Secret of the Qur'an in Umm Kulthūm's life]. *al-Jumhūrīyah*, January 31, 5.

——. 1969f. "3/4 milyūn ginīh īrād haflāt Umm Kulthūm fī Lībiyā yukhassis li munatḥtḥamat Fatḥ" [£E 3/4 million proceeds of Umm Kulthūm's concerts in Libya designated for Fatah]. *al-Jumhūrīyah*, March 10, 5.

——. 1969g. "3 ḥaflāt shahrīyan li Umm Kulthūm fī al-mawsim al-jadīd" [Umm Kulthūm's three monthly concerts in the new season]. *al-Jumhūrīyah*, June 26, 11.

——. 1969h. "Umm Kulthūm tughannī fī al-muḥāfatḥāt wa Lundun wa Bārīs wa Muntriyāl" [Umm Kulthūm sings in the provinces, London, Paris, and Montreal]. *al-Jumhūrīyah*, May 17, 8.

——. 1970. "Umm Kulthūm tabda' mawsimahā fī 7 yanāyir" [Umm Kulthūm starts her season January 7]. *al-Jumhūrīyah*, October 29, 10.

——. 1971a. "Umm Kulthūm taḥtall al-markaz al-awal fī Miṣr wa al-khārij" [Umm Kulthūm occupies first place in Egypt and abroad]. *al-Jumhūrīyah*, September 7, 6.

——. 1971b. "Wazīr al-Thaqāfah yaftataḥ mathaf Umm Kulthūm fī 'īd milādihā al-qādim" [Minister of Culture to open Umm Kulthūm museum on her next birthday]. *al-Jumhūrīyah*, July 31, 6.

Darwīsh, Ṣalāḥ, and Salāmah al-'Abbāsī. 1969. "Sha'b al-Gharbīyah tashar ma'a Umm Kulthūm ḥatā al-ṣabāḥ" [The people of al-Gharbīyah stay up with Umm Kulthūm until morning]. *al-Jumhūrīyah*, May 9, 7.

Darwīsh, Ṣalāḥ, and Muḥammad Nudānī. 1968. "al-Sūdān yastaqbil Umm Kulthūm istiqbāl ru'asā' al-duwal" [Sudan gives Umm Kulthūm an official state reception]. *al-Jumhūriyyah*, December 28, 7.

Davis, Ruth. 2003. "'New Sounds, Old Tunes': Tunisian Media Stars Reinterpret the *Ma'luf*." In *Mediterranean Mosaic*, ed. Goffredo Plastino, 121–41. London: Routledge.

"Da'wat Umm Kulthūm lil-ghinā' fī Lundun" [Invitation for Umm Kulthūm to sing in London]. 1967. *al-Dustūr*, November 12, 6.

Dawoud, Khaled. 1997. "Children of the Setback." *al-Ahram Weekly*, June 5, http://weekly.ahram.org.eg/archives/67-97/sup13.htm (accessed August 11, 2008).

Dāwud, 'Abd al-Salām. 1968. "Umm Kulthūm tuṣallī fī ashhar masjid fī Tūnis" [Umm Kulthūm prays in the most famous mosque in Tunisia]. *al-Akhbār*, June 7, 1.

——. 1969. "Akhbār al-nās" [The people's news]. *al-Akhbār*, February 9, 8.

"Dhikrayāt 'an Umm Kulthūm yarwīhā Sa'īd Farīhah" [Sa'īd Farīhah tells his memories of Umm Kulthūm]. 1975. *al-Anwār*, February 9, 1, 7.

Dirks, Anna Marie. "Annalog Blog Archive: Jabrin Taxi, 1." http://www.chillonia.org/blog/?p=171 (accessed July 16, 2007).

al-Disūqī, Muḥammad. 1978. "Umm Kulthūm." *al-Kawākib*, February 7, 55.

——. 1992. "Shams al-ghinā' 'ind al-aṣīl: Umm Kulthūm mātat marratayn; rūḥīyān yawm al-hazīmah, jasdīyān yawm al-raḥīl" [The Sun of Singing before sunset . . . Umm Kulthūm died twice: in spirit the day of the defeat, in body the day of her passing]. *al-Kifāḥ al-'arabī*, August 3, 45–46.

al-Disūqī, Muḥammad, and Ṣalāḥ Darwīsh. 1970a. "al-Mudhakkirāt al-khāṣṣah li Umm Kulthūm" [Umm Kulthūm's private memoirs]. *al-Jumhūrīyah*, January 1, 7.

——. 1970b. "Qiṣṣat ḥayāt Umm Kulthūm" [Umm Kulthūm's biography]. *al-Jumhūrīyah*, January 15, 7.

Doll, Susan M. 1998. *Understanding Elvis: Southern Roots vs. Star Image*. New York: Garland.

"Les 12 Reves." http://perso.wanadoo.fr.ihf/jarre/jarre_concerts_mega_concerts_les12reves.htm (accessed May 4, 2005).

Downes, Stephen C. 1996. "Szymanowski and Narcissism." *Journal of the Royal Musical Association* 121 (1): 58–81.

Dudley, Shannon. 2001. "Ray Holman and the Changing Role of the Steelband, 1957–72." *Latin American Music Review* 22 (2): 183–98.

——. 2008. *Music from behind the Bridge: Steelband Spirit and Politics in Trinidad and Tobago*. New York: Oxford University Press.

Dyer, Richard. 1998. *Stars*. London: BFI Publishing. First published 1979.

"Egyptian Court OKs Pyramid Party." 1999. *BBC News*, December 28, http://news.bbc.co.uk/1/hi/world/middle_east/580891.stm (accessed December 8, 2006).

"Egypt's Breath-taking Celebrations of the Seventh Millenium." 2000. *Egypt Magazine*, 20, http://www.sis.gov.eg/public/magazine/iss020e/html/mag04.htm (accessed May 12, 2003).

Eisenstein, Zillah. 2000. "Writing Bodies on the Nation for the Globe." In *Women, States, and Nationalism: At Home in the Nation?*, ed. Sita Ranchod-Nilsson and Mary Ann Tétrault, 35–53. London: Routledge.

Elliot, Anthony. 1999. *The Mourning of John Lennon*. Berkeley: University of California Press.

Erlich, Haggai. 1989. *Students and University in Twentieth Century Egyptian Politics*. London: Frank Cass.

Euroarabe. 2006. "Was Om Kulthoum a Big Dyke?" September 6, http://www.euroarabe.com/2006/09/ (accessed December 1, 2006; subsequently redesigned).

F., Ch. 1968. "Oum Kalthoum a quitte le Maroc." *Le petit Marocain/Le progres marocain,* March 21, 3.

Fahmī, Tharwat. 1975. "Naḥnu jamī 'an ta'allamnā al-ghinā' fī madrasat Umm Kulthūm" [All of us learned in the school of Umm Kulthūm]. *Ākhir sā'ah*, February 12, 49.

Fairchild, Charles. 2007. "Building the Authentic Celebrity: The 'Idol' Phenomenon in the Attention Economy." *Popular Music and Society* 30 (3): 355–75.

al-Falasteenyia. 2006. "Oum Kalthoum and the Liberation of Palestine." November 29, http://alfalasteenyia.blogspot.com/2006/11/oum-kalthoum-and-liberation-of.html (accessed June 20, 2009).

"al-Fannānah Umm Kulthūm taḥyī ūlá ḥaflātahā bi al-Sūdān wa tushayyid bi dawr al-sha'b azā' al-qaḍīyah al-'arabīyah" [The artist Umm Kulthūm gives the first of her concerts in Sudan and praises the role of the people in the pursuit of the Arab cause]. 1968. *al-Ra'ī al-'āmm*, December 27, 1.

"Fannānūnā qālū 'an Umm Kulthūm" [Our artists said about Umm Kulthūm]. 1975. *al-Idhā'ah wa al-talfazah*, February 15, 20.

Farag, Fatemah. 2000a. "Bitter-sweet Roots." *al-Ahram Weekly*, February 3, http://www.ahram.org.eg/weekly/2000/467/umm8.htm (accessed 27 May 2000).

———. 2000b. "The Heritage of Sound." *al-Ahram Weekly*, February 3, http://www.ahram.org.eg/weekly/2000/467/umm4.htm (accessed May 27, 2000).

———. 2000c. "Until the Very End." *al-Ahram Weekly*, February 3, http://www.ahram.org.eg.weekly/2000/467/umm7.htm (accessed 27 May 2000).

Farghalá, Sayyid. 1967. "Yā arḍ yā masjūnah sijnuki raḥa yazūl" [Oh captive land, your imprisonment begins to come to an end]. *al-Kawākib*, June 6, 4–5.

———. 1969. "Umm Kulthūm tughannī 'alá masraḥ al-tārīkh" [Umm Kulthūm sings on the stage of history]. *al-Kawākib*, June 24, 2–5.

———. 1970. "Umm Kulthūm allatī tanqul nabḍ Miṣr ilá Mūskū" [Umm Kulthūm takes the pulse of Egypt to Moscow]. *al-Kawākib*, September 14 (*Dār al-Hilāl* clippings file 65).

"Farḥat al-jamāhīr wa hiya tushāhid tasāqaṭ ṭā'irāt al-'udwān" [The public's joy upon seeing the downing of the enemy's planes]. 1967. *Ākhir sā'ah*, June 7, 49.

Farid, Abdel Majid. 1994. *Nasser: The Final Years*. Reading (UK): Ithaca Press.

al Faruqi, Lois Ibsen. 1985. "Music, Musicians, and Muslim Law." *Asian Music* 17 (1): 3–36.

Fawaz, Leila. 1998. "Swimming against the Tide: Personal Passions and Academic Fashion," *Middle East Studies Association Bulletin* 32 (1): 2–10.

Fay, Mary Ann. 2001a. Introduction to *Auto/Biography and the Construction of Identity and Community in the Middle East*, ed. Mary Ann Fay, 1–8. New York: Palgrave.

———. 2001b. Shawikar Qadin: Woman of Power and Influence in Ottoman Cairo. In *Auto/Biography and the Construction of Identity and Community in the Middle East*, ed. Mary Ann Fay, 95–108. New York: Palgrave.

Feiler, Gil. 2003. *Economic Relations between Egypt and the Gulf Oil States, 1967–2000: Petro Wealth and Patterns of Influence*. Sussex: Academic Press.

Fishkoff, Sue. 1996. "Diva Redux." *Jerusalem Post*, July 12, 8.

"Flood Waters Breach High Ground." 1968. *Minerva* 7 (1–2): 268–79.

Frishkopf, Michael. 2003. "Some Meanings of the Spanish Tinge in Contemporary Egyptian Music." In *Mediterranean Mosaic*, ed. Goffredo Plastino, 143–77. London: Routledge.

Frontani, Michael R. 2007. *The Beatles: Image and the Media*. Jackson: University Press of Mississippi.

Fu'ād, Ni'māt Aḥmad. 1975. "Umm Kulthūm wa Umm Ḥūrus wa īzīs!" [Umm Kulthūm, the mother of Horus, and Isis] *al-Idhā'ah wa al-tilīfizyūn*, February 8, 19.

——. 2000. *Umm Kulthūm wa aṣr min al-fann* [Umm Kulthūm and an era of art]. Cairo: Dār al-Hilāl. First published 1976 by al-Hay'ah al-Miṣrīyah al-'Ammah lil-Kitāb.

Fu'ād, Sakīnah. 1967. "al-Sayyidah al-'aṭhīmah tataḥaddathu 'an" [The great lady talks about . . .]. *al-Idhā'ah wa al-tilīfizyūn*, December 9, 5.

——. 1968. "Umm Kulthūm fī mufakkirat 5 mudhī'āt" [Umm Kulthūm in the notebook of five broadcasters]. *al-Idhā'ah wa al-tilīfizyūn*, June 29, 5–9 (*Dār al-Hilāl* clippings file 65).

Gale, Maggie B., and Viv Gardner, eds. 2004. *Auto/biography and Identity: Women, Theatre, and Performance*. New York: Manchester University Press.

Gartner, Scott. 1990. "The Corporeal Imagination: The Body as the Medium of Expression and Understanding in Architecture." In *The Architecture of the In-Between: The Proceedings of the 1990 ACSA Annual Conference*, 83–89. San Francisco: ACSA Press.

"Ghadan yaqūl al-sha'b kalimatahu 'Na'm'" [Tomorrow the people speak their word "Yes"]. 1968. *Ākhir sā'ah*, May 1, 1.

Gharībah, Muḥammad Aḥmad. 1968. "Yā Fataḥ" [Oh Fataḥ]. *Ākhir sā'ah*, March 27, 45.

Giammusso, Maurizio. 2004. "Teatro: Elisabetta Pozzi interpreta la Callas d'Egitto/Ansa; Uno spettacolo dedicato ad una gloria Araba, Umm Khultum." Notiziario Generale in Italiano, May 12.

Gier, Christina. 2008. "Gender, Politics, and the Fighting Soldier's Song in America during World War I." *Music & Politics* 2 (1): 1–20.

Gledhill, Christine. 1991. "Signs of Melodrama." In *Stardom: Industry of Desire*, ed. Chrstine Gledhill. London: Routledge.

Goldenberg, Suzanne. 2003. "Email from Baghdad." *Guardian Newspapers*, March 9, http://www.buzzle.com/editorials/3-9-2003-36990.asp (accessed May 5, 2005).

Goldman, Albert. 1988. *The Lives of John Lennon*. New York: William Morrow.

Golley, Nawar al-Hassan. 2003. *Reading Arab Women's Autobiographies: Shahrazad Tells Her Story*. Austin: University of Texas Press.

Golley, Nawar al-Hassan, ed. 2007. *Arab Women's Lives Retold: Exploring Identity through Writing*. Syracuse, NY: Syracuse University Press.

Gordon, Joel. 2003. "Singing the Pulse of the Egyptian-Arab Street: Shaaban Abd al-Rahim and the Geo-pop-politics of Fast Food." *Popular Music* 22 (1): 73–88.

de Groot, Rokus. 2005. "Perspectives of Polyphony in Edward Said's Writing." *Alif: Journal of Comparative Poetics* 25: 219–42.

Guindi, Maurice. 1998. "My Darling, My Song-bird." *al-Ahram Weekly*, December 24, http://www.ahram.org.eg/weekly/1998/409/fe2.htm (accessed May 27, 2000).

Guindy, Hosny, and Hani Shukrallah. 2000. "Liberating Nasser's Legacy." *al-Ahram Weekly*, September 28, http://weekly.ahram.org.eg/2000/501/nasser2.htm (accessed July 7, 2008).

Habib, Nadia. 1995. "Umm Kulthum wa bint al-balad (Umm Kulthum and a Daughter of the Country): Narratives of Identity, Location, and Displacements." Master's thesis, York University.

Ḥāfiṭh, Abū al-Ḥajjāj. 1973. "Umm Kulthūm fī zayārat Dār al-Taḥrīr" [Umm Kulthūm in her visit to Dār al-Taḥrīr]. *al-Jumhūrīyah*, June 18, 3.

"Hal kāna Isrā'īlīyan?" [Was he an Israeli?]. 1967. *al-Jumhūrīyah*, December 15, 10.

Halasa, Malu. 2003. "Out of the Shadows." *Guardian*, March 29, http://www.guardian.co.uk/artanddesign/2003/mar/29/art.iraqandthearts (accessed June 20, 2009).

el-Hamamsy, Laila Shukry. 1975. "The Assertion of Egyptian Identity." In *Ethnic Identity: Cultural Continuities and Change*, ed. George de Vos and Lola Romanucci-Ross, 276–306. Palo Alto: Mayfield Publishing.

Hammond, Andrew. 1999. "The Eternal Lady." *Cairo Times*, March 4, http://www.cairotimes.com (accessed November 28, 2003).

———. 2007. *Popular Culture in the Arab World: Arts, Politics, and the Media*. Cairo: American University in Cairo Press.

Hampton, Wayne. 1986. *Guerrilla Minstrels: John Lennon, Joe Hill, Woody Guthrie, and Bob Dylan*. Knoxville: University of Tennessee Press.

Hassan, Azza. 2003. "The Next Big Thing? With Approval from on High and Songs about Palestine, Amal Maher Just May Go Far." *Cairo Times*, February 6, 27.

Ḥassanayn, 'Ādil. 1998. *Umm Kulthūm: Sīrat al-ḥubb* [Umm Kulthum: Story of love]. Cairo: Amādū.

Hatchett, Louis, and W. K. McNeil. 2005. "'There's a Star Spangled Banner Waving Somewhere': The Story behind Its Success." In *Country Music Goes to War*, ed. Charles K. Wolfe and James E. Akenson, 33–42.

Hatina, Meir. 2004. "History, Politics, and Collective Memory: The Nasserist Legacy in Mubarak's Egypt." In *Rethinking Nasserism: Revolution and Historical Memory in Modern Egypt*, ed. Elie Podeh and Onn Winckler, 100–125. Gainesville, FL: University Press of Florida.

Hawkins, Stan, and John Richardson. 2007. "Remodeling Britney Spears: Matters of Intoxication and Mediation." *Popular Music and Society* 30 (5): 605–29.

"Ḥayāt Umm Kulthūm: Awwal aflām hādhā al-'ām" [Life of Umm Kulthūm: First of this year's films]. 1970. *al-Akhbār*, July 25, 13.

Helm, Sarah. 1994. "Jews Get in Tune with the Arabs." *Independent* (London), October 2, 16.

Ḥījāzī, Ibrāhīm. 2001. "Khārij dā'irat al-ḍaw'" [Beyond the lights]. *al-Ahrām*, July 13, http://www.ahram.org.eg/archive/Index.asp (accessed November 19, 2003).

Ḥijāzī, Muḥammad. 1969. "Akthar min fikrah" [More than an idea]. *al-Idhā'ah wa al-tilīfizyūn*, August 16, 2.

Hinnebusch, Jr., Raymond A. 1985. *Egyptian Politics under Sadat: The Post-Populist Development of an Authoritarian-Modernizing State*. Cambridge: Cambridge University Press.

al-Ḥiwān, Muḥammad. 1970. "Yawm al-arbi'ā' tughannī Umm Kulthūm fī Mūskū" [Wednesday Umm Kulthūm sings in Moscow]. *al-Jumhūrīyah*, September 25, 6.

——. 1971. "Umm Kulthūm wa 2 milyūn ginīh" [Umm Kulthūm and £E 2 million]. *al-Jumhūrīyah*, January 6, 10.

"Hiya tughannī fī Tūnis lī awwal marrah" [She sings in Tunis for the first time]. 1964. *al-Kawākib*, December 15 (*Dār al-Hilāl* clippings file 65).

Hollander, Edwin. 1958. "Conformity, Status, and Idiosyncrasy Credit." *Psychological Review* 65 (2): 117–27.

Horowitz, Amy. 2005. "Dueling Nativities: Zehava Ben Sings Umm Kulthum." In *Palestine, Israel, and the Politics of Popular Culture*, ed. Rebecca L. Stein and Ted Swedenburg, 202–30. Durham: Duke University Press.

"Hujūm 'alá Umm Kulthūm" [Attack on Umm Kulthūm]. 1967. Middle East News Agency. November 18 (*al-Ahrām* clippings file 110).

Hunsberger, Alice C. 2000. *Nasir Khusraw, the Ruby of Badakhshan: A Portrait of the Persian Poet, Traveller, and Philosopher*. London: Tauris.

Hussein, Mahmoud. 1977. *Class Conflict in Egypt: 1945–1970*. Translated by Michel and Susanne Chirman, et al. New York: Monthly Review Press.

Ibrāhīm, Fārūq. 1967. "'Indamā khāṭibat Umm Kulthūm al-jamāhīr" [When Umm Kulthūm spoke to the masses]. *Ākhir sā'ah*, December 20, 10.

Ibrāhīm, Ibrāhīm Mūsá. 1975. "Qīthārat al-Samā' wa al-kawkab alladhī mā saṭa'a mithalu Umm Kulthūm" [The Lyre of Heaven and the unmatched star Umm Kulthūm]. *al-Anbā'* (Jerusalem), February 21, 6.

al-Idhā'ah wa al-talfazah. 1975. February 15, 5.

al-Idhā'ah wa al-tilīfizyūn. 1967. August 5, 11.

"Idhā'at Faransā saharat ma'a Umm Kulthūm ḥatā al-ṣabāḥ [Radio France stays up with Umm Kulthūm until morning]. 1967. *al-Jumhūrīyah*, November 17, 3.

"In Front of Pyramids, Jarre Amazes the World!" http://mitglied.lycos.de/espacejarre/12reves.html (accessed May 12, 2003).

Inglis, Ian. 1996. "Ideology, Trajectory, and Stardom: Elvis Presley and the Beatles." *International Review of the Aesthetics and Sociology of Music* 27 (1): 53–78.

Inhorn, Marcia C. 1996. *Infertility and Patriarchy: The Cultural Politics of Gender and Family Life in Egypt*. Philadelphia: University of Pennsylvania Press.

"al-'Irāq wa Umm Kulthūm" [Iraq and Umm Kulthūm]. 1970. *al-Akhbār*, May 6, 10.

'Iṣmat, Nabīl. 1968a. "Ba'd ghiyāb 18 shahran ta'ūd Umm Kulthūm al-laylah li taltaqī bi jumhūrihā fī ḥaflah ʿāmmah" [After an absence of eighteen months Umm Kulthūm returns tonight to meet her public in a general concert]. *al-Akhbār*, December 5, 5.

———. 1968b. "Mā alladhī faʿalat Umm Kulthūm fī al-Kuwayt wa fī al-Khalīj al-ʿArab bi usarihā?" [What was it that Umm Kulthūm did in Kuwait and the Arab Gulf with its people?]. *al-Akhbār*, May 5, 8.

———. 1968c. "Maʿa Umm Kulthūm fī al-Kuwayt" [With Umm Kulthūm in Kuwait]. *al-Akhbār*, April 23, 8.

———. 1968d. "60 kilu dhahab wa 53 alf ginīh min al-Kuwayt lil-majhūd al-ḥarbī" [60 kilograms of gold and £53,000 from Kuwait for the war effort]. *al-Akhbār*, May 6, 8.

———. 1969. "'Alf Laylah wa Laylah' fī 20 yawm faqaṭ" ["1001 Nights" in just twenty days]. *al-Akhbār*, February 6, 5.

———. 1971. "'al-Qalb Yaʿshaq Kull Jamīl' allatī tughannīhā Umm Kulthūm al-laylah maqāmuhā bayyātī ʿalá darajat al-hussaynī" ["al-Qalb Yaʿshaq Kull Jamīl" that Umm Kulthūm sings tonight: its mode is bayyātī on hussaynī], *al-Akhbār*, February 4, 1971, 8.

ʿIṣmat, Nabīl, and Samīr Tawfīq. 1968a. "al-Kuwayt tashar laylat al-ʿamr maʿa Umm Kulthūm" [Kuwait spends the night of its life with Umm Kulthūm]. *al-Akhbār*, April 26, 11.

———. 1968b. "Qabl rafaʿa al-sitār bi laḥatḥāt wāfaqat Umm Kulthūm ʿalá idhāʿat al-ḥaflah" [Moments before the curtain rose, Umm Kulthūm agreed to broadcast the concert]. *al-Akhbār*, April 27, 13.

"Istaqbalathā al-ʿawāṣim kamā al-zuʿamā'" [The Arab capitals received her as they did political leaders]. 1988. *al-Anbā'*, February 7 (Umm Kulthūm Museum Library vol. 9, 159).

Jacquemond, Richard. 1997. "Egypt's Intellectuals Rediscover Nasser." *Le Monde diplomatique*, July, http://mondediplo.com/1997/07/egypt (accessed April 4, 2008).

Jādū, Muḥammad Ṣadīq. 1967. *al-Idhāʿah wa al-tilīfizyūn*, March 25, 2.

Jalāl, Muḥammad. 1967. "'Alāmat istifhām" [Question mark]. *al-Idhāʿah wa al-tilīfizyūn*, July 1, 24

———. 1968. "'Alāmat istifhām" [Question mark]. *al-Idhāʿah wa al-tilīfizyūn*, June 1, 58.

al-Jawādī, ʿAbd al-Karīm ʿAbd al-ʿAzīz. 1985. *Umm Kulthūm Sayyidat al-Ghinā' al-ʿArabī: Ḥayātuhā wa aghānīhā* [Umm Kulthum, the Lady of Arabic Song: Her life and her songs]. Baghdad: Maṭbaʿat Ishbilīyah al-Ḥadīthah.

Jawdat, Ṣāliḥ. 1967. "Thalāth ḥikāyāt" [Three stories]. *al-Kawākib*, June 27, 8–9.

———. 1968. "Hal tughannī Umm Kulthūm li hādhā al-shāʿir?" [Will Umm Kulthūm sing for this poet?]. *al-Muṣawwar*, June 28, 24.

———. 1970. "Ghannī yā Umm Kulthūm" [Sing Umm Kulthūm]. *al-Muṣawwar*, October 30, 41.

Jelinek, Estelle C., ed. 1980. *Women's Autobiography: Essays in Criticism*. Bloomington: Indiana University Press.

Jighām, Ṣāliḥ. 1975a. "Ḥafl arbaʿīnat Umm Kulthūm" [Celebration of the forty days after the passing of Umm Kulthūm]. *al-Idhāʿah wa al-talfazah*, April 1, 26–27.
———. 1975b. "Mātat Umm Kulthūm wa māta maʿahā yawm al-khamīs" [Umm Kulthūm died and Thursday died with her], *al-Idhāʿah wa al-talfazah*, February 15, 10, 16.
Johnson, Fred. 2004. "U2, Mythology, and Mass-Mediated Survival." *Popular Music and Society* 27 (1): 79–99.
Jones, John Bush. 2006. *The Songs That Fought the War: Popular Music and the Home Front, 1939–1945*. Waltham, MA: Brandeis University Press.
Jumjūm, Salwá. 1981. "Saʿdīyah: Hal hiya ibnat Umm Kulthūm?" [Saʿdīyah: Is she Umm Kulthūm's daughter?]. *al-Kawākib*, February 3, 46.
———. 1983. "al-Khayr fī ḥayāt Umm Kulthūm" [Charity in the life of Umm Kulthūm]. *al-Kawākib*, February 1, 42.
"Kānat fī khilāf maʿa Jīhān al-Sādāt" [She was in a dispute with Jīhān al-Sādāt]. 1975. *al-Idhāʿah wa al-talfazah*, February 15, 20.
Kanovsky, Eliyahu. 1970. *The Economic Impact of the Six-Day War*. New York: Praeger.
Karīm, Sāmiḥ. 1969a. "Aʿṭham wadāʿ li aʿṭham ziyārah fannīyah" [Greatest farewell for the greatest artistic visit]. *al-Idhāʿah wa al-tilīfizyūn*, January 11, 27.
———. 1969b. "ʿIndamā tughannī Ifrīqiyā bi lughah wāhidah" [When Africa sings with one language]. *al-Idhāʿah wa al-tilīfizyūn*, January 4, 16–17.
Kashak, Jalāl. 1975. "Widāʿan Sitt al-Kull" [Farewell, Lady of Them All]. *al-Anwār*, February 5, 8.
al-Kassim, Dina. 2008. "Sexual Epistemologies, East in West." In *Islamicate Sexualities: Translations across Temporal Geographies of Desire*, ed. Kathryn Babayan and Afsaneh Najmabadi, 297–340. Cambridge: Harvard University Press.
Kasson, Joy S. 2000. *Buffalo Bill's Wild West: Celebrity, Memory, and Popular History*. New York: Hill and Wang.
"Kayf yastaʿad al-Sūdān li istiqbāl Umm Kulthūm wa al-istimāʿ ilayhā?" [How does Sudan prepare to receive Umm Kulthūm and listen to her?]. 1968. *al-Jumhūrīyah*, December 19, 11.
Kenton, Egon. 1967. *Life and Works of Giovanni Gabrieli*. N.p.: American Institute of Musicology.
Khalidi, Ahmed S. 1973. "The War of Attrition." *Journal of Palestine Studies* 3 (1): 60–87.
Khalīl, ʿAbd al-Nūr. 1967. "Maʿa Umm Kulthūm fī Bārīs" [With Umm Kulthūm in Paris]. *al-Kawākib*, November 21, 6–8.
———. 1992. *Rijāl fī ḥayāt Umm Kulthūm* [Men in the life of Umm Kulthum]. Cairo: Maṭābiʿ Rūz al-Yūsuf al-Jadīdah.
Khalil, Nevine. 1999. "Celebrating a Galaxy of Stars" *al-Ahram Weekly*, June 10, http://weekly.ahram.org.eg/1999/433/eg3.htm (accessed June 4, 2003).
al-Khalīsī, ʿAbd al-Ruʾūf. 1968. "Fī ʿīdinā al-khālid Umm Kulthūm tughannī laylat al-fann al-khālid [On our eternal holiday Umm Kulthūm sings a night of eternal art]. *al-Idhāʿah wa al-talfazah*, June 15, 20–23, 58.

"15 alf dīnār īrād ḥafl Umm Kulthūm al-laylah fī al-Kuwayt" [15,000 Kuwaiti dinars—proceeds of Umm Kulthūm's concert tonight in Kuwait]. 1968. *al-Jumhūrīyah*, April 25, 12.

al-Khatābī, Muḥammad al-ʻAhlī. 1968. "Fiʻl al-qadrah al-drāmīyah ʻind Umm Kulthūm" [Impact of the dramatic power of Umm Kulthūm]. *al-ʻAlam* (Rabat), March 18. Reprinted in al-Marīnī 1975, 162–63.

al-Khaṭṭīb, Muḥammad ʻAdnān. 1975. *Umm Kulthūm muʻjizat al-ghinā' al-ʻarabī: Ḥayātuhā, mudhakkirātuhā, kifāḥuhā* [Umm Kulthūm, the miracle of Arabic song: Her life, her memoirs, and her struggle]. Damascus: N.p.

al-Khūrī, Jūrj Ibrāhīm. [1971]. "al-Haramayn: Umm Kulthūm wa Muḥammad ʻAbd al-Wahhāb" [The two pyramids: Umm Kulthūm and Muḥammad ʻAbd al-Wahhāb]. Undated supplement to *al-Shabakah*, 32–33.

———. 2000. *Ḥakāyatī maʻa Umm Kulthūm* [My stories with Umm Kulthum]. Beirut: Jarrus Press.

Kimche, David, and Dan Bawly. 1968. *The Sandstorm: The Arab-Israeli War of June 1967: Prelude and Aftermath.* New York: Stein and Day.

Kingsbury, Henry. 1988. *Music, Talent, and Performance: A Conservatory Cultural System*. Philadelphia: Temple University Press.

Kirshenblatt-Gimblett, Barbara. 1995. "Theorizing Heritage." *Ethnomusicology* 39 (3): 367–80.

Knittel, Kristen M. 1998. "Wagner, Deafness, and the Reception of Beethoven's Late Style." *Journal of the American Musicological Society* 51 (1): 49–82.

Kramer, Martin, ed. 1991. *Middle Eastern Lives: The Practice of Biography and Self-Narrative*. Syracuse, NY: Syracuse University Press.

"Kull bins aw sint yuʻtā li-Isrā'īl yumkinū taḥwīl ilá raṣāṣah li-qatl ʻArabī" ["Every penny given to Israel can be transformed into a bullet to kill an Arab]. 1967. *al-Jumhūrīyah*, November 10, 7.

al-Kurdī, Fāyiz. 1975. "Kalimat rithā' ilá rūḥ Umm Kulthūm" [Elegiac words for the spirit of Umm Kulthūm]. *al-Anbā'*, February 14, 6.

Labīb, Fūwmīl. 1967a. "Aḍwā al-madīnah min ajl al-musharradīn wa al-ḍaḥāyā" [City lights for the sake of the refugees and victims]. *al-Kawākib*, July 25, 10–11.

———. 1967b. "Kalimat ḥaqq: Ayn ʻAbd al-Wahhāb wa Farīd al-Aṭrāsh?" [A word of truth: Where are ʻAbd al-Wahhāb and Farīd al-Aṭrāsh?]. *al-Kawākib*, June 27, 12–13.

———. 1967c. "Umm Kulthūm min Ṭammāy al-Zahāyrah ilá Bārīs" [Umm Kulthūm from Ṭammāy al-Zahāyrah to Paris]. *al-Kawākib*, November 14, 5–9.

———. 1973. "Thalāth waṣlāt maʻa Umm Kulthūm" [Three suites with Umm Kulthūm]. *al-Muṣawwar*, March 16, 5.

———. 1975. "Ākhir ḥadīth li qīthārat al-samā'" [Last interview with the Lyre of Heaven]. *al-Muṣawwar*, February 7, 2.

Lacouture, Jean. 1973. *Nasser: A Biography*. Translated by Daniel Hofstadter. New York: Knopf.

Lake, Ed. 2008. "Diva Inspiration." *The National*, November 22, http://www.thenational.ae/article/20081122/ART/901916733/1007 (accessed June 20, 2009).

"Lamaḥāt min ḥayāt Sayyidat al-Ghinā' al-'Arabī Umm Kulthūm" [Glimpses of the life of the Lady of Singing Umm Kulthūm]. 1975. *al-Ayyām*, February 2, 12.

Lambert, Tom. 1967. "Nasser Reign Ended, Political Experts Say." *Los Angeles Times*, June 10, 15.

Lanier, Daniel. 2001. "Bus Stop Sharm el-Sheikh." *Tour Egypt Monthly* 2 (5), http://egyptmonth.com/mag05012001/mag11.htm (accessed September 23, 2006).

"Laqaṭāt" [Snapshots]. 1968. *al-Idhā'ah wa al-tilīfizyūn*, April 27, 65.

Larbi, L. 1968. "5,000 spectateurs ont "vécu" Oum Kalthoum." *La presse de Tunisie*, June 2, 7.

"Laylat ḥubb sama'hā Abū al-Hawl wa ibtisama lihā al-qamar" [A night of love that the Sphinx listened to and the moon smiled upon]. 1969. *al-Akhbār*, June 21, 13.

al-Laythī, Sāmī. 1952. "Qiṣṣat al-mawsim" [The story of the season]. *Rūz al-Yūsuf*, March 24, 34.

"Life and Songs of Om Kalthoum." 1975. *Kuwait Times*, February 5, 4.

"Li mādhā manaḥat Bākistān Umm Kulthūm Wisām al-Imtiyāz?" [Why did Pakistan award Umm Kulthum the Order of Excellence?] 1968. *al-Jumhūrīyah*, March 20, 10.

Lowe, Melanie. 2003. "Colliding Feminisms: Britney Spears, 'Tweens,' and the Politics of Reception." *Popular Music and Society* 26 (2): 123–40.

"Ma'a fannānat al-sha'b fī al-liqā' al-thānnī min ajl al-'ushsh al-akbar" [With the Artist of the People in the second encounter for the sake of the biggest gift]. 1967. *al-Jumhūrīyah*, September 2, 6.

"Ma'a lajnat al-fannānīn li jam' tabarru'āt al-dhahab" [With the committee of artists for the collection of gold donations]. 1967. *al-Akhbār*, July 19, 8.

"Mādhā tamma min yunyū 1967 ilá yunyū 1968?" [What was completed from June 1967 to June 1968?]. 1968. *al-Idhā'ah wa al-tilīfizyūn*, June 1, 1.

al-Maḥallāwī, Ḥanafī. 1994. *Sayyidatān min Miṣr: Umm Kulthūm wa Jīhān* [Two women of Egypt: Umm Kulthūm and Jīhān]. Cairo: Dār al-Shabāb al-'Arabī.

———. 1999a. *Umm Kulthūm: al-Ḥubb al-zawāj al-aṣdiqā'* [Umm Kulthum: Love, marriage, friends]. Cairo: Nahdat Miṣr lil-Ṭibā'ah wa al-Nashr wa al-Tawzī'.

———. 1999b. *Umm Kulthūm wa khamsūn sanat siyāsah* [Umm Kulthūm and fifty years of politics]. Cairo: al-Dār al-Miṣrīyah al-Lubnānīyah.

al-Maḥdī, Ṣāliḥ. 1993. *al-Mūsīqā al-'Arabīyah: Maqāmāt wa dirāsāt* [Arabic music: modes and studies]. Beirut: Dār al-Gharb al-Islāmī.

Mahfoudh, Mohamed. 1975. "Oum Kalthoum n'est plus." *La presse de Tunisie*, February 3, 1.

Maḥfūẓ, Najīb. 1989. *Midaq Alley*. Translated by Trevor Le Gassick. 2nd ed. Washington, D.C.: Three Continents Press.

Māhir, Aḥmad. 1971a. "70 alf ginīh li fīlm Umm Kulthūm" [£E 70,000 for Umm Kulthūm's film]. *al-Jumhūrīyah*, April 24, 7.

———. 1971b. "Umm Kulthūm tabda' mawsimahā bi shi'r al-Fayṣal" [Umm Kulthūm starts her season with Faysal's poetry]. *al-Jumhūrīyah*, December 11, 8.

———. 1971c. "Umm Kulthūm tughannī fī Abū Ṭhābī" [Umm Kulthūm sings in Abu Dhabi]. *al-Jumhūrīyah*, December 1, 10.

Maḥmūd, Sayyid. 2003. "Fī dhikrayātihā: al-Qur'ān awwal mudarris wa Ṭaha Ḥussayn afḍal kātib" [In her memoirs: The Qur'ān is my first teacher and Ṭaha Ḥ ussayn is my favorite writer]. *al-Ahrām al-riyāḍī*, February 12, 43 (*Dār al-Hilāl* clippings file 65).

Maḥsab, Ḥasan. 1969a. "Awwal fīlm ghanā'ī mulawwan 'an ḥayāt Fanānat al-Sha'b" [First color vocal film on the life of the Artist of the People]. *al-Idhā'ah wa al-tilīfizyūn*, May 24, 10–12.

——. 1969b. "Ḥadīth al-ḥubb fī riḥāb al-Sayyid al-Badawī" [Talk about love in the sacred precinct of al-Sayyid al-Badawī]. *al-Idhā'ah wa al-tilīfizyūn*, May 17, 24, 26.

——. 1969c. "Umm Kulthūm kamā yarāhā kātib shāb" [Umm Kulthūm as a young writer sees her]. *al-Idhā'ah wa al-tilīfizyūn*, August 16, 20.

al-Makāwī, Muḥammad. 2003. "'Wa Allāhi Zamān Yā Silāḥī'" ["It's Been a Long Time, Oh Weapon of Mine"]. *al-Kawākib*, April 1, 9–10.

Makdisi, Jean Said. 2006. *Teta, Mother, and Me: Three Generations of Arab Women*. New York: W. W. Norton.

Mäkelä, Janne. 2004. *John Lennon Imagined: Cultural History of a Rock Star*. New York: Peter Lang.

al-Malākh, Kamāl. 1966. "3 naṣā'iḥ min Umm Kulthūm ilá al-qāri'āt" [Three pieces of advice from Umm Kulthūm to Qur'an reciters]. *al-Ahrām*, December 9, 8.

——. 1967a. "5 ālāf ginīh min 'Abd al-Wahhāb wa majmū'ah min ḥila Nahlah lil-majhūd al-ḥarbī" [£E 5,000 from 'Abd al-Wahhāb and a collection of Nahlah's jewelry for the war effort]. *al-Ahrām*, July 15, 8.

——. 1967b. "Lil-marrah al-thānīyah tuqaddim Umm Kulthūm 16 kīlūjrām dhahab" [For the second time Umm Kulthūm presents sixteen kilograms of gold]. *al-Ahrām*, August 4, 8.

——. 1967c. "Shīk bi 20 alf ginīh istarlīnī min Umm Kulthūm" [Umm Kulthūm presented a check for £20,000]. *al-Ahrām*, June 20, 8.

——. 1967d. "Umm Kulthūm: tataghannā bi-'awdat al-rūḥ wa quwwat al-īmān" [Umm Kulthūm sings for the return of spirit and strength of belief]. *al-Ahrām*, July 6, 8.

——. 1967e. "Umm Kulthūm tataḥaddath ilá al-mar'ah al-'āmilah thumma ilá rabbāt al-buyūt" [Umm Kulthūm talks to working women and then to housewives]. *al-Ahrām*, July 21, 8.

——. 1967f. "Umm Kulthūm tubī' muntajāt al-tajammu' fī maṭār al-Qāhirah" [Umm Kulthūm sells products of the assembly in Cairo airport]. *al-Ahrām*, September 27, 8.

——. 1967g. "Umm Kulthūm tusallim 2,000 ginīh al-dhahab ilá al-bank" [Umm Kulthūm presents £2,000 in gold to the bank]. *al-Ahrām*, July 18, 8.

——. 1985. "Kayf ashhar umm ghannat amām ashhar ab fī sharqinā al-awṣat" [How the most famous mother sang in front of the most famous father in our Middle East]. *al-Ahrām*, January 31 (*Dār al-Hilāl* clippings file 65).

Maland, Charles J. 1989. *Chaplin and American Culture: The Evolution of a Star Image*. Princeton, NJ: Princeton University Press.

"Māmā Thūmah." 2000. *Nisf al-dunyā*, February 6, 106–11.

"Manḥ Umm Kulthūm jā'izat al-dawlah al-taqdīrīyah" [Awarding of state award to Umm Kulthūm]. 1968. *al-Jumhūrīyah*, February 14, 1.

al-Manṣūrī, Fu'ād. 1998. "'Abqarīyat al-Sitt" [The lady's genius]. *al-Kawākib*, February 3, 10–14.

"Maria Angers Umm Kalthoum's Heirs." 2007. *Yallabina*, March 14, http://www.yallabina.com/Music/Local/mariakalthoum.aspx (accessed March 25, 2007).

"Maria Vows Never to Seduce." 2007. *Albawaba*, March 15, http://www.albawaba.com/en/entertainment/210877 (accessed June 3, 2007).

al-Marīnī, Abū Bakr. 1975. *Umm Kulthūm: Mu'jizat al-qarn al-'ishrīn fī 'alam al-nagham wa al-talḥīn* [Umm Kulthūm: Miracle of the twentieth century in the world of melody and composition]. Casablanca: Dār al-Sulaymī Aḥmad lil-Ta'līf wa al-Tarjamah wa al- Ṭibā'ah wa al-Tawzī'.

Marsot, Afaf Lutfi al-Sayyid. 2002. "An Egyptian Childhood." In *Remembering Childhood in the Middle East: Memoirs from a Century of Change*, ed. Elizabeth Warnock Fernea, 100–111. Austin: University of Texas Press.

"Mashrū' Umm Kulthūm lil-salām" [Umm Kulthūm's project for peace]. 1970. *Sabāḥ al-Khayr*, April 30 (Umm Kulthūm Museum Library vol. 5, 88).

"Masraḥ kabīr yaḥmil ism Umm Kulthūm" [A large theater carries Umm Kulthūm's name]. 1975. *al-Akhbār*, February 6, 6.

Massad, Joseph. 2007. *Desiring Arabs*. Chicago: University of Chicago Press.

Maṭar, Sayyid Mīhūb. 1967. "Umm Kulthūm fī al-ma'rakah" [Umm Kulthūm in the battle]. *al-Akhbār*, July 20, 8.

"Mātat al-shādīyah al-miṣrīyah Umm Kulthūm" [The Egyptian singer Umm Kulthūm died]. 1975. *al-Hudá*, February 7, 4.

"Mātat Umm Kulthūm" [Umm Kulthūm died]. 1975. *al-Ayyām*, February 4, 12.

McLeese, Don. 2008. "Seeds Scattered by Katrina: The Dynamic of Disaster and Inspiration." *Popular Music and Society* 31 (2): 213–20.

Meital, Yoram. 2003. "Who Is Egypt's 'Hero of War and Peace'? The Contest over Representation." *History and Memory* 15 (1): 150–83.

Melligi, Tahar. 1975. "La Tunisie organisera des festivals sous le nom d'Oum Kalthoum." *La presse de Tunisie*, February 7, 3.

Mernissi, Fatima. 1988. *Doing Daily Battle: Interviews with Moroccan Women*. Translated by Mary Jo Lakeland. London: Women's Press.

Merton, Robert. 1946. *Mass Persuasion: The Social Psychology of a War Bond Drive*. New York: Long, Harper and Brothers.

Michael, Maggie. 2003. "Critics May Sneer, but Anti-War Song Strikes a Chord." *San Francisco Chronicle*, April 6, http://www.sfgate.com/cgi-bin/article.cgi?f=/news/archive/2003/04/06/international0149EDT0426.DTL (accessed April 8, 2003).

Miller, H. D. 2002. "Mother of Us All." *Travelling Shoes (The Zine)*, April 2, http://travellingshoe2.blogspot.com (accessed May 5, 2005).

"Min albūm Umm Kulthūm" [From Umm Kulthūm's album]. 1978. *al-Kawākib*, February 7, 12–19.

Moftah, Mohamed. 2002. "Language and Its Whims," *al-Ahram Weekly*, February

28, http://www.ahram.org.eg/weekly/2002/575/li1.htm (accessed October 17, 2002).
Moghadam, Valentine M. 2003. *Modernizing Women: Gender and Social Change in the Middle East*. 2nd ed. Boulder: Lynne Rienner.
Monaco, James. 1978. "Celebration." In *Celebrity: Who Gets It, How They Use It, Why It Works*, ed. James Monaco, 3–14. New York: Delta Books.
Monioudis, Perikles. N.d. *Land*. Translated by Melissa Woods Nelson, http://www.monioudis.de/Landengl.html (accessed April 20, 2005; site now discontinued).
Monson, Ingrid. 2007. *Freedom Sounds: Civil Rights Call Out to Jazz and Africa*. New York: Oxford University Press.
Morris, Joe Alex, Jr. 1967. "Angry Mobs March in Beirut and Cairo." *Los Angeles Times*, June 11, 1.
"La mosque d'el Menzah portera le nom d'Oum Kalthoum." 1975. *La presse de Tunisie*, February 6, 1.
"Mourning in Kuwait." 1975. *Kuwait Times*, February 5, 1.
Mubārak, Muḥammad Ḥusnī. 1995. Preface to *Oum Kalsoum*, by Ysabel Saïah, 6–7. Paris: Denoël.
al-Muhāmī, Muḥammad Rif'at. 1979. *Mudhakkirāt Aḥmad Rāmī wa qiṣṣat ḥubbihi li Umm Kulthūm: Asrār tudhā'u li-awwal marrah* [The memoirs of Aḥmad Rāmī and the story of his love for Umm Kulthūm: Secrets revealed for the first time]. Sayda/Beirut: Manshūrāt al-Maktabah al-'Aṣrīyah.
Muḥammad, Jalāl. 1991. *Ma'rakat marīḍ al-idz* [The struggle of the man sick with AIDS]. Cairo: Maktabat al-Nahḍah al-Miṣrīyah.
Muḥammad, Muḥassan. 1969. "Ma'a al-āthār al-qadīmah" [With the ancient monuments]. *al-Akhbār*, March 27, 12.
"al-Muḥāwalāt lā tazāl mustamirrah li inqādh sayyidat al-ghinā' al-'arabī" [Attempts still continuing to save the Lady of Arabic Song]. 1975. *al-Ittiḥād*, February 2, 8.
Munro, Alan. 2000. "Egypt: The Post-Nasser Revival," *Royal United Services Institute Journal* 145 (5): 66–72.
"Musalsalat thūmah" [The series "Thūmah"]. 1975. *al-Ayyām*, February 4, 12.
Muṣṭafá, Zakī. 1975. *Umm Kulthūm: Ma'bad al-ḥubb* [Umm Kulthūm: Temple of love]. Cairo: Dār al-Ṭibā'ah al-Ḥadīthah.
"Mu'tamar ṣaḥafī li Umm Kulthūm fī Bārīs" [Umm Kulthūm's press conference in Paris]. 1967. *al-Jumhūrīyah*, November 13, 3.
"Muṭhāhara fannīyah fī Wikālat al-Balaḥ" [An artistic demonstration in Bulaq]. 1967. *al-Kawākib*, August 1, 4–5.
Nahās, Jacqueline. 1970. "Ḥiwār hādi' ma'a Umm Kulthūm" [A quiet conversation with Umm Kulthūm]. *al-Ḥayāt*, July 9, 1, 7.
Najmabadi, Afsaneh. 2005. *Women with Mustaches and Men without Beards: Gender and Sexual Anxieties of Iranian Modernity*. Berkeley: University of California.
al-Najmī, Kamāl. 1992. *Muḥammad 'Abd al-Wahhāb: Mutrib mi'at 'ām* [Muḥammad 'Abd al-Wahhāb: Singer of the Century]. al-Muhandisīn: Awrāq lil-Nashr wa al-Abḥāth wa-al-I'lām.
———. 1993. *Turāth al-ghinā' al-'arabī bayn al-Mawṣilī wa Ziryāb wa Umm Kulthūm*

wa ʿAbd al-Wahhāb [The heritage of Arab song from al-Mawṣilī and Ziryāb to Umm Kulthūm and ʿAbd al-Wahhāb]. Cairo: Dār al-Shurūq.

"Nancy Ajram Alf Leyla Wa Leyla." All comments, http://www.youtube.com/comment_servlet?all_comments&v=iCoXIZB4JrM&fromurl=/watch%3Fv%3DiCoXIZB4JrM (accessed July 17, 2007).

al-Naqqāsh, Rajāʾ. 1969. "Umm Kulthūm wa al-fidāʾiyīn" [Umm Kulthūm and the freedom fighters]. *al-Muṣawwar*, March 28, 36–37.

——. 1978. *Lughz Umm Kulthūm wa kalimāt ukhrá* [The secret of Umm Kulthūm and other words]. Cairo: Dār al-Hilāl.

——. 2000. *Lughz Umm Kulthūm* [The secret of Umm Kulthūm]. Cairo: al-Hayʾah al-Miṣrīyah al-ʿĀmah lil-Kitāb.

Nāṣif, Ṣafīyah. 1968a. "Dumūʿ Umm Kulthūm" [Umm Kulthūm's tears]. *al-Hawāʾ*, June 15 (*Dār al-Hilāl* clippings file 65).

——. 1968b. "Umm Kulthūm fī al-Kuwayt" [Umm Kulthūm in Kuwait]. *al-Kawākib*, May 7, 23.

——. 1968c. "Umm Kulthūm tughannī 4 alḥān jadīdah" [Umm Kulthūm sings four new songs]. *al-Muṣawwar*, May 3, 60–61.

——. 1968d. "Umm Kulthūm tuṣallī fī Masjid al-Zaytūnah" [Umm Kulthūm prays in the al-Zaytūnah Mosque]. *al-Muṣawwar*, June 14, 4.

——. 1969. "Kayf iḥtafala al-Sūdān bi Umm Kulthūm?" [How did Sudan celebrate with Umm Kulthum?]. *al-Muṣawwar*, January 3, 54–55.

Nasr, Zeina. 2006. "French-Moroccan Singer Sapho Thrills Audience with Her Modern Rendition of Timeless Classics." *Daily Star*, November 2, http://www.dailystar.com.lb (accessed May 25, 2007).

Naṣrī, Samīr. 1975. Ṭabaq mahlabīyah dakhala al-tārīkh [A plate of mahlabīyah enters history]. In *Umm Kulthūm: Qīthārat al-ʿArab*, 1975, 18–26.

Nassib, Sélim. 1994. *Oum*. Paris: Balland.

——. 1996. *Ti ho amato per la tua voce*. Translated by Barbara Ferri. Rome: Edizioni E/O.

——. 1999. *Um*. Translated by Habit Bat-ʿAdah. Tel Aviv: Asyah.

——. 2006. *I Loved You for Your Voice*. Translated by Alison Anderson. New York: Europa.

Naṯhamī, Īrīs. 1968. "Kayf ʿāshat Baʿalabakk layālī Umm Kulthūm?" [How did Baalbek experience the nights of Umm Kulthūm?]. *Ākhir sāʿah*, July 17, 38–39.

Negus, Keith. 1997. *Popular Music in Theory: An Introduction*. Hanover, NH: University Press of New England.

Nelson, Cynthia. 1996. *Doria Shafik, Egyptian Feminist: A Woman Apart*. Gainesville, FL: University Press of Florida.

——. 2002. "Writing Culture, Writing Lives: Fictional Boundaries." In *Auto/Biography and the Construction of Identity and Community in the Middle East*, ed. Mary Ann Fay, 201–14. New York: Palgrave.

Nicholson, Stuart. 1995. *Billie Holiday*. Boston: Northeastern University Press.

"al-Niḍāl mustamirr" [The battle is continuing]. 1967. *Ākhir sāʿah*, July 26, 1–2.

"'Nightingale of the Nile' Out." 1975. *Kuwait Times*, February 4, 1.

"Niṣf milyūn min al-bashr yuwaddi'ūna Umm Kulthūm" [Half a million people bid farewell to Umm Kulthūm]. 1975. *al-'Umān*, February 15, 7.

Nūr al-Dīn, Īmān. 2003. "Hal aṣbaḥa khalīfat Ḥalīm?" [Did he become the successor to Ḥalīm?]. *al-Kawākib*, April 1, 62.

"Omkolthoum-iraq." http://www.youtube.com/watch?v=n6O3Adpz30g (accessed July 17, 2007).

"Omm Kalthoum-Inta Omri," http://www.youtube.com/watch?v=vjfH8a8wDOU (accessed July 16, 2007).

Oren, Michael B. 2002. *Six Days of War: June 1967 and the Making of the Modern Middle East*. New York: Oxford University Press.

"Oriental Music." Jerusalem Sounds, http://www.jerusalemshoppe.com/oriental.html (accessed May 25, 2005).

Osborne, Richard. 2007. *Rossini: His Life and Works*. 2nd ed. New York: Oxford University Press.

"Oum Kalthoum a célébré l'Aid el adha au sein d'une famille nécessiteuse." 1968. *Le Petit Marocain/Le Progres Marocain*, March 11, 1, 3.

Oweis, Khaled Yacoub. 2003. "Iraqis Don't Buy U.S. Vow to Target Only Army." *Independent Online*, March 20, 2003, http://www.iol.co.za/index.php?sf=2813&set_id=&sf=2813&click_id=3&art_id=qw1048174561405B262&set_id=1 (accessed July 20, 2007).

Palti, Michal. 2000. "Special Pope: My Song Is a Song of Peace." *Haaretz*, May 9.

"Paris: De nombreux marocains pour Oum Kalthoum a l'Olympia." 1967. *Le petit Marocain/Le petit marocain*, November 17, 2.

Peterson, V. Spike. 2000. "Sexing Political Identities/Nationalism as Heterosexism." In *Women, States, and Nationalism: At Home in the Nation?*, ed. Sita Ranchod-Nilsson and Mary Ann Tétrault, 54–80. London: Routledge.

Podeh, Elie. 2004. "The Lie That Won't Die: Collusion 1967." *Middle East Quarterly* 11 (1): 1–11.

Pomerleau, Cynthia S. 1980. "The Emergence of Women's Autobiography in England." In Jelinek 1980, 21–38.

Postlewait, Thomas. 1989. "Autobiography and Theatre History." In *Interpreting the Theatrical Past: Essays in the Historiography of Performance*, ed. Thomas Postlewait and Bruce A. McConachie, 248–72. Iowa City: University of Iowa Press.

Qābīl, Muḥammad. 1999. *Mustaqbal al-ughnīyah al-miṣrīyah* [The future of Egyptian singing]. Cairo: Dār al-Aḥmadī lil-Nashr.

"Qālat Umm Kulthūm fī tilīfizyūn al-Sūdān" [On Sudanese television, Umm Kulthūm said. . .]. 1969. *al-Kawākib*, January 21, 38–40, 47.

Qandīl, Muḥammad Wajdī. 1967. "Ayn taqaf al-mar'ah al-miṣrīyah min qaḍāyā waṭanihā?" [Where do Egyptian women stand on their homeland's struggle?]. *Ākhir sā'ah*, November 15, 11.

——. 1968a. "Ayyām ma'a al-safīrah Umm Kulthūm fī al-khalīj" [Days with the ambassador Umm Kulthūm in the gulf]. *Ākhir sā'ah*, May 1, 41–43.

——. 1968b. "Hādhā al-sha'b yaqūl 99.989% bi al-ijmā'" [With 99.989 percent agreement, these people say. . .]. *Ākhir sā'ah*, May 8, 11.

———. 1968c. “Mā hiya al-fikrah al-jadīdah allatī bada’athā Umm Kulthūm ma‘a al-sanah al-ghanā’īyah” [What is the new idea that Umm Kulthūm started with the vocal season?]. *Ākhir sā‘ah*, December 11, 32–33.

———. 1968d. “al-Qur’ān bi sawt Umm Kulthūm” [The Qur’ān in the voice of Umm Kulthūm]. *Ākhir sā‘ah*, May 22, 31–32.

———. 1968e. “Yawm ma‘a Umm Kulthūm bayn mu‘ālim dhikrayātihā” [A day with Umm Kulthūm among the landmarks of her memories]. *Ākhir sā‘ah*, February 7, 35–37.

———. 1969a. “Umm Kulthūm tujannid ṣawtahā lil-fidā’iyīn” [Umm Kulthūm enlists/drafts her voice for the freedom fighters]. *Ākhir sā‘ah*, March 19, 58–60.

———. 1969b. “Umm Kulthūm wa ḥadīth fī al-siyāsah” [Umm Kulthūm and a conversation about politics]. *Ākhir sā‘ah*, May 14, 38–40.

———. 1999. “Asrār Umm Kulthūm” [Umm Kulthūm’s secrets]. *al-Nujūm*, February 6, 8–18.

Qaṭāmish, Bākīnām. 2000. “I‘tirāf khaṭīr li ibn Aḥmad Rāmī” [Important admission by Aḥmad Rāmī’s son]. *al-Kawākib*, February 29, 29–30.

“Qiṣṣat Dār Umm Kulthūm wa kayf nāmat fī al-adrāj” [The story of the Umm Kulthūm Foundation and how its plans slept in the desks]. 1982. *al-Akhbār*, January 23, 13.

Qureshi, Regula Burckhardt. 2006. Female Agency and Patrilineal Constraints: Situating Courtesans in Twentieth-Century India. In *The Courtesan’s Arts: Cross-Cultural Perspectives*, ed. Martha Feldman and Bonnie Gordon, 312–31. New York: Oxford University Press.

Racy, Ali Jihad. 1981. “Music in Contemporary Cairo: A Comparative Overview.” *Asian Music* 13 (1): 4–26.

———. 1991. “Creativity and Ambience: An Ecstatic Feedback Model from Arab Music.” *World of Music* 33 (3): 7–28.

———. 2003. *Making Music in the Arab World: The Culture and Artistry of Tarab.* Cambridge: Cambridge University Press.

Raḍwān, Kamāl. 2000. *Umm Kulthūm bayn al-ittihām wa al-ḥaqīqah* [Umm Kulthūm between accusation and reality]. Cairo: Maṭba‘ah al-Yawm/Muḥammad Sayyid Muḥammad.

“Rajul al-shāri‘ yaqūl” [The man of the street says]. 1967. *al-Kawākib*, May 30, 33.

Rakha, Youssef. 2000. “The Other Umm Kulthoum.” *al-Ahram Weekly*, February 3, http://weekly.ahram.org.eg/2000/467/umm11.htm (accessed May 27, 2000).

Rakha, Youssef, and Nevine el-Aref. 2001. “Umm Kulthoum Superstar.” *al-Ahram Weekly*, December 27, http://weekly.ahram.org.eg/2001/566/cu2.htm (accessed March 24, 2007).

Ramaḍān, Sa‘d Sāmī. N.d. *Umm Kulthūm: Ṣawt fī tārīkh ummah* [Umm Kulthūm: Voice in a nation’s history]. Tunis: Ma‘had al-Mūsīqá al-‘Arabīyah.

al-Rāmī, Muḥammad Ḥasan. 1968. “Sirr ‘athamat Umm Kulthūm” [The secret of Umm Kulthūm’s greatness]. *al-Anbā’*, March 6, 6. Reprinted in al-Marīnī 1975, 185–86.

al-Ramlī, Linin. 1982. *Inta Ḥurr* [You are free]. Cairo: Rūz al-Yūsuf.

Rashīd, Muḥammad al-Zabīd. 1975. "Yā Umm Kulthūm" [Oh Umm Kulthūm]. *al-Ayyām*, February 6, 12.

Rathey, Marcus. 2007. "Celebrating Patriotism: Carl Philipp Emanuel Bach's Compositions for the Militia in Hamburg." *Eighteenth-Century Music* 4 (2): 265–83.

Regester, Charlene. 2000. "The Construction of an Image and the Deconstruction of a Star: Josephine Baker Racialized, Sexualized, and Politicized in the African-American Press, the Mainstream Press, and FBI Files." *Popular Music and Society* 24 (1): 31–84.

Regev, Motti. 1995. "Present Absentee: Arab Music in Israeli Culture." *Public Culture* 7: 433–45.

Regev, Motti, and Edwin Seroussi. 2004. *Popular Music and National Culture in Israel*. Berkeley: University of California Press.

Rice, Timothy. 1987. "Toward the Remodeling of Ethnomusicolgy." *Ethnomusicology* 31 (3): 469–88.

"Riḥlātuhā min ajl al-majhūd al-ḥarbī" [Her trips for the sake of the war effort]. 1975. *al-Ayyām*, February 4, 12.

Rojek, Chris. 2001. *Celebrity*. London: Reaktion Books.

Rose, Chris. 2005. "Where Home Is," http://www.learnenglish.org.uk/stories/refugee_story.html (accessed May 3, 2005).

Rosenbaum, Gabriel M. 2004. "Nasser and Nasserism as Perceived in Modern Egyptian Literature through Allusions to Songs." In *Rethinking Nasserism: Revolution and Historical Memory in Modern Egypt*, ed. Elie Podeh and Onn Winckler, 324–42. Gainesville, FL: University Press of Florida.

Royce, Anya Peterson. 1982. *Ethnic Identity: Strategies of Diversity*. Bloomington: Indiana University Press.

Ryan, Curtis R. 2001. "Political Strategies and Regime Survival in Egypt." *Journal of Third World Studies* 18 (2): 25–46.

"Sab'a nidā'āt li Umm Kulthūm" [Umm Kulthum's seven appeals]. 1967. *al-Kawākib*, May 30, 31.

Sabra, Hanan. 2000. "Small Screen, Big Success," *al-Ahram Weekly*, February 3, http://www.ahram.org.eg/weekly/2000/467/umm9.htm (accessed May 27, 2000).

Sa'd, Maḥmūd. 2003. Untitled contribution to *al-Kawākib*, April 1, 2.

Sa'd, Muḥammad. 1967. "Umm Kulthūm taqūl" [Umm Kulthūm says]. *al-Idhā'ah wa al-tilīfizyūn*, July 29, 16.

———. 1970. "Fūnūghrāf al-'umda wa ḥanjarat Umm Kulthūm" [The mayor's phonograph and Umm Kulthūm's throat]. *al-Idhā'ah wa-al-tilīfizyūn*, August 8, 6–9.

al-Sādāt, Sakīnah. 1967. "Umm Kulthūm tunādī kull muwāṭin 'arabī" [Umm Kulthūm calls all the Arab citizens]. *al-Muṣawwar*, August 4, 34.

Ṣādiq, 'Ādil. 2003. "'Ālamīyat al-fannān al-miṣrī" [The internationalism of the Egyptian artist]. *al-Ahrām*, May 26, http://www.ahram.org.eg/archive/Index.asp (accessed November 19, 2003).

Ṣādiq, Ṣalāḥ. 1968. "Katā'ib lil-muqāwamah al-sha'bīyah 'alá khatt al-nār" [Popular resistance corps at the front line]. *Ākhir sā'ah*, May 1, 6.

al-Saʿdnī, Maḥmūd. 1975a. "al-Fallāḥah allatī faraḍat nafsahā ʿalā al-ʿarab" [The fellaha who thrust herself on the Arabs]. In *Umm Kulthūm: Qīthārat al-ʿArab* (1975), 8–17. Beirut: Maktabat al-Jamāhīr.

———. 1975b. Tafattat al-aḥjār [The stones crumbled]. In *Umm Kulthūm: Qīthārat al-ʿArab* (1975), 90–93. Beirut: Maktabat al-Jamāhīr.

Ṣāghīyah, Ḥāzim. 1991. *al-Hawá dūna ahlihi Umm Kulthūm sīrratan wa naṣṣan* [Love minus its folks, Umm Kulthūm as biography and text]. Beirut: Dār al-Jadīd.

Saḥḥāb, Ilyās. 1980. *Difāʿan ʿan al-ughnīyah al-ʿarabīyah* [In defense of Arabic song]. Beirut: al-Muʾassasah al-ʿArabīyah lil-Dirāsāt wa al-Nashr.

Saḥḥāb, Fiktūr. 1997. *Muʾtamar al-mūsīqá al-ʿarabīyah al-awwal* [First conference on Arabic music]. Beirut: al-Sharikah al-ʿĀlamīyah lil-Kitāb.

Saḥḥāb, Fiktūr, and Ilyās Saḥḥāb. 2003. *Umm Kulthūm*. Hazimiyah, Lebanon: Mūsīqá al-Sharq.

Said, Edward. 1983. Introduction to *Days of Dust*, by Halim Barakat. Translated by Trevor Le Gassick. Washington, D.C.: Three Continents Press.

———. 1993. *Musical Elaborations*. New York: Columbia University Press.

———. 1999. "Farewell to Tahia." *al-Ahram Weekly*, October 7, http://weekly.ahram.org.eg/1999/450/cu4.htm (accessed February 25, 2005).

al-Saʿīd, Labīb. 1968. "al-Talḥīn al-mūsīqī lil-qurʾān ḥarām" [Musical composition of the Qurʾān is forbidden]. *al-Akhbār*, January 5, 4.

Saʿīd, Muḥammad. 2002. *Ashhar māʾah fī al-ghināʾ al-ʿarabī* [The hundred most famous people in Arab song], vol. 1. Cairo: al-Hayʾah al-Miṣrīyah al-ʿAmmah lil-Kitāb.

Sajrawy, Michel. http://www.michelsajrawy.com/html_ver/htmlver/index.htm (accessed August 25, 2007).

Ṣalāḥ. 1969. "Umm Kulthūm," *al-Dustūr* (letter from a reader), March 16, 2.

Ṣalāḥ, Maḥmūd. 2000. "Qiṣṣat ḥubb majhūlah bayn Amīr al-Muʿjabāt wa Umm Kulthūm" [Unknown love story between the Prince of the Fans and Umm Kulthūm]. *Ākhir sāʿah*, August 30, 19–23 (*Dār al-Hilāl* clippings file 65).

Ṣāliḥ, Aḥmad. 1970. "Mādhā ḥadatha laylat Umm Kulthūm fī Baʿalabakk?" [What happened on Umm Kulthūm's night in Baalbek?]. *Ākhir sāʿah*, July 22, 28–30.

Ṣāliḥ, Rushdī. 1967. "al-Tilīfizyūn yaʿruḍ baʿd ghad ūlá haflāt Umm Kulthūm fī Bārīs" [Day after tomorrow television presents first of Umm Kulthūm's concerts in Paris]. 1967. *al-Akhbār*, December 26, 2.

———. 1968. "Liqāʾ maʿa Umm Kulthūm taftatah bihi al-idhāʿah barāmij Ramaḍān" [Radio opens Ramadan program with a meeting with Umm Kulthūm]. *al-Akhbār*, November 20, 2.

Sālim, Ḥilmī. 1981. "Qiṣṣat ḥubb wa zawāj Umm Kulthūm wa Maḥmūd al-Sharīf" [The story of love and marriage of Umm Kulthūm and Maḥmūd al-Sharīf]. *al-Kawākib*, February 3, 14–17.

Sālim, Maḥmūd. 1967. "Min wa ilá" [From and to]. *al-Idhāʿah wa al-tilīfizyūn*, July 1, 7.

——. 1968. "Rafḍ al-hazīmah" [Refusal of the defeat]. *al-Idhā'ah wa al-tilīfizyūn*, June 1, 12.
——. 1969. "Ṣuwar min riḥlat Umm Kulthūm" [Photographs from Umm Kulthūm's trip]. *al-Idhā'ah wa al-tilīfizyūn*, March 29, 14–17.
Salmāwī, Muḥammad. 1997. "Umm Kulthūm fī al-ma'rakah!" [Umm Kulthūm in the fight]. *al-Ahrām*, March 6 (Umm Kulthūm Museum Library vol. 10, 163–66).
——. 2000. "Ma aghfalathu ḥalaqāt Umm Kulthūm!" [What the episodes of Umm Kulthūm left out]. *al-Ahrām*, January 24, http://www.ahram.org.eg/archive/Index.asp (accessed August 30, 2008).
"Sanafir Hotel—Sharm el Sheikh." Sun Tours, http://www.suntours.com.jo/sanafir.htm (accessed June 8, 2007).
Santelli, Robert. 1999. "The Rock and Roll Hall of Fame and Museum: Myth, Memory, and History." In *Stars Don't Stand Still in the Sky: Music and Myth*, ed. Karen Kelly and Evelyn McDonell, 237–43. New York: New York University Press.
"Ṣawtī hibah min Allāh.'" [My voice is a gift from God]. 1968. *al-Akhbār*, May 11, 13.
"Ṣawt Umm Kulthūm yaghzū Bārīs li awwal marrah" [The voice of Umm Kulthūm conquers Paris for the first time]. 1967. *Ākhir sā'ah*, November 15, 52.
"al-Sayyidah Umm Kulthūm qadamat 16 kīlū dhahab bi ism tajammu' al-muwāṭinīn" [Umm Kulthūm presented sixteen kilograms of gold in the name of the assembly of citizens]. 1967. *al-Akhbār*, July 18, 3.
Scheppler, Bill. 2006. *Al-Biruni: Master Astronomer and Muslim Scholar of the Eleventh Century*. New York: Rosen.
"Security Problems Likely at Umm Kalthoum Funeral." 1975. *Kuwait Times*, February 5, 1.
Shaaban, Bouthaina. 1988. *Both Right and Left Handed: Arab Women Talk about Their Lives*. London: Women's Press.
al-Shādhilī, Farūq. 1969. "6 ālāf ṭālib wa ṭālibah taqaddamuu li ikhtibārāt al-qudrāt" [6,000 students took aptitude exams]. *al-Akhbār*, September 23, 8.
al-Shādhilī, Muḥammad. 2000. "Umm Kulthūm: Mādhā yabqā minhā: Hal kāfiyan li yukrimhā?" [Umm Kulthūm: What remains of her: Is it sufficient to honor her?]. *al-Wafd*, February 21, 56 (*Dār al-Hilāl* clippings file 65).
Shahātih, 'Alī. 1969. "Umm Kulthūm fī al-Qāhirah al-yawm" [Umm Kulthūm in Cairo today]. *al-Akhbār*, March 22, 13.
Shalabī, Karam. 1968. "Laylat al-sahrah" [Night of the performance]. *al-Idhā'ah wa al-tilīfizyūn*, December 7, 19.
el-Shawan, Salwa Aziz. 1980. "al-Musika al-'Arabīyah: A Category of Urban Music in Cairo, Egypt, 1927–1977," PhD diss., Columbia University, 1980.
Shehata, Samer S. 1992. "The Politics of Laughter: Nasser, Sadat, and Mubarek in Egyptian Political Jokes." *Folklore* 103 (1): 75–91.
Shelemay, Kay Kaufman. 2001. "Toward an Ethnomusicology of the Early Music

Movement: Thoughts on Bridging Disciplines and Musical Worlds." *Ethnomusicology* 45 (1): 1–29.

Shemesh, Moshe. 1996. *The Palestinian Entity, 1959–1974: Arab Politics and the PLO*, 2nd rev. ed. London: Frank Cass.

Shukrallah, Hani. 1989. "Political Crisis/Conflict in post-1967 Egypt." In *Egypt under Mubarak*, ed. Charles Tripp and Roger Owen, 53–102. London: Routledge.

Shūshah, Muḥammad al-Sayyid. 1976. *Umm Kulthūm: Ḥayāt naghm* [Umm Kulthūm: A life of melody]. Cairo: Maktabat Rūz al-Yūsuf.

al-Sibāʿī, Yūsuf. 1968a. "Li mādhā al-istiftāʾ wa li mādhā 'Naʿm'?" [Why the referendum and why "Yes"?]. *Ākhir sāʿah*, May 1, 2–5.

———. 1968b. "Mādhā baʿd an qāla al-shaʿb 'Naʿm'?" [What after the people said "Yes"?]. *Ākhir sāʿah*, May 8, 4.

Sonbol, Amira al-Azhary. 1995. "Adoption in Islamic Society: A Historical Survey." In *Children in the Muslim Middle East,* ed. Elizabeth Warnock Fernea, 45–67. Austin: University of Texas Press.

Souief, Ahdaf. 1992. *In the Eye of the Sun*. New York: Pantheon.

Stein, Rebecca Luna. 2000. "Spatial Fantasies: Israeli Culture after Oslo." *Middle East Report* 216: 36–38.

Stephens, Robert Henry. 1971. *Nasser: A Political Biography*. London: Allen Lane.

Stokes, Martin. 2002. "Sentimentalism and Its Futures: The Vocal Art of Zeki Müren and Abd al-Halim Hafez." *Musica e storia* 10 (2): 581–98.

Stone, Christopher. 2008. *Popular Culture and Nationalism in Lebanon: The Fairouz and Rahbani Nation*. London: Routledge.

Strich, Jo. 1996. "Zehava Ben, Switching Camps to Sing for Peace." *Agence France-Presse*, May 20.

Suleiman, Michael W. 1983. "Values and Societal Development: Education and Change in Nasser's Egypt." In *Political Behavior in the Arab States*, ed. Tawfic Farah, 93–106. Boulder: Westview Press.

Surk, Barbara. 2008. "Arab Diva's Necklace Sold at Auction for $1.3M." April 29, http://www.foxnews.com/wires/2008Apr29/0,4670,DubaiUmmKulthoumNecklace,00.html (accessed May 6, 2008).

Surūr, Amal. 2000. "Umm Kulthūm hiya allatī rafaḍat al-zawāj min Rāmī!" [Umm Kulthūm was the one who refused to marry Rāmī]. *Nisf al-dunyā*, February 6, 35.

"Ṣuwar min riḥlat Umm Kulthūm" [Photographs from Umm Kulthūm's trip]. 1969. *al-Idhāʿah wa al-tilīfizyūn*, March 29, 6–7.

Sweeney, Regina M. 2001. *Singing Our Way to Victory: French Cultural Politics and Music during the Great War*. Middletown, CT: Wesleyan University Press.

Tabārak, Muḥammad. 1968. "Laylah min layālī al-ʿamr fī al-Khārtūm" [A night of the life in Khartoum]. *al-Akhbār*, December 28, 13.

———. 1969a. "Umm Kulthūm ghayyarat kull kalimāt al-ughnīyah allatī tabdaʾ bi ḥarf al-qāf" [Umm Kulthūm changed all the words of the song that begin with *qaf*]. *al-Akhbār*, December 6, 13.

———. 1969b. "Umm Kulthūm tughannī lil-Masjid al-Shahīd" [Umm Kulthūm sings about the mosque]. *al-Akhbār*, August 23, 13.

———. 1969c. "Umm Kulthūm waḥduhā—ayn baqiyat al-muṭribāt?" [Umm Kulthūm alone—where are the other singers?]. *al-Akhbār*, March 8, 13.

———. 1971a. "Fī ākhir waqt ajarat taʿdīlan fī 'al-Thulāthīyah al-Muqaddassah'" [At the last moment Umm Kulthūm made modification to "al-Thulāthīyah al-Muqaddassah"]. *al-Akhbār*, October 23, 13.

———. 1971b. "Ilāh al-hubb ʿalá mīdālīyat Umm Kulthūm al-dhahabīyah" [Cupid on gold medal of Umm Kulthūm]. *al-Akhbār*, May 1, 13.

———. 1974. "al-Ḥamdu lillāh. . . anā bi khayr" [Thank God . . . I am well]. *al-Akhbār*, April 13, 9.

———. 1975. "Riḥlātuhā min ajl al-majhūd al-ḥarbī baʿd al-naksah" [Her trips for the sake of the war effort after the Naksah]. *al-Akhbār*, February 1, 9.

———. 1990. *Dhikrayāt ʿāshiq: Rāmī wa Umm Kulthūm* [Memories of a fan: Rāmī and Umm Kulthūm]. Cairo: Mu'assasat Akhbār al-Yawm.

al-Tābiʿī, Muḥammad. 1967. "Bank al-dhahab" [Gold bank]. *al-Akhbār*, June 21, 8.

"al-Tajammuʿ al-Waṭanī yubīʿu fasātīn al-sahrah fī al-sūq al-ḥurrah" [The National Assembly sells evening dresses in the duty-free market]. 1967. *al-Ahrām*, December 17, 10.

Tanner, Henry. 1967. "An Arab Singer Stirs Pandemonium in Paris Hall," *New York Times*, November 17, 43.

Ṭanṭāwī, Mursī. 1967. "Umm Kulthūm tazūr al-muḥāfatḥāt li jamʿ tabarruʿāt al-dhahab" [Umm Kulthūm visits the governorates to collect gold donations]. *Ākhir sāʿah*, July 26, 28.

Tarasti, Eero. 1995. *Heitor Villa-Lobos: The Life and Works, 1887–1959*. Jefferson, NC: McFarland.

"Tataghannā Umm Kulthūm fī Bārīs li muqābil 14 alf ginīh istarlīnī" [Umm Kulthūm sings in Paris for £14,000 in compensation]. 1966. *al-Ahrām*, September 29, 10.

Tawfīq, Samīr. 1967. "Umm Kulthūm tu'ajjil ʿawdatahā ilá yawm al-khamīs likay tarkab ṭā'irah miṣrīyah" [Umm Kulthūm postpones her return until Thursday in order to take an Egyptian plane]. *al-Akhbār*, November 21, 5.

———. 1968a. "ʿIndamā ghannat Umm Kulthūm ʿalá dufūf al-qabā'il fī Marākash" [When Umm Kulthūm sang to the drums of the tribes in Marrakesh]. *Ākhir sāʿah*, March 27, 31–32.

———. 1968b. "Mahrajān multahib min ajl al-waḥdah al-ʿarabīyah yaḥtafil bi Umm Kulthūm fī al-Maghrib" [Festival fired up for the sake of Arab unity welcomes Umm Kulthūm in Morocco]. *al-Akhbār*, March 14, 3.

Tawfīq, Samīr, and Farūq Ibrāhīm. 1967. "Faransā kulluhā tataḥaddath ʿan ṣawt Umm Kulthūm" [All of France talks about the voice of Umm Kulthūm]. *al-Akhbār*, November 13, 3.

Tawfīq, Samīr, and Yaḥyá Shafīq. 1967a. "Akbar ḥadath tārīkhī lil-fann al-miṣrī fī

Bārīs" [Biggest historical event for Egyptian art in Paris]. *al-Akhbār*, November 20, 3.

———. 1967b. "al-Tilīfizyūn al-ʿarabī yuqaddimu fī ramaḍān ḥaflāt Umm Kulthūm fī Bārīs" [In Ramadan Arab television presents Umm Kulthūm's concerts in Paris]. *al-Akhbār*, November 30, 4.

al-Ṭāwīl, Fārūq. "Quwātunā taqdī ʿalá hujūm al-ʿudū wa mudarraʿātunā tatawaghghal dākhil Isrāʾīl" [Our forces thwart the enemy's attacks and armored vehicles penetrate deeply inside Israel]. 1967. *Ākhir sāʿah*, June 7, 6.

"Telegram d'Oum Kalthoum au peuple Tunisien." 1968. *L'Action*, May 29, 1.

Terrill, W. Andrew. 2001. "The Political Mythology of the Battle of Karameh." *Middle East Journal* 55 (1): 91–111.

"30 alf ginīh īrād ḥaflat Umm Kulthūm" [£E 30,000 in proceeds from Umm Kulthūm's concert]. 1967. *al-Akhbār*, August 6, 1.

"Thalāth iqtirāḥāt min ʿAbd al-Wahhāb li takrīm Umm Kulthūm" [Three suggestions from ʿAbd al-Wahhāb for honoring Umm Kulthūm]. 1975. *al-Akhbār*, February 5, 3.

Ṭirād, Majīd. 1999. *Umm Kulthūm: Ḥayātuhā wa aghānīhā* [Umm Kulthūm: Her life and her songs]. Tripoli, Lebanon: al-Muʾassasah al-Ḥadīthah lil-Kitāb.

Tribe, Ivan M. 2005. "Purple Hearts, Heartbreak Ridge, and Korean Mud: Pain, Patriotism, and Faith in the 1950–53 'Police Action.'" In *Country Music Goes to War*, ed. Charles K. Wolfe and James E. Akenson, 126–42.

"Tudfan bi jawār wālidatahā fī maqburah ashrafat ʿalā iqāmatihā" [She is buried near her mother in a cemetery that overlooked her house]. 1975. *al-Ahrām*, February 4, 5.

Tuohy, William. 1970. "Oum Kolthoum: She's Nightingale of the Nile." *Los Angeles Times*, July 24, H14.

Turkiya, Salīm (Nessib). 1999. *Kāna ṣarḥān min khiyāl* [It was an imaginary castle]. Translated by Bissām Hajjār. Beirut: al-Massār lil-Nashr wa al-Abḥāth wa al-Tawzīʿ.

"Ughnīyah jadīdah li Umm Kulthūm" [Umm Kulthūm's new song]. 1967. *al-Kawākib*, August 1, 38.

"Ughnīyah min Bārīs" [A song from Paris]. 1967. *al-Idhāʿah wa al-tilīfizyūn*, December 9, 46.

"Ughnīyat Umm Kulthūm qunbulah tharīyah" [Umm Kulthūm's song is an atomic bomb]. 1967. *Ākhir sāʿah*, June 7, 12.

"Ukhtī Wafā'." Palestinian Media Watch, http://pmw.org.il/asx/PMW_wafa.asx (accessed June 8, 2007).

"Umm Kalthoum—In Memorium." 1975. *Kuwait Times*, February 4, 3.

"Umm Kolthoum." Egyptian State Information Service, http://www.sis.gov.eg/En/Arts&Culture/Music&Singing/Music&SingingStars/070602000000000001.htm (accessed August 13, 2007).

Umm Kulthūm. 1967. "Risālah ilā Jamāl" [A letter to Jamāl]. *al-Kawākib*, June 13, 18.

"Umm Kulthūm aʿṭham ḥadath fī tārīkh al-mūsīqā" [Umm Kulthūm is the greatest event in the history of music]. 1967. *al-Jumhūrīyah*, November 16, 12.

"Umm Kulthūm al-qalb al-ḥanūn" [Umm Kulthūm the tender heart]. 1969. *al-Akhbār*, December 4, 12.
"Umm Kulthūm al-yawm 'alá kull al-maḥaṭṭāt wa kull al-mawjāt" [Umm Kulthūm today on every station and every airwave]. 1967. *al-Akhbār*, November 15, 6.
"Umm Kulthūm amām rijāl al-ṣiḥāfah" [Umm Kulthūm in front of the press]. 1968. *al-Idhā'ah wa al-talfazah*, March 3. Reprinted in al-Marīnī 1975, 196.
"Umm Kulthūm: Fannānat al-Sha'b fī al-ma'rakah" [Umm Kulthūm: Artist of the People in the battle]. 1967. *al-Muṣawwar*, August 25, 44–45.
"Umm Kulthūm fī al-Fījārū" [Umm Kulthūm in Figaro]. 1967. *al-Kawākib*, May 30, 24.
Umm Kulthūm fī al-Ittiḥād al-Sūviyatī. 1970. Zamalek: Foreign Press and Information Services.
"Umm Kulthūm fī Faransā" [Umm Kulthūm in France]. 1967. *al-Akhbār*, November 10, 1.
"Umm Kulthūm fī kalimāt" [Umm Kulthūm in words]. 1970. *al-Anwār* supplement, July 12, 12.
"Umm Kulthūm ghannat "Amal Hayātī,' 'al-Aṭlāl,' 'Fāt al-Mi'ād' al-ummah al-'arabīyah istama'at ilá Umm Kulthūm min jamī' idhā'ātinā" [Umm Kulthūm sang "'Amal Hayātī," "al-Aṭlāl," and "Fāt al-Mi'ād," the Arab nation listened to Umm Kulthūm through all of our broadcasting]. 1967. *al-Ahrām*, November 16, 8.
"Umm Kulthūm ism al-qariyah allatī wulidat fīhā" ["Umm Kulthūm" is the name of the village in which she was born]. 1975. *al-Idhā'ah wa al-talfazah*, February 15, 20.
Umm Kulthūm: Qiṣṣat ḥayātihā wa mukhtārāt min aghānīhā [Umm Kulthūm: The story of her life and portions of her songs]. 1977. Beirut: al-Maktab al-Tijārī lil-Ṭibā'ah wa al-Nashr wa al-Tawzī'.
Umm Kulthūm: Qīthārat al-'Arab [Umm Kulthūm: Lyre of the Arabs]. 1975. Beirut: Maktabat al-Jamāhīr.
Umm Kulthūm: Qīthārat al-'Arab [Umm Kulthūm: Lyre of the Arabs]. 1978. Beirut: Dār al-'Afaq al-Jadīdah.
"Umm Kulthūm sallamat ams 2,000 ginīh istarlīnī dhahab" [Yesterday Umm Kulthūm presented 2,000 pounds sterling in gold]. 1967. *al-Jumhūrīyah*, July 18, 6.
"Umm Kulthūm sallamat 15,050 ginīhan li Wazīr al-Shu'ūn hadiyat al-'īd lil-mahjarīn fī al-'īd" [Umm Kulthūm gives £E 15,050 to minister of social affairs as gift to the immigrants on the feast day]. 1969. *al-Akhbār*, December 10, 8.
"Umm Kulthūm taftatiḥ mawsimahā al-ghanā'ī al-yawm min Bārīs" [Umm Kulthūm opens her singing season today from Paris]. 1967. *al-Jumhūrīyah*, November 15, 1, 3.
"Umm Kulthūm taqūl bi idhā'at Lundun: ṣawtī hibbah min Allāh" [Umm Kulthūm says to London radio, "My voice is a gift from God"]. 1968. *al-Akhbār*, May 11, 13.
"Umm Kulthūm taqūl ṣawtunā fī al-intikhāb huwa ṣawt Miṣr" [Umm Kulthūm says our voice in the selection is the voice of Egypt]. 1968. *al-Akhbār*, April 1, 1, 6.
"Umm Kulthūm tatabarra' 5,000 ginīh" [Umm Kulthūm donates 5,000 pounds]. 1967. *al-Ahrām*, May 27, 12.

"Umm Kulthūm tataghannā bi al-jihād ilá ummat al-'arab" [Umm Kulthūm sings for jihad to the Arab nation]. 1967. *al-Ahrām*, May 27, 12.
"Umm Kulthūm tataghannā taḥīyat al-'awda: 'Dum al-sha'b'" [Umm Kulthūm sings a greeting of his return: "Dum al-Sha'b"]. 1967. *al-Kawākib*, June 20, 5.
"Umm Kulthūm tughannī fī Kanadā" [Umm Kulthūm sings in Canada]. 1969. *al-Jumhūriyyah*, January 18, 1.
"Umm Kulthūm tughannī wa al-Iskandarīyah tuqaddim mā'at alf ginīh" [Umm Kulthūm sings and Alexandria presents £E 100,000]. 1967. *al-Kawākib*, September 5, 3.
"Umm Kulthūm tukhātib al-junūd wa usarahā min khilāl al-tilīfizyūn wa al-idhā'ah" [Umm Kulthūm addresses the soldiers and their families on television and radio]. 1967. *al-Jumhūrīyah*, July 18, 6.
"Umm Kulthūm tuqabbil Umm Kulthūm" [Umm Kulthūm kisses Umm Kulthūm]. 1969. *al-Kawākib*, January 21, 40.
"Umm Kulthūm tuqaddim dawr bint murdi'at al-nabī" [Umm Kulthūm plays the daughter of the Prophet's wet nurse]. 1965. *al-Jumhūrīyah*, August 14 (*Dār al-Hilāl* clippings file 65).
"Umm Kulthūm tuqarrir al-Tajammu' al-Waṭanī lil-Mar'ah al-Miṣrīyah" [Umm Kulthūm establishes the National Assembly of Egyptian Women]. 1967. *al-Akhbār*, July 11, 8.
"Umm Kulthūm tusāfir ilá al-Sa'ūdīyah wa al-Kuwayt li jam' al-tabarru'āt" [Umm Kulthūm travels to Saudi Arabia and Kuwait to collect donations]. 1967. *al-Akhbār*, July 22 (*al-Ahrām* clippings file 110).
"Umm Kulthūm wa ashhar 50 sayyidah fī al-'ālam" [Umm Kulthūm and the fifty most famous women in the world]. 1971. *al-Akhbār*, November 27, 1.
"Umm Kulthūm wa ḥamalāt al-khayr" [Umm Kulthūm and the benevolent campaign]. 1971. *al-Jumhūrīyah*, June 14, 10.
"Umm Kulthūm wa qiṣṣat al-ṣawt al-sāḥir" [Umm Kulthūm and the story of the enchanting voice]. 1975. *al-Anwār*, January 31, 7.
"Umm Kulthūm 'wishsh al-khayr' fī Ba'alabakk" [Umm Kulthūm a good blessing in Baalbek]. 1968. *al-Jumhūrīyah*, July 18, 5.
'Uthmān, Ḥussayn. 1977. "Mawāqif waṭanīyah li Umm Kulthūm" [Umm Kulthūm's patriotic stances]. *al-Manṣūrah*, February, 24–26.
'Uthmān, Sa'īd. 2000. *Kawkab al-Sharq Umm Kulthūm: Ḥayātuhā wa aghānīhā* [The Star of the East Umm Kulthūm: Her life and her songs]. Cairo: Dār al-'Ālamīyah lil-Kitāb wa al-Nashr.
Van Nieuwkerk, Karin. 1995. *A Trade like Any Other: Female Singers and Dancers in Egypt*. Austin: University of Texas Press.
Veal, Michael. 2000. *Fela: The Life and Times of an African Musical Icon*. Philadelphia: Temple University Press.
Victor, Barbara. 1994. *A Voice of Reason: Hanan Ashrawi and Peace in the Middle East*. New York: Harcourt Brace & Company.
"Wa 'ādat Umm Kulthūm ilá al-Qāhirah" [Umm Kulthūm returned to Cairo]. 1967. *al-Jumhūrīyah*, November 25, 12.

"Wafūd 'arabīyah taṣil al-Qāhirah li-tabi' janāzat Fannānat al-Sha'b al-yawm" [Arab delegations arrive in Cairo to walk in the funeral of the Artist of the People today]. 1975. *al-Anbā'*, February 5, 1.

"al-Wajh al-khayrī li Umm Kulthūm" [The charitable side of Umm Kulthūm]. 1975. *al-Anwār*, February 5, 10.

Wallach, Janet, and John Wallach. 1997. *Arafat: In the Eyes of the Beholder*. Secaucus, NJ: Carol Publishing Group.

Waterbury, John. 1983. *The Egypt of Nasser and Sadat: The Political Economy of Two Regimes*. Princeton, NJ: Princeton University Press.

Weidman, Amanda J. 2006. *Singing the Classical, Voicing the Modern: The Postcolonial Politics of Music in South India*. Durham, NC: Duke University Press.

White, Bob W. 2008. *Rumba Rules: The Politics of Dance Music in Mobutu's Zaire*. Durham, NC: Duke University Press.

Wilson, David A. 2005. "Ulster Loyalism and Country Music, 1969–85." In *Country Music Goes to War*, ed. Charles K. Wolfe and James E. Akenson, 192–207.

Witzleben, J. Lawrence. 2002. "Music in the Hong Kong Handover Ceremonies: A Community Re-Imagines Itself." *Ethnomusicology* 46 (1): 120–33.

"Wizārat al-Thaqāfah tashtarī istawānāt Umm Kulthūm al-qadīmah" [Ministry of Culture buys Umm Kulthūm's old recordings]. 1970. *al-Jumhūrīyah*, June 10, 8.

Wolfe, Charles K. 2005. "'Bloody War': War Songs in Early Country Music." In *Country Music Goes to War*, ed. Charles K. Wolfe and James E. Akenson, 26–32.

Y., Dh. 1968. "Hiya al-rūḥ wa ḥalāwat al-rūḥ" [She is soul and euphoria]. Supplement to *al-Anwār*, July 21, 17.

Yaḥyá, 'Afāf. 1968a. "Afrāḥ al-Sūdān bi Umm Kulthūm mustamirrah" [Sudan's celebrations with Umm Kulthūm continue]. *al-Akhbār*, December 29, 2.

———. 1968b. "2,500 isṭawānah lil-Sūdān min 'Hādhihi Laylatī'" [2,500 recordings of "Hādhihi Laylatī" for Sudan]. *al-Akhbār*, December 31, 2.

———. 1968c. "Wufūd 18 dawlah taḥḍar ḥafl Umm Kulthūm al-laylah fī al-Khārtūm" [Groups from eighteen states attend Umm Kulthūm's concert tonight in Khartoum]. *al-Akhbār*, December 30, 2.

———. 1969a. "Hadīth maftūḥ ma'a Sayyidat al-Ghinā' al-'Arabī" [Open conversation with the Lady of Arabic Song]. *al-Akhbār*, January 10, 2.

———. 1969b. "Masraḥ fī al-Qāhirah li Umm Kulthūm" [A theater in Cairo for Umm Kulthūm]. *al-Akhbār*, February 24, 2.

Yūnis, Ibrāhīm. 1968. "Umm Kulthūm tughannī fī Baghdād min ajl al-naṣr" [Umm Kulthūm sings in Baghdad for the sake of victory]. *al-Akhbār*, June 27, 1.

Yūsuf, Ḥasb Allāh al-Ḥājj. 1968. "*al-Ra'ī al-'Āmm* tarhab bi Ṣanājat al-Sharq Umm Kulthūm" [*al-Ra'ī al-'Āmm* welcomes Bayonet of the East Umm Kulthūm]. *al-Ra'ī al-'Āmm*, December 25, 3.

Zakariyā, Zakariyā Hāshim. 1983. *Umm Kulthūm: Tuḥfat al-'aṣr wa mu'jizat al-dahr* [Umm Kulthūm: Gem of the era and miracle of the age]. Cairo: Matba'at al-Taqaddum.

al-Zarārī, Nūr al-Dīn. 1969. "Umm Kulthūm taqūl: al-Mustami' al-'arabī wāḥid fī kull al-aqṭār" [Umm Kulthūm says, The Arab listener is one in all the nations]. *al-Jumhūrīyah*, March 10, 5.

Zarrūq, Ḥasan al-Ṭāhir. 1969. *Muwaḥḥidat al-'Arab: al-Sayyidah Umm Kulthūm* [The Uniter of the Arabs: Umm Kulthūm]. Khartoum: n.p.

"Zehava Ben to Sing on al-Jazeera TV." 2003. *Jerusalem Post*, November 13, 6.

Zonis, Marvin. 1991. "Autobiography and Biography in the Middle East: A Plea for Psychopolitical Studies." In *Middle Eastern Lives: The Practice of Biography and Self-Narrative*, ed. Martin Kramer, 60–88. Syracuse, NY: Syracuse University Press.

Zuhur, Sherifa. 2000. *Asmahan's Secrets: Woman, War, and Song*. Austin: University of Texas Press.

Audio Recordings

'Abd al-Nāṣir, Jamāl. 1992a. *Jamāl 'Abd al-Nāṣir*, vol. 5. Cairo: Mūjīfūn. Audiocassette.

———. 1992b. *Jamāl 'Abd al-Nāṣir*, vol. 8. Cairo: Mūjīfūn. Audiocassette.

'Abd al-Raḥīm, Sha'bān. 2003. *al-Ḍarb x al-'Irāq*. Cairo: al-Wādī lil-Intāj al-fannī. 35/2003. Audiocassette.

Aghānī Waṭanīyah li Sayyidat al-Ghinā' al-'Arabī Umm Kulthūm, vol. 1. Ṣawt al-Qāhirah 00/031/401, D00/1015. Audiocassette.

Aghānī Waṭanīyah li Sayyidat al-Ghinā' al-'Arabī Umm Kulthūm, vol. 2. Ṣawt al-Qāhirah 00/032/401, D00/1016. Audiocassette.

"Allah Ma'ak." 1967. June 1. Qaṣr al-Nīl, Cairo. Egyptian State Radio library. Reel 4907N.

"Amal Ḥayātī." 1968. Morocco. Egyptian State Radio library. Reels 50384N and 50385N.

"Asbaḥa 'Indī al-Ān Bundūqīyah." *Aghānī Waṭaniyah*, vol. 2. Ṣawt al-Qāhirah. 00/032/401. Audiocassette.

"al-Aṭlāl." 1966. December 1. Qaṣr al-Nīl, Cairo. Egyptian State Radio library. Reels 46958N, 46959N, and 46960N.

"al-Aṭlāl." 1967. January 5. Qaṣr al-Nīl, Cairo. Egyptian State Radio library. Reels 47253N, 47254N, and 47255N.

"al-Aṭlāl." 1968. Morocco. Egyptian State Radio library. Reels 50386N, 50387N, and 50388N.

Attieh, Elie. 2004. *Inta Omri*, Take 5 Music T5M 4103 390 162. Compact disc.

"Ba'īd 'Anak: Ḥaflat Tūnis." Ṣawt al-Qāhirah. SC81115/901. Audiocassette.

"Fakkarūnī." 1968. Tunis. Egyptian State Radio library. Reels 52030N and 52031N.

"Hādhihī Laylatī." 1969. May 8. Egyptian State Radio library. Reel 54259N.

"Ḥadīth al-Rūḥ" 1967. June 1. Qaṣr al-Nīl, Cairo. Egyptian State Radio library. Reels 4924N and 4925N.

"Ḥadīth al-Rūḥ." Ṣawt al-Qāhirah. 94 SDCD01 B67. Compact disc.

al-Ḥakīm, Wajdī. N.d. "Ayyām fī Ḥayāt Umm Kulthūm" [Days in the life of Umm Kulthūm]. Audiocassette.

"Istiqbāl al-Munaṭhṭhimāt al-Nisā'īyah al-Sudānīyah" [Reception of the Sudanese women's organizations for Umm Kulthūm]. Egyptian State Radio library. Reel 52015R.

Khalīl, Yaḥyá. *Nagham*. Ṣawt al-Qāhirah. 93002/401. Audiocassette.

The Mother of the Arabs. 2005. EMI International. 31662. Compact disc.

Murād, Sa'īd. 2001. *Two Thousand and One Nights: Remixes by Said Mrad*. Alam el Phan TC213 722/2001A. Audiocassette.

"Nahj al-Burdah." Ṣawt al-Qāhirah. 94 SDCD 01B74. Compact disc.

"Nidā'āt al-Naṣr" [Calls of victory]. 1967. Recorded May 23. Egyptian State Radio library. Reel 39723N.

"al-Qalb Ya'shaq Kull Jamīl: Ḥaflat Dawlat al-Imārāt al-'Arabiyyah." Ṣawt al-Qāhirah. 9910/401. Audiocassette.

"Risālat Jamāl 'Abd al-Nāṣir." 1970. November 18. Egyptian State Radio library. Reel 57914R.

Ṣādiq, Sāmīyah. N.d. "Sahrat Umm Kulthūm al-Juz' al-Thānī" [An evening with Umm Kulthūm, part 2]. Egyptian State Radio library. Reel N68421.

Sagrawy, Michel. 2006. *Yathrib*. Ozella Music. OZ010CD. Compact disc.

"Salū Qalbī." 1967. June 1. Egyptian State Radio library. Reels 4922N and 4923N.

"Salū Qalbī." Ṣawt al-Qāhirah. 94 SDCD01B06. Compact disc.

"al-Thulāthīyah al-Muqaddasah." Ṣawt al-Qāhirah. 94 SDCD 01B82. Compact disc.

Ughniyāt Waṭanīyah Ṣawt al-Qāhirah. 82025/602 D1454 1981. Audiocassette.

"Wa Dārit al-Ayyām." 1971. January 7. Egyptian State Radio library. Reels 56343N and 56344N.

Films and Video Recordings

'Alī, In'ām Muḥammad. 2001. *Umm Kulthūm*. Lebanon: Sabbah Media Corp. DVD.

Alkassim, Sami. 1996. *Far from You*. N.p.: Puti Productions. Videocassette.

'Arafah, Sharīf. 2006. *Ḥalīm*. Riyadh: Rūtānā. DVD.

Bitton, Simone. 1996. *Oum Kalsoum: Egypte 1902–1975*. N.l: n.n. Videocassette.

Fāḍil, Muḥammad. 2000. *Kawkab al-Sharq* [Star of the East]. Cairo: Funūn lil-Sīnamā wa al-Fīdiyū. Videocassette.

"Firqat 'Abd al-Ḥalīm Nuwīrah lil-Mūsīqā al-'Arabīyah ma'a Amāl Māhir 17 February 2003." Cairo Opera House Library. Videocassette 1244.

Goldman, Michal. 1996. *Umm Kulthūm: A Voice Like Egypt*. Waltham, MA: Filmmakers Collaborative. Videocassette.

"Hādhihī Laylatī." 1968. Sudan. Video on computers at the Umm Kulthūm Museum.

Laufer, Erez. 1998. *Zehava Ben—The Solitary Star*. Ergo Media. Videocassette.

"Riḥlat Umm Kulthūm ilá Bārīs" [Umm Kulthūm's trip to Paris]. Egyptian State Television library. Tape 1435 digital 94.

"Riḥlat Umm Kulthūm ilá Lībiyā" [Umm Kulthūm's trip to Libya]. Egyptian State Television library. Tape 1436 digital 94.

"Riḥlat Umm Kulthūm ilá al-Maghrib wa al-Dār al-Bayḍā' wa Tūnis" [Umm Kulthūm's trip to Morocco, Casablanca, and Tunisia]. Egyptian State Television library. Videotape 1579 digital 94.
"Umm Kulthūm: 'Min Ajli 'Aynayk' and 'Aghadān Alqāk'." Videocassette no. 1. Anaheim, CA: Sawt wa Soorah.

Index

MUSIC/CULTURE

A series from Wesleyan University Press

Edited by Harris M. Berger and Annie J. Randall

Originating editors: George Lipsitz, Susan McClary, and Robert Walser

Listening to Salsa: Gender, Latin Popular Music, and Puerto Rican Cultures
by Frances Aparicio

Jazz Consciousness: Music, Race, and Humanity
by Paul Austerlitz

Metal, Rock, and Jazz: Perception and the Phenomenology Musical Experience
by Harris M. Berger

Identity and Everyday Life: Essays in the Study of Folklore, Music, and Popular Culture
by Harris M. Berger and Giovanna P. Del Negro

Monument Eternal: The Music of Alice Coltrane
by Franya J. Berkman

Bright Balkan Morning: Romani Lives and the Power of Music in Greek Macedonia
by Dick Blau and Charles and Angeliki Keil

Musical Childhoods and the Cultures of Youth
edited by Susan Boynton and Roe-Min Kok

Music and Cinema
edited by James Buhler, Caryl Flinn, and David Neumeyer

My Music
by Susan D. Crafts, Daniel Cavicchi, Charles Keil, and the Music in Daily Life Project

Born in the USA: Bruce Springsteen and the American Tradition
by Jim Cullen

Presence and Pleasure: The Funk Grooves of James Brown and Parliament
by Anne Danielsen

Echo and Reverb: Fabricating Space in Popular Music Recording, 1900–1960
by Peter Doyle

Recollecting from the Past: Musical Practice and Spirit Possession on the East Coast of Madagascar
by Ron Emoff

Locating East Asia in Western Art Music
edited by Yayoi Uno Everett and Frederick Lau

Black Rhythms of Peru: Reviving African Musical Heritage in the Black Pacific
by Heidi Feldman

"You Better Work!" Underground Dance Music in New York City
by Kai Fikentscher

The Hidden Musicians Music-Making in an English Town
by Ruth Finnegan

The Other Side of Nowhere: Jazz, Improvisation, and Communities in Dialogue
edited by Daniel Fischlin and Ajay Heble

Empire of Dirt: The Aesthetics and Rituals of British "Indie" Music
by Wendy Fonarow

The 'Hood Comes First:
Race, Space, and Place in Rap and Hip-Hop
by Murray Forman

Wired for Sound:
Engineering and Technologies in Sonic Cultures
edited by Paul D. Greene and
Thomas Porcello

Sensational Knowledge:
Embodying Culture Through Japanese Dance
by Tomie Hahn

Voices in Bali:
Energies and Perceptions in Vocal Music and Dance Theater
by Edward Herbst

Traveling Spirit Masters:
Moroccan Gnawa Trance and Music in the Global Marketplace
by Deborah Kapchan

Symphonic Metamorphoses:
Subjectivity and Alienation in Mahler's Re-Cycled Songs
by Raymond Knapp

Umm Kulthūm:
Artistic Agency and the Shaping of an Arab Legend, 1967–2007
by Laura Lohman

A Thousand Honey Creeks Later:
My Life in Music from Basie to Motown—and Beyond
by Preston Love

Music and Technoculture
edited by René T.A. Lysloff
and Leslie C. Gay, Jr.

Songs, Dreamings, and Ghosts:
The Wangga of North Australia
by Allan Marett

Phat Beats, Dope Rhymes:
Hip Hop Down Under Comin' Upper
by Ian Maxwell

Some Liked It Hot:
Jazz Women in Film and Television, 1928–1959
by Kristin A. McGee

Carriacou String Band Serenade:
Performing Identity in the Eastern Caribbean
by Rebecca S. Miller

Global Noise:
Rap and Hip-Hop outside the USA
edited by Tony Mitchell

Popular Music in Theory:
An Introduction
by Keith Negus

Upside Your Head!
Rhythm and Blues on Central Avenue
by Johnny Otis

Coming to You Wherever You Are:
MuchMusic, MTV, and Youth Identities
by Kip Pegley

Singing Archaeology:
Philip Glass's Akhnaten
by John Richardson

Black Noise:
Rap Music and Black Culture in Contemporary America
by Tricia Rose

The Book of Music and Nature:
An Anthology of Sounds, Words, Thoughts
edited by David Rothenberg
and Marta Ulvaeus

Angora Matta:
Fatal Acts of North-South Translation
by Marta Elena Savigliano

Making Beats:
The Art of Sample-Based Hip-Hop
by Joseph G. Schloss

Dissonant Identities:
The Rock 'n' Roll Scene in Austin, Texas
by Barry Shank

Among the Jasmine Trees:
Music and Modernity in Contemporary Syria
by Jonathan Holt Shannon

Banda:
Mexican Musical Life across Borders
by Helena Simonett

Global Soundtracks:
Worlds of Film Music
edited by Mark Slobin

Subcultural Sounds:
Micromusics of the West
by Mark Slobin

Music, Society, Education
by Christopher Small

Musicking:
The Meanings of Performing and Listening
by Christopher Small

Music of the Common Tongue:
Survival and Celebration
in African American Music
by Christopher Small

Singing Our Way to Victory:
French Cultural Politics and Music
During the Great War
by Regina M. Sweeney

Setting the Record Straight:
A Material History of Classical Recording
by Colin Symes

False Prophet:
Fieldnotes from the Punk Underground
by Steven Taylor

Any Sound You Can Imagine:
Making Music/Consuming Technology
by Paul Théberge

Club Cultures:
Music, Media and Sub-cultural Capital
by Sarah Thornton

Dub:
Songscape and Shattered Songs
in Jamaican Reggae
by Michael E. Veal

Running with the Devil:
Power, Gender, and Madness
in Heavy Metal Music
by Robert Walser

Manufacturing the Muse:
Estey Organs and Consumer Culture
in Victorian America
by Dennis Waring

The City of Musical Memory:
Salsa, Record Grooves, and Popular Culture in
Cali, Colombia
by Lise A. Waxer

ABOUT THE AUTHOR

Laura Lohman is an associate professor in the Department of Music at California State University, Fullerton.